Beyond the Cutting Edge?

Beyond the Cutting Edge?

Yoder, Technology, and the Practices of the Church

PAUL C. HEIDEBRECHT

☙PICKWICK *Publications* · Eugene, Oregon

BEYOND THE CUTTING EDGE?
Yoder, Technology, and the Practices of the Church

Copyright © 2014 Paul C. Heidebrecht. All rights reserved. Except for brief quotations in critical publications or reviews, no part of this book may be reproduced in any manner without prior written permission from the publisher. Write: Permissions, Wipf and Stock Publishers, 199 W. 8th Ave., Suite 3, Eugene, OR 97401.

Pickwick Publications
An Imprint of Wipf and Stock Publishers
199 W. 8th Ave., Suite 3
Eugene, OR 97401

www.wipfandstock.com

ISBN 13: 978-71-62032-811-8

Cataloguing-in-Publication data:

Heidebrecht, Paul C.

    Beyond the cutting edge? : Yoder, technology, and the practices of the church / Paul C. Heidebrecht.

    xx + 232 pp. ; 23 cm. Includes bibliographical references and index.

    ISBN 13: 978-71-62032-811-8

    1. Technology—Religious aspects—Christianity. 2. Yoder, John Howard. I. Title.

BR115.T42 H45 2014

Manufactured in the U.S.A.

For Carmen

Contents

Acknowledgments | ix

Introduction | xi

1 The Theological Significance of Technology | 1

2 Using the Work of John Howard Yoder as a Resource for Engaging Technology | 37

3 The Moral Vision Embodied and Encouraged by Three Particular Technologies | 72

4 Conscientiously Engaging Technology Through the Practices of the Church | 114

5 Not Engineering, but Doxology? | 155

6 Continuing to Test Yoder With Technology | 176

Bibliography | 205

Index | 229

Acknowledgments

THIS BOOK IS THE culmination of a journey, and as I release this text to a larger audience, I am reminded of the significance of the process that led to the words on the pages that follow. I am also reminded of the many gifts I have received along the way.

If I had to pick a starting point for my journey, it would be the Mennonite Central Committee guest house in Dhaka, Bangladesh, where I discovered a dusty old copy of John Howard Yoder's book *The Politics of Jesus*. At the time I was an engineering student keenly interested in improving the world through the appropriate use of technology, and I was struggling to find hope given the enormous challenges of life in Bangladesh. This journey continued several years later at the Anabaptist Mennonite Biblical Seminary in Elkhart, Indiana, where I found myself reacting against the "Yoderian air" that seemed to permeate every course in the curriculum. Nonetheless, I was encouraged to find alternative conversation partners, and to pursue my interest in thinking theologically about technology.

Thus I must begin by acknowledging the gifts I have received from my church, which made transformational experiences in higher education and overseas service possible. In addition, I am indebted to the particular congregations who have nurtured my faith, and, more recently, walked with me as I dedicated myself to studying and applying theology. In this regard I am particularly thankful for the friendship and support of my brothers and sisters at Milwaukee Mennonite Church.

The journey toward this book intensified as I explored my interests in the context of doctoral studies at Marquette University. From the outset I appreciated the ecumenical spirit of the Department of Theology, although I had no idea that conversations with teachers and colleagues at a Catholic, Jesuit university would end up rekindling my interest in the work of a Mennonite theologian. For this I express special thanks to Dr. Michael Duffey and Fr. Bryan Massingale. In addition, there was no way I could have anticipated the extent to which Dr. Jame Schaefer would make it possible for me to pursue my interest in technology at Marquette; I am grateful for all I learned through assignments both as her student and her teaching assistant. I am also grateful for the enthusiastic participation of Dr. Stephen Long and Dr. Therese Lysaught on my dissertation committee, especially since it began before they had a chance to settle into their offices at Marquette. A final unexpected gift during my time at Marquette was the opportunity to work as a Graduate Writing Consultant in the Department of Theology. My own approach to writing was aided enormously by what I learned, and I want to thank Dr. Paula Gillespie for the significant role she played in this experience.

I must also acknowledge that I was able to take full advantage of the gifts offered by these mentors because of the financial support I received during my studies. I thank the Department of Theology and the Graduate School at Marquette University for a Teaching Assistantship, the President's Council at Marquette University for the Rev. John P. Raynor, SJ, Dissertation Fellowship, and the trustees of the Charles M. Ross Trust for an additional scholarship.

Finally, I want to acknowledge the immeasurable support of Carmen Brubacher. Without Carmen's passion for and commitment to the mission of the church, it is unlikely that I would have taken the initial steps on the journey toward this project. And without her encouragement and willingness to make sacrifices, I most certainly would not have pursued doctoral studies. Most significantly, I am thankful that I can share with her the joy of parenting Conrad, Sophia, Nathan, and Jesse, who are an inspiration for my work.

In addition to conversations with professors and colleagues at Marquette, this project has been enriched by feedback I received on papers presented at York College of Pennsylvania, the University of Dayton, the American Society of Church History, the Upper Midwest Regional Meeting of the American Academy of Religion, Anabaptist Mennonite Biblical Seminary, the University of Toronto, Elizabethtown College, and Loyola University Chicago. Furthermore, several sections of this book include revised versions of previously published material in which I explored the topic of technology and/or the theology of John Howard Yoder. These sources include: "Not Engineering, But Doxology? Re-examining Yoder's Perspective on the Church," in *Power and Practices: Engaging the Work of John Howard Yoder*, ed. Anthony Siegrist and Jeremy Bergen (Scottdale, PA: Herald, 2009); Review of *Real American Ethics*, by Albert Borgmann, *Conrad Grebel Review* 26/1 (2008) 130–33; "Walking With Yoder Toward a Theological Approach to the Automobile from a Mennonite Perspective," *Conrad Grebel Review* 24/2 (2006) 59–80; and "A Prescription for the Ills of Modernity? Understanding A. James Reimer's Approach to Theology," *Mennonite Quarterly Review* 80/2 (2006) 229–48. All material is reprinted by permission.

Introduction

A QUICK SCAN OF any newsstand is enough to confirm the North American—if not global—preoccupation with technological change. As a myriad of articles and advertisements demonstrate, not only are we preoccupied with technology, but we are bombarded with numerous reminders that the cutting edge is in constant motion. More specifically, it appears we are preoccupied with finding technological solutions to all our problems, including the very problems that particular technologies have created. Even stories that assume a very different tone, for example, those that draw attention to social or environmental consequences resulting from the widespread use of our gadgets, often end up perpetuating the same assumption. Indeed, it seems that many if not most people are convinced that the salvation of the environment—not to mention the eradication of famine and poverty, the resolution of longstanding public health issues, and even the defeat of terrorism—depends upon new technology.

TECHNOLOGY HAS COME TO DEFINE PROGRESS

Due in part to this preoccupation with finding technical fixes, technological change has become the most visible and authoritative indication of our historical location. Changes in technological devices, systems, and ways of thinking have become *the* key factor in marking the passage of time. Just as we can date a photo by looking at the artifacts in the background, we date events in our lives according to the experiences made possible by new technologies, not to mention the distance we have traveled from technologies of old. Technology has become the embodiment of progress.

This introduction is deliberately setting out to frame technology in a non-controversial way, seeking to avoid typical—and typically polarizing—debates about whether technology is good or bad. It seems to me that pinning people down as either optimists or pessimists when it comes to technology is much too simplistic, even though it seems to be a practice that is almost reflexive. Certainly some scholars do fall neatly into one of these two camps, excelling at either utopian or dystopian hyperbole. Yet many more seek to overcome these extremes and articulate a more moderate view, describing their attitude toward technology with terms such as contextualist, intermediate, or realistic. Furthermore, at times thinkers within the same intellectual tradition have exhibited the full spectrum of attitudes toward technology, making it difficult to clearly discern the issues at play.

Defining Technology

One of the issues that can lead to divergent depictions of technology is semantic; the way technology is defined often leads people to talk past each other. Perhaps this should not come as a surprise, given that the English word "technology" has not been in use for long, and that its meaning has evolved.[1] Indeed, the political scientist Langdon Winner has traced a shift in the meaning of technology "from something relatively precise, limited, and unimportant, to something vague, expansive, and highly significant" not only in academic reflection, but in linguistic convention over the course of the twentieth century.[2] Winner points out that in *Webster's New International Dictionary* (1909) technology is said to mean "industrial science, the science or systematic knowledge of the industrial arts, especially of the more important manufactures." In *Webster's Third New International Dictionary* (1961), however, this definition was expanded to include "the totality of the means employed by a people to provide itself with the objects of material culture."[3] Thus for some, technology refers simply to tools or instruments, and they remain focused on material artifacts. Some narrow this focus further by restricting the definition of technology to modern artifacts, the

---

1. According to the *Oxford English Dictionary* (1989), the earliest known use of the English term "technology" was in 1615. However, popular usage of the term has been linked to the publication of Jacob Bigelow's *Elements of Technology* in 1829—see Segal, *Technological Utopianism in American Culture*, 78.

2. Winner, *Autonomous Technology*, 8–9.

3. Mitcham has noted that the first use of the Greek term *technologia* is actually found in Aristotle, where it was associated with the study of grammar and rhetoric. It does not appear that medieval interpreters of Aristotle made use of the Latin equivalent, *tecnologia*, since the earliest source located by Mitcham is from the sixteenth-century philosopher Peter Ramus (1515–72). The more common Greek term used by classical philosophers, *technē*, was translated into Latin by medieval interpreters as *ars*, which is typically translated into English as either "art" or "craft." See *Thinking Through Technology*, 117–29.

assumption being that there is a clear and qualitative distinction to be made with pre-modern artifacts that are not derived from scientific knowledge.[4] For others technology is shorthand for the pattern or paradigm that guides our approach to reality. Still others attempt to overcome any ambiguity by proposing their own, more precise definition for the term.[5]

While I am not interested in creating a new definition for technology, it is important to be clear about my own use of terms throughout this book. When I use the word *technology*, I will usually mean more than simply tools, instruments, or material artifacts. As will soon become clear, I am interested in the interactions and connections between various technologies, and so I will frequently refer to *technological systems*, which includes networks of tools and instruments, as well as the processes and institutional structures that make it possible for systems to function. Furthermore, I am interested in drawing attention to the techniques, methods, or ways of thinking that make the development of modern technology, not to mention the operation of modern societies, possible. Thus in what follows I will also be discussing *technological ways of thinking*.[6] However, the term *technology* will often serve as shorthand to refer collectively to technological artifacts, systems, and ways of thinking.

---

4. The helpfulness of this distinction is another significant point of contention in reflections on technology that I will be attempting to sidestep, in part because attempting to discern qualitative differences between types of technologies is a neverending exercise. Distinctions are now made not only between pre-modern and modern or preindustrial and industrial technologies, but between modern and postmodern or industrial and postindustrial technologies. I do not deny that these distinctions are significant, but I do want to resist the tendency to prioritize the significance of one particular historical shift or to distill the essential nature of a particular technological epoch.

5. Examples of definitions of technology intended to narrow or redirect our focus include: "practical implementations of intelligence" (Ferré, *Philosophy of Technology*, 26); "the application of organized knowledge to practical tasks by ordered systems of people and machines" (Barbour, *Ethics in an Age of Technology*, 3); and "humanity at work" (Pitt, *Thinking About Technology*, 11).

6. This parallels Mitcham's examination of types of technology as "object" (artifacts or hardware), as "activity" (systems of production and use), and as "knowledge" (technique or methodology) in chapters 7–9 of *Thinking Through Technology*. Mitcham's typology builds upon McGinn's "What Is Technology?" 179–97, and Kline's "What Is Technology?," 215–18, and he goes on to consider types of technology as "volition" in chapter 10 in order to ground his analysis in a comprehensive philosophical anthropology (technology is manifest in independent objects, through bodily activities, in the mind, and in the will). However, in the end technology as volition ends up being inseparable from the first three types of technology for Mitcham, and serves simply to highlight that technology is never value (or intention) neutral.

Defining Progress

Returning now to the connection between technology and progress, numerous books have been published on the topic of progress over the past century, but most authors agree that the idea evolved from a Judeo-Christian, linear view of time. More specifically, it emerged in eighteenth-century Europe and America as a result of the age of Enlightenment. Indeed, Enlightenment thought is often summed up by two key characteristics: faith in reason and faith in progress.[7] Despite the great confidence gained in the power of human reason during this time, a confidence gained through the successes of the scientific revolution, the idea that people were rational creatures was not new. What *was* truly new was the idea that the present age was more enlightened than the past.

In his classic early twentieth-century work on the history of the idea of progress, the British historian J.B. Bury (1861–1927) argues that progress was "based on an interpretation of history which regarded people as slowly advancing . . . in a definite and desirable direction." This direction is "desirable" because "a condition of general happiness will ultimately be enjoyed, which will justify the whole process of civilization."[8] Bury was convinced that the idea of progress provided an alternative to the religious notion of providence—to the idea that God was in control of history and would make everything work out in the end. In other words, he thought this idea highlighted a fundamental shift from a theocentric to an anthropocentric worldview.[9] The crucial point to note here is that early enthusiasts of progress were not only interested in building a better civilization, but in making better people. Eighteenth-century Enlightenment thinkers talked not just about the gradual perfection of society, but about the gradual perfection of humanity. Human nature itself, it was thought, was gradually improving; we were not nearly as savage as our ancestors, or the so-called "uncivilized" peoples of the world.

This idea of progress as the perfecting of human nature didn't last very long, at least in North America. One of the reasons was that moral progress, or the "perfectibility of man," as it was called, clearly failed to keep pace

---

7. May, *Enlightenment in America*, xiv. See also Koselleck, *Futures Past*; Hazard, *European Mind, 1680–1715*; Cassirer, *Philosophy of the Enlightenment*; and Gay, *Enlightenment, an Interpretation*.

8. Bury, *Idea of Progress*, 5.

9. Not all contemporary historians agree with Bury on this point. Robert Nisbet, for example, argues for the antiquity of the idea of progress, insisting that it depends upon the premise of historical continuity. See *History of the Idea of Progress*. Nonetheless, Bury's perspective is shared by most contemporary studies of progress, and is a significant reference point for all of them. See, for example, the essays collected in Marx and Mazlish, eds., *Progress*.

with the explosion in scientific knowledge that occurred in the nineteenth century. It is ironic that some religious leaders, particularly those anxious to preserve a conservative Calvinist understanding of human nature as unchanging and sinful, actively supported this growing enthusiasm for science as the sole marker of progress.[10]

Of course, any utopian visions about scientific progress also came to be undermined, in this case by the threats of nuclear and environmental catastrophe that emerged in the twentieth century. As a result, the idea of progress had to latch on to something else once again. In a more recent study of the idea, historian and social critic Christopher Lasch stresses that the appeal of progress owes less to a "millennial vision of the future"—to the "promise of a secular utopia that would bring history to a happy ending"—than to "the promise of steady improvement with no foreseeable ending at all."[11] According to Lasch, progress today is not about where we are going as much as where we are coming from. Following Lasch then, it would seem that progress in our age has less to do with the advance of science than it does with changes in technology. Indeed, theologian Brent Waters argues that this shift from scientific to technological progress—he actually refers to the latter as a concern with "process"—is the defining feature of the shift from a modern to a postmodern worldview.[12]

An earlier book by another theologian, David Hopper, shares Lasch's perspective, suggesting that technology "provides a lesser hope." It is a distraction from the earlier hopes raised by science, and, as Hopper writes, any "disillusion which it breeds is less acute" because "its promise is concrete but also vague."[13] The acceleration of technological change and the subsequent impact those changes have on our culture give the impression that we are rapidly leaving the past behind. Where we are headed, no one seems to know, but we are certainly headed somewhere in a hurry. In the words of the Czech novelist Milan Kundera, technology is "organized forgetting."[14]

This is the picture that characterizes our time: the march of technology enables us to not only distinguish ourselves from those who came before us,

---

10. See Miller's *Brief Retrospect of the Eighteenth Century*.

11. Lasch, *True and Only Heaven*, 39, 47.

12. See "The Late Modern Landscape," chapter 1 in *From Human to Posthuman*. Caldecott also sees the prominence of technology, especially technology that serves individual rather than national interests, as a defining feature of the postmodern period—see "New Sins: Technology and Catholic Social Teaching," 490–92. Others see the connection between progress and technology as being crucial from the start of the Enlightenment—see Wright's *Short History of Progress*, 4.

13. Hopper, *Theology, Technology, and the Idea of Progress*, 74.

14. Kundera, *The Book of Laughter and Forgetting*, 235–36.

but also to elevate ourselves above those who came before us, not to mention those who fail to keep up with our prowess. In making this claim I am insisting that there is good reason for anyone, but perhaps especially those in the Christian tradition, to pay attention to the topic of technology. However, in pointing out that technological change has come to define progress, I am *not* arguing that technology determines history. I am *not* arguing that there are no other factors at play in our context that are also crucial and worthy of theological investigation, factors such as economics, politics, race, and gender. Finally, I am not yet making any claims about whether contemporary understandings of progress are good or bad—that is, whether technological change really is progress.[15] As I did earlier when defining technology, I am attempting to set the stage for a theological examination of technology without getting side-tracked by long-standing debates.

THE BOOK IN OUTLINE

The overall argument of this book is that the work of one of the most prominent Mennonite theologians of the twentieth century, John Howard Yoder (1927-1997), demonstrates that the practices of the church make it possible for Christians to conscientiously engage—rather than simply object or acquiesce to—technological artifacts, systems, and ways of thinking. Goals established at the outset of this project included providing a clear articulation of the theological significance of technology, addressing the need for reflection on technology that moves beyond analysis and theory, creating space for a conversation between theologians and those who not only use, but who develop new technology, and creatively applying the thought of one particular theologian to a new realm. To put it most simply, this was intended to be an exercise in thinking theologically about technology.

As ambitious as this project may be, its structure is relatively straightforward. Chapter 1 goes beyond the above comments on the general significance of technology in our contemporary context to build a case for the *theological* significance of technology. Obvious places to look for support for this argument are the fields of religion and science and bioethics, and yet, as highlighted by the first section of this chapter, efforts to think theologically about technology in these fields have tended to fall short. The second section goes on to argue that technology is not morally neutral, and it is

---

15. This is often the crux of the matter when philosophers and historians of technology start talking about progress—see, for example, Marx and Mazlish, eds., *Progress*; Newman, "Technology and Progress," chapter 3 in *Religion and Technology*; and Visser, *Beyond Fate*.

the inherently moral nature of technology that is of greatest theological relevance. Technological artifacts, systems, and ways of thinking do not simply meet human needs and desires, but come to shape our needs and desires, and thus our vision of what is good. Support for this perspective is found in the work of a wide range of philosophers and historians of technology, who, interestingly enough, are also the thinkers who have tended to raise the most interesting theological questions about technology. This chapter then concludes with two illustrations. The first is an overview of official Catholic teaching in order to highlight the tendency among theologians to overlook the moral thrust of technology. The second illustration is an overview of attempts to appropriate the Amish approach to technology, which highlights the fact that the theological implications of technology are not always evident even to those who agree that technology is not morally neutral.

Chapter 2 argues that the work of John Howard Yoder has significant technological implications. Although this is not a topic that Yoder addressed directly, this chapter begins by noting some hints to the relevance of his theology, as well as some of the challenges involved in reading his work. It then takes on two common criticisms of Yoder, charges that would seem to call into question the possibility that his work could have any bearing on the theological engagement of technology. The first critique is that Yoder was sectarian. In response, this chapter argues that, far from separating himself from larger social concerns, Yoder encouraged the church to conscientiously engage these concerns. The second critique—one that is especially common in Mennonite circles—is that Yoder reduced theology to ethics. In response, this chapter offers a clarification of Yoder's understanding of the relationship between theology and ethics, and argues that his discussion of Christian practices represented a significant theological contribution. The final section moves beyond a defensive posture to explore the most direct connection with technology that can be found in Yoder's work. This connection is found in the places where Yoder pointed to the work of one of the best known contemporary critics of technology, Jacques Ellul, which suggest that Yoder's discussion of the biblical concept of principalities and powers speaks directly to the topic of technology.

Chapter 3 develops the argument that technology is not morally neutral, an argument that was introduced in chapter 1. It does this by focusing on the way particular manifestations of technology embody and encourage particular ideals, ideals that have come to assume the status of moral imperatives. Picking up on Yoder's preference for particularity, however, the intent of this chapter is not to make a general or systematic argument about the moral nature of technology. Rather, the purpose is to provide a more focused study of three particular examples of technology: the automobile, genetically modified food, and the Internet. In each case, the state of recent debates in the literature surrounding these technologies is examined, and the tendency for positions to become polarized around extreme views is noted. It is then argued that this polarization is not the result of differing assessments of scientific, economic, or political data as much as it is due to differing moral visions. Thus the discussion of each example is concluded by highlighting three key technological ideals that are intrinsic to the technology under consideration, and that these technologies subsequently come to nurture in those who use them.

Chapter 4 is the crucial chapter of this book. Now that previous chapters have brought together the theology of John Howard Yoder and the topic of technology, and highlighted the moral vision of three particular technologies, this chapter argues that each of these technologies needs to be understood in a new way. The first section of this chapter reviews the automobile, genetically modified food, and the Internet through the lens of Yoder's depiction of the marks of the church, marks that provide a striking contrast to the technological ideals discussed in the previous chapter. The second section attempts to demonstrate that the technological implications of Yoder's theology are made clear in his discussion of church practices. By bearing witness to the marks that distinguish it from the technological ideals of the automobile, genetically modified food, and the Internet, the church is able to conscientiously engage these technologies rather than simply reject or embrace them. The church is able to resist their seductive power by testifying to the fact that, like all principalities and powers, technological systems and ways of thinking are necessary, fallen, and capable of being transformed by the power of Christ. The church is thus able to re-describe technology in light of the things we do as Christians, rather than allowing the things we do with technology to re-describe what it means to be a Christian.

Chapter 5 begins to use the topic of technology to test and extend Yoder's thought. The first section of this chapter highlights the several places in Yoder's work where he is critical of an engineering approach to problem-solving, an approach he contrasts with the witness of doxology. This is especially striking because, as noted in the next section of this chapter, Yoder himself appears to have the mind of an engineer, especially when he writes about the history of the church. The third section takes a closer look at the practice of engineering, and, with this enriched understanding, it becomes clear that Yoder's criticism of engineering is misguided. In fact, the concluding section of this chapter suggests that a good theologian can be properly seen as an engineer of the church—as being concerned with not only the history and direction of the church, but with the formation of followers of Christ. In this regard, theologians might have something to learn from engineers about how to resist the power of technological systems and ways of thinking in the church.

Chapter 6, the final chapter, continues the task that was started in chapter 5. More specifically, it moves on to explore two ways we need to go beyond Yoder in order to further the conscientious engagement of technology that his work compels us to pursue. First, Yoder's focus on the church as the locus for the transformation of principalities and powers such as technology does not seem to fully appreciate the complex ways in which these powers are able to exert themselves. Yoder's perspective thus needs some nuance in order to be able to recognize the pervasive influence of technological systems and ways of thinking, especially within the church. Second, Yoder's discussion of the practices of the church not only needs to be enriched by addressing the formative nature of these practices as discussed in chapter 5, but it needs to be expanded to include the everyday life of church communities. The bulk of this chapter is composed of a discussion of additional tactics that can enable the church to conscientiously engage the automobile, genetically modified food, and the Internet. These tactics are properly viewed as Christian practices not simply because they are grounded in the Christian tradition, but because they are capable of nurturing the marks of the church.

1

The Theological Significance of Technology

THE PRIMARY AIM OF this chapter is to make a convincing case that theologians have something relevant to say about technology. It is an attempt to answer the basic question: Why would someone focus on the topic of technology in a project in theology? At first glance, it might appear the more difficult challenge would be convincing a broader, non-theological audience this is a worthwhile project. However, as will become clear in what follows, the biggest hurdle may actually be convincing *theologians* it is important for them to reflect on technology. These are the first steps toward demonstrating that theological reflection on technology is important because a theological perspective provides insights into technology that would not otherwise be possible.

This chapter begins by highlighting shortcomings in attempts to grapple theologically with technology as found in fields such as religion and science and bioethics. It then argues that technology *is* theologically significant because it is *not* morally neutral—it does not simply meet human needs and desires, but comes to shape us in profound ways by determining our needs and desires. Thus, as demonstrated by prominent philosophers and historians of technology, the analysis of technology compels theological consideration. This chapter then concludes with two illustrations that provide further evidence for this latter point: an overview of official Catholic teaching on technology, and attempts to appropriate the Amish approach to technology.

beyond the cutting edge?

RECENT ATTEMPTS TO GRAPPLE THEOLOGICALLY WITH TECHNOLOGY FALL SHORT

The word "technology" can be found sprinkled throughout the works of several of the most prominent twentieth-century philosophers and theologians, including Martin Heidegger and Paul Tillich.[1] Although Heidegger can be credited with inspiring a new philosophical specialty or sub-discipline devoted to technology, for Tillich technology was of secondary importance to his larger concern with science and culture. Other prominent contemporary theologians who touch on the topic of technology but also see it as symptomatic of more significant underlying methodological issues include James Gustafson, Douglas John Hall, Bernard Lonergan, Oliver O'Donovan, and Stanley Hauerwas.[2] Perhaps then it should not be surprising that, in contrast to the many self-identified philosophers of technology who have emerged over the past forty years (not to mention the related associations, conferences, and publications), the expression "theology of technology" is rarely found in theological discourse. In fact, one is much more likely to find philosophers or even historians discussing moral and theological issues raised by technology in general.

To be sure, there have been a handful of anthologies over the past few decades that serve as reminders of attempts to spark theological discussion in this area. For example, a conference in Europe on technology in the early 1960s led to the publication of one collection of essays.[3] In addition, one of the leading American philosophers of technology, Carl Mitcham, included a section on religious critiques of technology in a widely-used anthology on philosophy and technology.[4] After Mitcham became convinced that the central questions about technology were ultimately theological in nature, a few years later he helped to assemble another collection of essays that were explicitly theological. This second anthology, *Technology and Theology: Essays in Christian Analysis and Exegesis*, was the outgrowth of a symposium on "Philosophy, Technology, and Theology" at a meeting of the fledgling Society of Philosophy and Technology held in conjunction with the American Catholic Philosophical Association annual meeting in 1979.[5] Given this

---

1. Heidegger, *Question Concerning Technology*; Tillich, *Spiritual Situation*.

2. See, for example, Gustafson, *Intersections*; Hall, *Thinking the Faith*; Lonergan, *Method in Theology*; O'Donovan, *Begotten or Made?*; and Hauerwas, *Suffering Presence*.

3. White, *Christians in a Technological Era*.

4. Mitcham and Mackey, eds., *Philosophy and Technology*.

5. An earlier, lesser known collection of essays that also grew out of events in a Catholic setting (in this case a lecture series at Catholic University of America) can be found in Mohan, ed., *Technology and Christian Culture*.

context, it should come as no surprise, however, that only a third of the contributions came from theologians.[6] It is also interesting to note that most of the recent monographs on religion and technology have been written by philosophers, not theologians, and they all reference the now rather dated essays in the above collections when they are looking for what theologians have to say about technology.[7]

When technology is discussed in contemporary theological discourse, it is most often encountered in the relatively new interdisciplinary fields of religion and science and bioethics. These fields contain a significant and growing body of literature that reflects upon the impact of recent advances in technology on scientific or medical practice, and on the significance of this impact for theology. In my view, however, there are significant shortcomings in these reflections.

Religion and Science

Examples of those touching on issues raised by technology in the interface between theology and the natural sciences include Ian Barbour, Willem Drees, and Philip Hefner. Barbour, one of the formative figures in this field, even devoted half of his Gifford lectures to the topic of technology and ethics.[8] Drees, the past president of the European Society for the Study of Science and Theology (ESSSAT), provided two significant contributions to an issue of *Zygon*, the preeminent journal in the field, devoted to "Human Meaning in a Technological Culture."[9] He underlined the way that issues raised by technology are fundamentally different from the issues that arise in attempts to relate religion and science—the latter are concerned with understanding reality, while the former are concerned with the transformation of reality. And a recent book by Hefner, the long-time editor of *Zygon* and past president of the Zygon Center for Religion and Science, demonstrates

---

6. A more recent—and more substantial—project edited by Mitcham is the *Encyclopedia of Science, Technology, and Ethics* that stretches to almost 2,400 pages, but includes just seventeen religion scholars or theologians out of a total of more than 450 contributors.

7. See Ferré, *Technology and Religion*; George, *Religion and Technology*; Newman, *Religion and Technology*; and Pattison, *Thinking About God*. Recent exceptions include works by two theologians: Herzfeld's *Technology and Religion* and Brock's *Christian Ethics in a Technological Age*.

8. Barbour, *Ethics in an Age of Technology*. Like many in the field of religion and science, Barbour received formal training in both science (a PhD in physics from the University of Chicago) and theology (a divinity degree from Yale), and has encouraged interdisciplinary studies.

9. Drees, "Religion in an Age of Technology"; and Drees, "'Playing God? Yes!'"

his interest in helping theologians keep pace with the ever-changing technological reality that surrounds them.[10]

However, the list does not stop with these three. Robert John Russell, the founder of the Center for Theology and the Natural Sciences, has enriched Barbour's threefold typology of Christian attitudes towards technology by adding two more distinct approaches.[11] In contrast to either a positive attitude which views technology as a liberator or a negative attitude which views technology as a threat, Barbour proposed that we adopt a middle-of-the-way or contextualist attitude that views technology as a powerful instrument that can be used for either good or evil. To these Russell adds Hefner's proposal to re-imagine humankind as "created co-creators,"[12] which assumes that technology is not something we can clearly distinguish from ourselves and thus adopt an attitude toward. For Hefner, technology is much more than an instrument, it is an extension of our very being, and thus is itself neither liberating or threatening. Finally, as a fifth alternative Russell proposes the attitude of an "eschatological companion." This attitude is based upon the assumption that God is at work transforming the world into a new creation, and technology "must ultimately serve as a means to express and help achieve this future, even in a rudimentary way." Technology itself is not a liberator, although it can contribute to liberation when we "mold technology in the service of Christ-like love: self-sacrificial, inclusive, and transformative."[13]

Other thinkers have covered similar terrain as Drees. For example, Ursula Goodenough, a biologist and past president of the Institute on Religion in an Age of Science, insists that science is all about "asking a question of Nature," while technology is all about "using an answer from Nature to develop a new way of doing things."[14] The point she wants to emphasize is that the domain of technology is inherently ethical: "whereas science brings us information that we have little choice but to absorb and reflect upon, technology is something that humans elect to do and, hence, can also elect not to do."[15] This clearly provides motivation for adding technology-religion

---

10. Hefner, *Technology and Human Becoming*.

11. Russell, "Five Attitudes Toward Nature and Technology." Since Barbour already associates the spectrum of attitudes toward technology with H. Richard Niebuhr's well-known *Christ and Culture* typology (see Barbour, *Ethics in an Age of Technology*, 19–20), it seems appropriate to distinguish five rather than three different attitudes.

12. Hefner's most extensive development of this anthropology is found in *The Human Factor*, although it clearly undergirds *Technology and Human Becoming*.

13. Russell, "Five Attitudes Toward Nature and Technology," 157.

14. Goodenough, "Reflections on Science and Technology," 6.

15. Ibid., 5.

dialogue to the field of science and religion. Rustum Roy, a leading materials scientist and past chair of the National Council of Churches' Committee on Science, Technology, and the Church, is even more pointed in emphasizing the importance of technology, insisting that attention needs to be paid to the relationship between religion and technology *rather* than religion and science. He argues that the "proper cognate" of science is theology, and that both science and theology are increasingly "applications-driven;" they are evaluated by their results. Thus the more fruitful realm of interaction is found by bringing together the fields of technology and religion, both of which "involve or control or limit human *practice* and *experience*."[16] In addition to these contributions, perhaps the best indication that technological issues are on the radar for theologians in this field is that in 2006 the "Religion and Science Group" at the American Academy of Religion was renamed the "Science, Technology and Religion Group."

What then is the problem with this body of literature? Where is the shortcoming? In the first place, while technology is clearly on the radar for some theologians and scientists interfacing theology and the natural sciences, it is still a secondary or subordinate interest. The few exceptions noted above prove the general rule that theologians tend to see science as the more foundational and therefore the more important topic. No doubt the growing understanding of the cosmos provided by scientific inquiry has raised significant metaphysical questions with obvious theological implications. For example, questions prompted by new knowledge about the origins of the universe or the evolution of life that challenge traditional Christian doctrines of God, creation, and anthropology. However, I would argue it is because of modern technology that humanity has an unprecedented ability to not only understand, but to manipulate our world, an ability that we have yet to fully come to grips with.[17]

Furthermore, even when technology is considered by people like Drees and Hefner, the discussion usually remains confined to theoretical issues such as the challenge technology poses to our understanding of the human person.[18] Once again, there are a few reasons why this may be

---

16. Roy, "Religion/Technology," 667. Roy has amplified this point in "Scientism and Technology as Religions."

17. This is similar to what Murray Jardine argues in *The Making and Unmaking of Technological Society*. Jardine's thesis is that modern Western societies are in the midst of a crisis due to the theoretical incoherence of liberal thought—i.e., we are unable to make moral sense of our capacity to change our environment through technology because our moral framework assumes that this environment is part of an unchanging natural order.

18. Barbour is an exception in this regard, as the bulk of his *Ethics in an Age of Technology* moves beyond theoretical issues to confront specific problems in three key

the case. First of all, theologians are typically more comfortable dealing with theories, both theological and scientific, than they are with practices, either Christian or technological. Secondly, technology is typically thought of as applied science, and so the more interesting and foundational questions are encountered in the history and philosophy of science. Technology is typically seen as the dependent descendant of science. The operating assumption in both cases is that theory and practice is related in a hierarchical fashion, and so if we get our thinking right, the correct course of action will naturally follow.

However, the more significant problem with this body of literature, in my view, is that the discussion assumes a reactive tone—the world, and possibly even humanity, is being transformed into something new, and the job of the theologian seems to be to contort religious faith to fit this new reality. One gets little sense when reading through the journal *Zygon* that the job of the theologian may also include making prescriptive statements about how Christians should seek to constrain or reshape this change.

Bioethics

Certainly bioethicists are at the forefront of trying to provide theological guidance for the direction of medical technologies such as reproductive techniques and stem cell research. Although the field has come to be dominated by philosophers and scientists, the roots of bioethics can be traced to the work of medical ethicists trained as Catholic moral theologians.[19] Furthermore, even though research and publications tend to be driven by public policy debates, prominent voices have insisted that theological issues

---

technological realms. In agriculture, environmental issues such as soil erosion and pollution from fertilizers and pesticides, and social issues such as the impact of mechanization on family farms are addressed. In energy generation, he focuses on the way our reliance on fossil fuels has contributed to global warming and economic inequalities, as well as the large-scale environmental risks posed by nuclear power. And when it comes to computers he raises questions about meaningful work and access to information. Barbour's critique is also more than academic hand-wringing—it is based on comparisons with alternative approaches that have become more prominent and viable since this book was first published in 1993. These include organic farming and vegetarian diets, conserving and relying on reliable sources of energy, and decentralized computer networks such as the Internet. Barbour has also noted that his separation of science and technology and religion and ethics had more to do with his pedagogical approach than with his acceptance of any real division between these realms.

19. Curran, "Catholic Moral Tradition in Bioethics." Some important voices, for example, Deane-Drummond, do not fit neatly within, but rather bridge the fields of religion and science and bioethics. See *Theology and Biotechnology*, and *Genetics and Christian Ethics*.

remain on the table. For example, the theologian Ronald Cole-Turner has sought to bring insights from the Christian tradition to bear upon public deliberations on human cloning. Instead of asking what we should think of the "'age of biological control,' with its promises of unprecedented power," or asking whether anything can control this technology, he asks how we submit our technology to God. After all, "God, not nature, defines the values and purposes of our actions . . . It is God's purposes for our offspring, not our own, that must regulate our use of technology to shape future generations."[20] Another theologian, Lisa Sowle Cahill, in an attempt to address the lament that theology has been marginalized even in explicitly Christian bioethics, has tried to help the discipline "recover its religiously distinctive prophetic voice and enter into policy debates as an energetic adversary of the liberal consensus."[21] Thus Cahill seeks to connect reflection on theoretical issues with activism—to develop a "participatory bioethics" that can "mediate between a Christian worldview . . . and the social practices and institutions that determine the concrete experiences of decline and dying."[22] She has also helpfully expanded the range of issues in bioethics under consideration in the Catholic tradition to include the economic and social realms as well as sexual ethics and personal morality.[23]

One shortcoming in this discourse is that, perhaps because of the need to keep pace with the rapidly changing terms of public debates, bioethicists have made little effort to explore connections or parallels with the more pervasive and mundane technologies that are actually of greater influence in the day-to-day lives of most people. As Eran P. Klein and Jennifer K. Walter, two chroniclers of the field put it: "bioethics tends to orient itself toward the future." The questions always being asked are: "What bioethical issues lie on the horizon? What can be done about them now?" Furthermore, "ongoing changes in medical technology and the exigencies of medical practice" make it necessary to view all contributions to bioethics as "works in transition."[24] While self-reflective tendencies are emerging in the field, I think bioethics will continue to be impoverished until there is more effort to place medical technologies in a larger context. Our responses to cutting-edge technological issues are shaped to a large extent by the way we have become accustomed to respond to technology on a daily basis.

20. Cole-Turner, "Toward a Theology for the Age of Biotechnology," 137–38.
21. Cahill, *Theological Bioethics*, 18.
22. Ibid., 130.
23. In addition to *Theological Bioethics*, see *Bioethics and the Common Good*.
24. Walter and Klein, *Story of Bioethics*, x–xi.

Brent Waters has made a similar point, arguing that disputes involving reproductive technology such as contraception and assisted reproduction "are not unrelated issues, but are dimensions of a larger issue on the extent to which humans should control the means and outcomes of their propagation."[25] Rather than allowing the terms of these disputes to be defined by what he sees to be the dominant view of "procreative liberty," Waters advocates that we step back and begin with a critique of "technology in general and its distorting influence on contemporary moral deliberation."[26]

A second reason why the field of bioethics is wanting is that focusing on cutting-edge issues perpetuates the myth that moral issues with technology are only encountered in rare or special cases. Lisa Sowle Cahill provided a good example of this kind of thinking at the 2007 Society of Christian Ethics Annual Meeting in Dallas, Texas, during her participation in a panel discussion about the ethical, religious, and legal issues related to genetic patenting.[27] She argued that patenting genetic material is bad because it harms the common good, and yet, since the genie is already out of the bottle, reforming the international patent system may actually hold great promise for financing the basic health infrastructure in developing nations. What was most interesting was that Cahill and the rest of the panel were consumed with making an argument for why patent systems should not be blind to moral concerns. In the case of genetic research and material, it does seem clear that both commodifying and restricting access to these inventions poses a threat to important moral traditions. Yet even if we seek to encourage the use of moral criteria to guide the way a few particular technologies are regulated in the public sphere,[28] Christians, in my view, should be starting with the assumption that *all* technologies and technological systems have moral implications.

25. Waters, *Reproductive Technology*, 90.

26. Ibid., 91. Waters's analysis is informed by the work of Oliver O'Donovan and George Grant, and his concern with technology in general is carried over to his subsequent volume, *From Human to Posthuman*.

27. Along with Cahill's paper on "Genetic Patents and Just Access," other panel participants included Audrey R. Chapman ("Ethical Dimensions of the Ownership and Control of Human Stem Cells") and Ronald W. Duty ("American and European Approaches to Genetic Patents: Ethical Dimensions"). The panel was moderated by Roger A. Willer, and was held on January 5, 2007.

28. In fact, the U.S. patent system makes moral judgments all the time when determining whether an application meets the requirement of "utility"—an invention must be functional, and in order to be functional, the use of the process, machine, manufacture, or "composition of matter" must not break any laws. Since laws evolve, sex toys and gambling machines are now patentable, while nuclear weapons technology and instruments of torture are not. See the U.S. Patent and Trademark Office's "General Information Concerning Patents."

Gerald McKenny is one theologian who seems to agree with me on this point, while also providing a critique of the dominant or "standard" view in bioethics. He does this by linking bioethics to the "Baconian project," to the imperative "to eliminate suffering and to expand the realm of human choice—in short, to relieve the human condition of subjection to the whims of fortune or the bonds of natural necessity."[29] Thus, McKenny argues, rather than challenging technological utopianism, bioethics tends to presuppose and support it.[30] The connections between those evaluating the latest and greatest medical technologies and the optimistic promoters of the industrial revolution run deep, and yet they have gone unexamined. In fact, McKenny disagrees with the many voices who insist that the novelty of new medical technologies presents issues that both medical and religious traditions never anticipated and are thus unable to address.[31] He is convinced that these issues are not unprecedented, but rather that modern technologies are only distinctive because of the "vastly greater scope of such intervention."[32] McKenny insists that the newness of our situation is not defined by what we are trying to do, or even by how we are trying to do it, but by the effectiveness or reach of our efforts.

Although they may be the most obvious, the fields of religion and science and bioethics are certainly not the only subdisciplines where one might expect to find theologians engaging the topic of technology. Indeed, examples can also be found, although not as readily, of references to technology in the fields of environmental ethics, economic ethics, and peace and

---

29. McKenny, *To Relieve the Human Condition*, 2. McKenny is certainly not the only like-minded thinker I could point to—see, for example, Shuman's critique of the way bioethics, like science and technology, is used by medicine to exert control over our lives in *The Body of Compassion*, and Lysaught's critique of the way the discourse of biomedical ethics functions as an agent of social regulation and the handmaiden of science in "Patient Suffering and the Anointing of the Sick," and "From Clinic to Congregation."

30. McKenny's discussion of technological utopianism (as contrasted with Marxist utopianism) echoes the discussion of progress in the previous section of this chapter: "The dynamics of modern technology overtake the human effort to realize—even to formulate—an objective ideal in history . . . The result is that modern technology is at once both utopian and nihilistic. It is utopian since it clings to the notion that humanity is yet to be realized. It is nihilistic since its imperviousness to any substantial ideal leaves it beyond good and evil . . . Modern technology, including biomedicine, moves toward no ideal to be realized, but simply keeps moving forward" (*To Relieve the Human Condition*, 49).

31. Ibid., 11. Chris K. Huebner makes a similar critique when he argues that "the need for bioethics grows out of the perception that a new space is opened up because technological possibilities outrun the capacity for ethical judgments" (see "Bioethics and the Church," 74).

32. McKenny, *To Relieve the Human Condition*, 5.

conflict studies. In these cases, however, technology is even more clearly of secondary concern, and here too, technology is typically discussed either because of its novelty or because it is assumed to be a given that we must respond to. To be clear, I am not arguing that engaging technology will provide the key to understanding what is really going on in the worlds of science, medicine, the environment, economics, or politics. Nor am I interested in starting another academic specialty. I have simply been trying to demonstrate that there are inadequacies with recent efforts by theologians to engage the topic of technology, and to explain why I have sought a different starting point.

TECHNOLOGY IS NOT MORALLY NEUTRAL

What this chapter is saying, briefly put, is that when we look inside the "black box" of a technology or technological system, we discover more than wires and batteries, more than precisely machined metals and highly refined synthetics, and more than bits and bytes. Indeed, we find much that is of theological significance. Theologians should be interested in technology not simply because of the uses that can be made of it by well or ill-intentioned individuals and communities. They should be interested in technology because the ideals that are embodied within a particular technology or system come to shape the moral character of the individuals or communities that use it. Thus in this section I will argue that technological artifacts, systems, and ways of thinking are not morally neutral because they are heavily laden with ideals that have deep moral implications. In short, technologies always come equipped with an inherent moral trajectory.

Over the past forty years this point has become accepted dogma among scholars who focus their attention on technology, including philosophers, historians, and others who contribute to the broad field of science and technology studies.[33] To be sure, there are fierce debates among and within these fields about the extent to which technology is shaped by, or comes to shape human thought and practice. At one end of the continuum are people like the French sociologist and theologian Jacques Ellul, the Canadian philosopher George Grant, and others influenced by Marx, Nietzche,

---

33. Many of the interdisciplinary Science and Technology Studies (or Science, Technology, and Values) courses that can now be found in most North American universities and colleges were pioneered in the 1960s by concerned philosophers, historians, and sociologists. Because of these courses (and, in some cases, minor or even major degree programs), it has become common to refer to Science and Technology Studies as a field of its own. Yet there are only a few doctoral programs in this field, and no overarching scholarly association to unite it.

and Heidegger who emphasize the autonomous nature of technology.[34] At the other end are people like Lynn White Jr., David Noble, and other historians of technology influenced by social constructivism who "emphasize contingency and choice rather than forces of necessity" in the development of technology.[35] In my view, both groups make helpful contributions. Technology is, to a certain extent beyond the control of its users. Yet technology is also, to a certain extent, influenced by those who develop it. Nonetheless, these debates do not preclude a common concern to emphasize that there is something going on *inside* the black boxes, complex networks, and ways of thinking that we rely on every day that is of moral relevance.[36]

---

34. Winner, *Autonomous Technology*; Illich, *Tools for Conviviality*; Mumford, *Technics and Civilization*; and Postman, *Technopoly*.

Marx, Nietzche, and Heidegger have each exerted significant influence on contemporary analyses of technology in general, and on the work of Ellul, Grant, and Albert Borgmann in particular. Other prominent philosophers whose influence lingers include Hannah Arendt, John Dewey, Jurgen Habermas, Herbert Marcuse, Leo Strauss, and Simone Weil. Since this is not a project in the philosophy of technology, however, I will confine myself to more contemporary voices. Indeed, one should consider the perspectives of Kant, Hume and Rousseau, not to mention Plato and Aristotle in order to thoroughly trace the roots of any contemporary philosophy of technology.

35. Winner, "Upon Opening the Black Box," 366–67. For an overview of the emergence of the history of technology as an academic discipline, see Staudenmaier, *Technology's Storytellers*; and Hughes, *Human-Built World*. For an overview of debates over the autonomous or deterministic nature of technology among historians of technology, see Smith and Marx, *Does Technology Drive History?*

36. In many summaries of the philosophy of technology a continuum is set up between "substantive," "autonomous," or "determinist" views of technology on the one hand, and "instrumentalist" or "neutral" views of technology on the other—see Feenberg, *Critical Theory of Technology*, 5–8.

The problem is that even though an instrumental view of technology may be assumed by many (if not most) people today, there are no contemporary philosophers that I am aware of who argue for this position. Furthermore, treating technology as a morally neutral set of tools does not *necessarily* preclude one from arguing that technology itself is of moral significance. For example, the political scientist Homer-Dixon makes a compelling argument for why we need to go beyond the search for technical fixes to all human problems in *The Ingenuity Gap*. In short, our modern tools exacerbate social and environmental problems because they "extend our *agency horizon*" (ibid., 119), and thus make it possible to create new problems faster than our ingenuity enables us to solve the old ones. Homer-Dixon's proposal for overcoming this ingenuity gap is that we nurture tacit, non-technical forms of knowledge, and this is "fundamentally an emotional, moral, and even spiritual matter" (ibid., 399).

It should also be noted that the ends of any continuum continue to shift. For example, some philosophers have recently suggested that we need to talk about the moral agency of technology itself. That is, since technological artifacts possess intentionality as well as functionality, they are best thought of as moral agents which, along with their creators and users, can be evaluated using standard philosophical accounts of agency and action. See Johnson and Powers, "Ethics and Technology."

beyond the cutting edge?

Technology is Autonomous: Jacques Ellul and George Grant

Ellul and Grant are undoubtedly two of the best known critics of technology, and while their popularity may have peaked in the 1970s, their work continues to be translated, republished, and engaged today. Both seek to draw attention not only to the material manifestations of technology, but (especially for Grant) to the systems that link technology together, and (especially for Ellul) to the ways of thinking that make it all possible. Indeed, Ellul's writings focus primarily on *technique*, on the "*totality of methods rationally arrived at and having absolute efficiency* (for a given stage of development) in *every* field of human activity."[37] While machines may be symptomatic of this pursuit of efficiency, Ellul argues that technique "has taken over all of [humankind's] activities, not just [its] productive activities."[38] Thus technological ways of thinking are also evident in social organizations ("the nation is essentially an affair to be managed"[39]) and in the lives of individuals ("training in sports makes of the individual an efficient piece of apparatus"[40]), and this dominance has led to nothing less than a state of tyranny. Ellul is clearly trying to describe the fundamental problem in modern society, and yet his all-encompassing definition makes it difficult to state clearly what human activity does *not* fall under the domain of technique. Technological ways of thinking are characterized by words and phrases as varied as rationality, artificiality, self-directedness, self-supporting growth, indivisibility, universality, and autonomy.[41] Nonetheless, Ellul's discussion of the autonomy of technique is informed by two important insights into the nature of technology: it is irreversible—once invented it cannot be un-invented, and it

---

37. This definition was added in a "Note to the Reader" in the American edition of *La Technique*. See Ellul, *Technological Society*, xxv. The English translation of this book does not alter Ellul's use of the word *technique*, however many people have argued, and most just assume that it is best translated "technology." See, for example, Mitcham and Mackey, "Jacques Ellul and the Technological Society," 105. Ellul himself, however, preferred that English-speakers "use 'Technique' with a capital *T* when it was a question of the totality of techniques" rather than the term technology—see Gill, "Jacques Ellul," 20. Subsequent volumes of Ellul's technology trilogy more specifically addressed technological systems and artifacts—see *Technological System* and *Technological Bluff*.

38. Ellul, *Technological Society*, 4.

39. Ibid., 263.

40. Ibid., 383.

41. In *The Technological System,* Ellul clarified his thoughts on the "characteristics of the technological phenomenon" in chapters on autonomy, unity, universality, and totalization. He also clarified his thoughts on the "characteristics of technological progress" in chapters on self-augmentation, automatism, casual progression and absence of finality, and the problem of acceleration.

develops exponentially rather than in a linear fashion. New technologies always give rise to new families of related technologies.

Like Ellul, George Grant is also interested in critiquing modernity, an era he describes as the "post-Enlightenment age"—a time in which Enlightenment thought has been taken to its logical conclusion in liberalism, and is characterized by the combination of individual freedom and technology.[42] He identifies the key intellectual shift that led to this age as the reduction of time to history.[43] Unlike the classical view of time which placed history within the context of an ontological or cosmic framework, in modernity human history became the only level of reality. Unlike the ancients, who were convinced, in Grant's words, that "we are not on our own,"[44] we moderns have decoupled ourselves from eternity and the divine and see no limits to our capacity to shape and control history, not to mention the natural world. Technology has become our ontology, our very mode of being.

Many have viewed this shift as an important gain, and Grant cites the famous aphorism on the tomb of Marx an example: "The philosophers have thought about the world long enough; now it is time to change it."[45] Marx got his wish, Grant says, and look at the results. After relatively few years of obsessive human action in the name of improving the world, the scale and scope of our problems threaten to overwhelm us. And yet, aside from the obvious political and environmental problems, Grant argues that modernity is a failure on its own terms, for technology, the product of our newfound human agency, has turned on its creators and threatens to subsume our freedom. It is a threat because it embodies a monolithic and homogenizing force—the instrumental rationality embodied in modern technology—that counters the diversity and pluralism promised by modernity. Instead of greater freedom, we actually have less.

A key illustration of this phenomenon for Grant is the computer. He wrote: "The simple characterization of the computer as a neutral instrument makes it sound as if instruments are now what instruments have always been, and so hides from us what is completely novel about modern instruments."[46] Unlike pre-modern technologies, computers tend "to hide the fact that their very capabilities entail that the ways they can be used are never neutral. They can only be used in homogenizing ways."[47] Indeed,

---

42. Grant, *Technology and Empire*, 114.
43. This thesis is most forcefully stated in Grant's *Time as History*.
44. Grant, "Conversation," 63.
45. Grant, *Time as History*, 23.
46. Grant, "Computer Does Not Impose," 121.
47. Ibid., 122.

these ways "must be at one with certain conceptions of political purposes [i.e. human freedom conceived of as autonomy] because the same kind of reasoning made the machines and formulated the purposes."[48] The end result is that societies, not to mention workplaces and homes, increasingly begin to resemble each other as they adopt the same technologies. They resemble each other not simply in their material form, but in the kinds of relationships they permit and in their patterns of thinking. For those skeptical about his claim that computers lead to increasing homogeneity, Grant points to the impact of the automobile: "Fifty years ago men might have said 'the automobile does not impose on us the ways it should be used.'"[49]

Although the analysis of Grant and Ellul is persuasive, it is also paralyzing. Indeed, many have pointed out that while these two are able to fill volumes with all that is wrong with contemporary life, they never tell us what we should do about it. In their eyes the future seems rather bleak. Thus it is interesting to note that Grant felt the same way about some of his own writings: "the purpose of the negations . . . [is] to clear away the junk of the modern era and to say how difficult it is to make positive affirmations . . . these essays are really attempts in the old manner of negative theology."[50] As a plethora of recent scholarship indicates, Grant's philosophical analysis of technology not only makes space for theological reflection, it demands a theological perspective if one is to have any hope.[51]

The same thing can be said for Jacques Ellul. Ellul divided his vast corpus of over forty books and eight hundred articles into distinct groups:

48. Ibid., 124.

49. Ibid., 123. A third influential philosophical critique of modernity that hinges on the analysis of technology is provided by Jonas in *The Imperative of Responsibility*. For Jonas, the essence of technology is power, and thus what is characteristic about modern technology is the way it has enhanced human power beyond anything known or even dreamed before, "lengthening the reach of our deeds." Jonas thinks that this novel situation demands a novel approach to ethics, as traditional natural law, utilitarian or deontological theories are inadequate when we simply cannot grasp all of the implications of our technology. Jonas argues that "responsibility is a correlate of power," and so ethical discernment *must* find its way into the realm of technology (ibid., x). Precisely because of the success of technology, this call to responsibility demands "a new kind of humility—a humility owed, not like the former humility to the smallness of our power, but to the excessive magnitude of it" (ibid., 58). To stimulate this humility, Jonas proposes that utopian dreams be replaced by the practice of an imaginative "heuristics of fear" that would consider worst-case scenarios before undertaking any technological project.

50. Grant, *George Grant Reader*, 23.

51. See Angus, *Athens and Jerusalem*; Athanasiadis, *George Grant and the Theology of the Cross*; Davis, *George Grant and the Subversion of Modernity*; Christian, *George Grant*; and O'Donovan, *George Grant and the Twilight of Justice*.

sociology or critical social thought, ethics, and biblical hermeneutics. While the latter two are explicitly theological, the first group of writings claim to be descriptive, and it is here that the bulk of Ellul's analysis of technology is found. Indeed, in the forward to *The Technological Society*, Ellul says he has used an "objective" method and "deliberately not gone beyond description."[52] On another occasion he made this point even more strongly:

> I have always tried to prevent "my" theology from influencing my sociological research and my comprehension of the world from distorting my reading of the Bible. These were two domains, two distinct interests. Only after the separation, one begins to perceive relationship.[53]

Ellul's dialectical approach has been challenged, however, and there seems to be widespread agreement that his "descriptive" work only becomes fully intelligible when it is read with his Christian faith in mind.[54] Indeed, his ultimate intent was to discover the meaning of the gospel for present times, which first required him to determine the character of these times. It was this end that his social analysis served.

As we have already seen, for Ellul, modern life was characterized by the phenomenon of technique—by the application of rational methods of efficient action, "the one best means," to every field of human activity. The fundamental problem we face then is technological tyranny, and in Ellul's naming of the problem we can already see his solution: the opposite of tyranny is freedom. Not surprisingly then, Ellul has written that "freedom is the location and condition and arena of all Christian ethics" because what we have gained in Christ is freedom.[55] Ellul's theology is thus at its very core a theology of technology, as our freedom, our very salvation depends upon being able to overcome technology. This is what the gospel message means for us today. Given that technology, technological systems, and technological ways of thinking are viewed by Ellul as autonomous, skeptical readers are left to wonder how the gospel message can be good news if what it seeks to remedy, technology, is beyond human control. Isn't the outcome, tyranny, an inevitable state of affairs? Why does he describe his work as "a call to

---

52. Ellul, *Technological Society*, xxvii.

53. Ellul, *Sources and Trajectories*, 4.

54. See Terlizzese, *Hope in the Thought of Ellul*; Fasching, "Dialectic of Apocalypse and Utopia"; Clendenin, *Theological Method in Ellul*; Gill, *Word of God in the Ethics of Ellul*; and John Wilkenson's "Translator's Introduction," in Ellul, *Technological Society*.

55. Ellul, *Ethics of Freedom*, 7. Despite his emphasis on freedom and attraction to Marxism, Ellul was critical of liberation theologies that advocated violence in their pursuit of political revolution. See Ellul, *Jesus and Marx*, 46–52.

the sleeper to awake"?[56] It is here that Ellul's vision is nothing but bleak for those who do not assume his theological framework, because, as he says in an earlier work, true freedom does not result from material change.[57] "It is not a question of getting rid of [technology], but, by an act of freedom, of transcending it."[58] Ellul can have hope because technology is ultimately "illusionary"—the "true situation of the world" becomes apparent when we begin with "the spiritual plane."[59]

To recap then, two of the best known exemplars of a pessimistic view of technology have insisted that technological artifacts, systems, and ways of thinking continue to develop autonomously. And yet, although they lie beyond the reach of human control, or better, *because* they lie beyond the reach of human control, our fate rests in the hands of the divine. Both Ellul and Grant provide ample justification for theologians to pay close attention to the topic of technology. However, interestingly enough, even those who reject their analysis and rail against any hint of technological determinism end up providing further justification for this kind of attention.

Technology is a Social Construction: Lynn White Jr. and David F. Noble

As mentioned above, historians of technology tend to emphasize that technology develops through a process filled with contingency and choice, even as they agree that technology is not morally neutral. This becomes readily apparent when we study the inner workings of technologies and the groups of people who develop them, and has led some historians to insist that technology requires theological knowledge in order to be fully understood. For example, Lynn White Jr., one of the first historians of technology, attempted to demonstrate that the character of modern technology was established in medieval times, and that Western Christianity was a significant factor in this process.[60] Monastic movements, for example, elevated the role of work to that of a spiritual discipline and thus became the driving force behind technical innovation. Western Christianity also placed humans at the center of creation, and understood time as unidirectional rather than cyclical. Here we have the roots of the typical

---

56. Ellul, *Technological Society*, xxxiii.
57. See ch. 2 ("Revolutionary Christianity") in Ellul, *Presence of the Kingdom*.
58. Ellul, *Technological Society*, xxxiii.
59. Ellul, *Presence of the Kingdom*, 25.
60. White, *Medieval Religion and Technology*.

Western self-centered, time and labor conscious worldview, or, as White famously put it, the "roots of our ecological crisis."[61]

The more recent study by another prominent historian of technology, David Noble, confirms that the relationship between Christianity and technology still has contemporary relevance—that technological development has accelerated whenever it was invested with religious significance.[62] In the ninth century this happened when the classical Christian disdain for the useful arts was replaced by an association with the possibility for renewed perfection, for redemption from earthly struggles. In the twentieth century this happened when humans began to exercise God-like powers. While it is often masked by a secular vocabulary, Noble points out the religious underpinnings of high-profile technologies such as atomic weapons, space exploration, artificial intelligence, and genetic engineering. In between, he describes the religious faith and practice that was the inspiration for scientists and inventors such as Robert Boyle, Isaac Newton and Joseph Priestly. The unifying thread throughout this history is the identification of technology with transcendence, an identification that is characteristically Christian:

> Christianity alone blurred the distinction and bridged the divide between the human and the divine. Only here did salvation come to signify the restoration of [human]kind to its original God-likeness.[63]

This is an identification that Noble believes is problematic:

> On the deeper cultural level, these [twentieth-century] technologies have not met basic human needs because, at the bottom, they have never really been about meeting them. They have been aimed rather at the loftier goal of transcending such mortal concerns altogether. In such an ideological context, inspired more by prophets than by profits, the needs neither of mortals nor of the earth they inhabit are of any enduring consequence. And it is here that the religion of technology can rightly be considered a menace.[64]

---

61. White, "Historical Roots of Our Ecological Crisis." Originally written in 1966, this article has been published with various titles on nine separate occasions—obviously White's thesis struck a chord.

62. Noble, *Religion of Technology*. Arnold Pacey is another historian of technology who has sought to emphasize the way in which ideas more than economic and other social factors have provided the driving force for technological change. See *Culture of Technology*; *Technology in World Civilization*; and *Maze of Ingenuity*.

63. Noble, *Religion of Technology*, 10.

64. Ibid., 206–7.

Thus Noble also provides a succinct explanation for why technology is not morally neutral, although for him this is because of the way that technology embodies the ideals of its creators more than the way it shapes the ideals of its users. Despite his hostility toward Christianity, his thesis underscores the need for a background in theology in order to fully understand technology. Located as I am within the Christian tradition, I would go beyond Noble to argue that, in addition to explaining the past, a theological exploration can provide guidance for human interaction with technology in the future.

It also needs to be pointed out that White and Noble's interpretation of history is problematic.[65] For example, while the work of other historians such as George Ovitt provides support for the premise that the roots of modern technology lie deeper than the Enlightenment, it also confirms that there is little consensus among medieval historians of technology regarding the role of religion in the transformation of Western attitudes toward technology.[66] Ovitt, like Noble, examines familiar Christian figures from the twelfth through fourteenth centuries: Benedictines such as Theophilus (twelfth century), Augustinians such as Hugh of St. Victor (1096–1141), Cistercians such as Joachim of Fiore (1135–1201), and Franciscans such as Roger Bacon (1214–94). The texts he reviews contain such a diversity of perspectives that overall they appear rather ambiguous in their assessment of technology, and lead him to wonder whether Christianity is more properly "seen as having adjusted itself to a world being altered by technology rather than being the decisive force behind such alteration." At most it was only when coupled with "other economic and social factors" that the attitudes supplied by Christianity could have helped "create a receptivity to technological change."[67]

My own study of Thomas Aquinas (1225–74) confirms this ambiguous relationship between Christian theology and the rise of technology in medieval times. In contrast to the frequent references to Aquinas's teacher and fellow Dominican Albertus Magnus (1193–1280) in most medieval histories of technology, when the name of the most significant theologian of the era is mentioned at all, it is typically as a historical place-keeper. For

65. For a survey of criticisms of White's "The Historical Roots of Our Ecological Crisis," see Mitcham, "Questions of Christianity and Technology."

66. Ovitt, "Cultural Context of Western Technology." In addition to the work of Lynn White, Ovitt discusses Benz, *Evolution and Christian Hope*; and Le Goff, *Time, Work, and Culture in the Middle Ages*. Ovitt's article was subsequently expanded to a book-length treatment of the topic in *Restoration of Perfection*. Several other studies have further complexified the picture, including Gimpel, *Medieval Machine*; Gies and Gies, *Cathedral, Forge, and Waterwheel*; and Smith and Wolfe, *Technology and Resource Use in Medieval Europe*.

67. Ovitt, "Cultural Context of Western Technology," 500.

example, White refers to "the contemporaries of Saint Thomas Aquinas," and "the time of Saint Thomas Aquinas."[68] Although Aquinas did not discuss issues relevant to technology to the same extent as the figures mentioned above, several pathways in his work lead to an informed discussion of the topic—for example, his discussion of the material realm, the role of humanity within nature, manual labor, and the mechanical arts.[69] And the bottom line is that Aquinas's ambiguity on these topics means he had little to do with the larger cultural transformation of attitudes toward technology during medieval times.

Finally, although the theologian Susan White argues that "liturgy as a social institution has influenced the course of technology," her study of calendars and clocks, in addition to advances in navigation, the printing press, the assembly line, and the computer demonstrates that these technologies have also shaped the development of Christian worship.[70] Thus she argues that a background in the history of technology is required in order to fully understand the practices of the church. Furthermore, Susan White demonstrates that we cannot generalize the church's response to technology, but must examine technologies on a case by case basis; indeed, we need to be wary of making any kind of general claims about the way technology develops.

All this is *not* intended to argue that David Noble, Lynn White, and other historians are unhelpful when they seek to uncover the intellectual and social factors that have influenced the growing embrace of technology. Like Ellul and Grant, they end up drawing attention to the relationship between theological convictions and technology, even though they are coming from a very different starting place. However, this section will conclude with a discussion of two thinkers who, like Susan White, have attempted to steer a middle course between the extremes of technological determinism on the one hand and technology as a social construction on the other.

---

68. White, *Medieval Religion and Technology*, 54, 222.

69. Of course, pathways are required to explore this theme in the work of any medieval author because a term akin to "technology" was several centuries away from common usage. In addition, all of these pathways have been utilized by historians and philosophers of technology in their study of medieval texts—see Whitney, *Paradise Restored*. To my knowledge the only sustained discussion of Aquinas on the theme of technology that has been published is found in the work of Paul T. Durbin, a prominent American philosopher of technology. See "Thomism and Technology"; and "Aquinas, Art, and Technology." As a philosopher Durbin is primarily concerned with the contemporary application of Thomist thought, not its historical significance.

70. White, *Christian Worship and Technological Change*, 10.

Technology is Formative and Formable: Don Ihde and Albert Borgmann

One of the more succinct explanations of just what is going on inside the black boxes of modern technology is provided by Don Ihde, the author of a widely used introductory text on the philosophy of technology.[71] In the process of reinterpreting the relationship between science and technology, Ihde points to an "instrumental epistemology" in which technologies "form the conditions for and are the mediators of much, if not all current scientific knowledge."[72] As an instrument, technology must have some concrete, material component, but it must also be used in some way, and it is in its use that technology becomes more than just a tool, but a way of revealing, a way of seeing.[73] For example, the use of early optical technologies such as telescopes and microscopes revealed unexpected worlds both cosmic and microscopic. Furthermore, Ihde writes:

> For every enhancement of some feature, perhaps never before seen, there is also a reduction of other features. To magnify some observed object, optically, is to bring it forth from a background into a foreground and to make it present to the observer, but it is also to reduce the former field in which it fit.[74]

While modern science has accentuated this transformative power, its roots lie deep within human history. Ihde points to the way in which "deep technologies" such as writing, calendars, clocks, and maps are examples of technological ways of seeing that became culturally embedded and dramatically shaped the development of civilizations. He provides a helpful corrective to the tendency of historians to concentrate on the productive dimension of technologies and thus overlook the deeper cultural factors that form and come to be formed by these same technologies.[75]

Albert Borgmann, another leading contemporary philosopher of technology, shares the desire of Ihde to highlight the formative influence that technology has had on our existence while remaining optimistic that a

---

71. Ihde, *Philosophy of Technology*.

72. Thus in his view science owes more to technology than technology owes to science—see Ihde, *Instrumental Realism*, 45. John Dewey (1859–1952) is credited with making a similar point—see Hickman, *John Dewey's Pragmatic Technology*.

73. Ihde acknowledges the influence of Heidegger, who first highlighted this "anthropological" dimension of technology. See Heidegger, *Question Concerning Technology*, 5–12.

74. Ihde, *Philosophy of Technology*, 111.

75. Ibid., 55–60. Ihde develops this position more thoroughly in *Technology and the Lifeworld*.

significant influence can also be exerted in the opposite direction by both the users and creators of technology. Like Ellul and Grant, Borgmann is convinced that technology raises moral issues, and like David Noble and Lynn White he is convinced that the particulars of technology matter just as much if not more than the phenomenon of technology in general.

When Borgmann talks about technology he is referring to something akin to Ellul's *technique*, to a technological way of thinking. Technology is a pervasive metaphor more than it is tools or systems; it is a shorthand way of describing the pattern or paradigm that guides our approach to reality. Technology is "not just an ensemble of machines and procedures, but a type of culture."[76] However, this way of thinking or culture is more explicitly focused on and grounded in—if not dependent on—our instruments and procedures. Borgmann is not as concerned with developing a critique of modern culture as he is with solving problems; for him our tools and systems are not simply a symptom of an underlying problem as much as they are the very source of the problem.

In his classic book, *Technology and the Character of Contemporary Life*, Borgmann introduced the notion of the device paradigm as the characteristic feature of our technological way of thinking:

> It is the division between the commodity, e.g. music, and the machinery, e.g. the mechanical and electronic apparatus of a stereo set, that is the distinctive feature of a technological device.[77]

Put another way, the separation of means and ends that is so characteristic of modern life contrasts sharply with the traditional life of engagement. Listening to a recording of a concert on a stereo is a fundamentally different experience from listening to performers creating the same sounds using musical instruments, as is lighting a fire in a wood stove when compared with adjusting the thermostat of a gas furnace. As technology develops, devices have a tendency to become concealed, to shrink—both literally and metaphorically—encouraging our disengagement with the world. Indeed, according to Borgmann, any device that eludes common understanding is suggestive of modern technology. And as our lives are increasingly characterized by interaction with these devices, we are distanced more and more from the reality of the world. While we may not need to be concerned about the way a stereo converts the digital information stored on a compact disc into the sound of music, use of this device also means we no longer need to

---

76. Borgmann, *Power Failure*, 7.

77. Borgmann, *Technology and the Character of Contemporary Life*, 4. This concept continues to be utilized by many philosophers today—see the proceedings of a symposium on Borgmann's thought in Higgs, Light, and Strong, *Technology and the Good Life?*

be concerned about our relationship with the performers. Similarly, while we may not need to be concerned about the way a furnace responds to an adjustment of the thermostat by warming our house, use of this device also means we no longer need to be as concerned about the natural resources that are expended.

Once again, it is important to note that Borgmann attempts to break through the paralysis and despair created by critiques of technology, even as he agrees a critique of technology is needed.[78] Unlike Ellul and Grant, Borgmann's solution to our problems does not lie in reformulating the way we think, as if once we have the correct philosophy, understanding of time, or theological perspective, the way we relate to the world would be reformed or even revolutionized. Like Noble and White, he is inclined to say that focusing on ends instead of means is the problem, not the solution. Thus Borgmann urges us to pay more, not less attention to the means we use, and makes a convincing argument that, provided the correct means are chosen, i.e., "focal things and practices" instead of devices, we will become more engaged with the world.[79] This emphasis on means clearly lends itself to the discussion of particular, concrete practices, and thus has a built-in ethical thrust. Furthermore, in a number of essays Borgmann suggests that Christianity is "the most promising response to technology," even as he makes it clear that it is grace that enables us to recognize the problems of our technological society in the first place.[80] Perhaps not surprisingly then, Borgmann's work will play a role in subsequent chapters of this book.[81]

---

78. In the words of Andrew Feenberg, "technology is not a destiny but a scene of struggle" (*Critical Theory of Technology*, 14).

79. Examples of focal practices that Borgmann discusses include jogging and preparing meals together with family and friends; in other words, practices where means become ends themselves. See Borgmann, *Technology and the Character of Contemporary Life*, 196–209.

80. Borgmann, *Power Failure*, 8. Additional writings by Borgmann that pursue this theme include: "Christianity and the Cultural Center of Gravity"; "Prospects for the Theology of Technology"; "Liberty, Festivity, and Poverty"; "Everyday Fortitude"; "Contingency and Grace"; "Technology and Trust."

81. I am certainly not the first theologian to draw on Borgmann's work. Examples of recent theological interaction include Rasmussen, *Moral Fragments and Moral Community*; Gaillardetz, *Transforming Our Days*; Jacobsen, *Sidewalks in the Kingdom*; Dawn, *Unfettered Hope*; Waters, *From Human to Posthuman*; and Boers, *Living Into Focus*. Interestingly, Boers, Dawn, and Jacobsen all became acquainted with Borgmann's work at the "Missoula Consultation with Albert Borgmann and Eugene Peterson" in March, 2001. Other notable participants in that consultation included: David Wood (see "Interview with Albert Borgmann"), Kathleen Cahalan (see "Technology and Temperance"), and Rodney Clapp (who went on to publish Borgmann's work at Brazos Press).

IS THIS REALLY A THEOLOGICAL CONCERN?

By now it should be clear that a wide array of philosophers and historians of technology, despite significant disagreements in other areas, agree that technology is not morally neutral. Furthermore, it is primarily for this reason that many go on to discuss related theological issues. Indeed, the prominent role that theological issues play in the work of these thinkers makes the lack of sustained attention to the topic of technology on the part of theologians all the more striking.

This chapter will conclude with two extended illustrations. First, it will briefly review the way technology is portrayed in official Catholic teaching. This portrayal provides an illustration of the first and second points that have been made in this book: technological change has come to define progress, and recent attempts to grapple theologically with technology fall short. Regarding this latter point, not only does Catholic teaching fall short when it addresses technology in the realm of bioethics, but it falls short because it assumes that technology is morally neutral. This provides a poignant example of how theologians would benefit enormously by paying attention to recent philosophical and historical insights into technology. Second, this concluding section will review the way members of another religious tradition, the Amish, have become the poster children for alternative approaches to technology in contemporary North American society.[82] To be clear, my objective with this final illustration is not to put the Amish on a pedestal. Rather, it is to qualify the thesis of this chapter—that the morally-laden nature of technology demonstrates its theological significance—by acknowledging that there are also many thinkers who agree that technology is not morally neutral, yet disagree that this has any theological implica-

---

82. The Amish church tradition emerged in 1693 when the follows of Jacob Amman split from the Swiss Mennonite church over the practice of shunning (also known as excommunicating or banning) church members who had been disciplined. Amman viewed the demise of this practice as a sign that the Mennonites were drifting away from the central tenants of Anabaptist faith. Nonetheless, there continue to be many theological and personal connections between the Amish and Mennonite churches. There are over 1,600 local Amish church districts or congregations in 400 different settlements in the United States and Canada, which are loosely organized into more than two dozen affiliations. Thus it is difficult to speak of *the* Amish in a generalized way. However, the vast majority of these churches and affiliations (both "Old Order" and "New Order" Amish groups) share certain practices such as the use of a horse and buggy for local transportation, and reject the use of electricity from public utility lines, telephones, televisions, and computers in their homes (exceptions include the "Beachy" Amish and "Amish Mennonites"). Other widespread Amish distinctives include plain dress, beards for men, ending formal education at the eighth grade, meeting in homes for worship every other Sunday, and lay leadership. See Kraybill's *Riddle of Amish Culture*.

tions. In short, some of the biggest fans of the Amish, mistakenly, in my view, attempt to downplay the extent to which the theology of the Amish plays a necessary role in their approach to technology. They are mistaken because, as the Amish demonstrate, there are some insights into technology that would not be possible without a theological lens.

Official Catholic Teaching

One of the benefits of the Catholic church's embrace of its teaching office is that it provides a great deal of material for theologians (as well as the laity) to sift through on a myriad of topics. One place to get a glimpse into official Catholic teaching related to the topic of technology is to consult the index to the *Compendium of the Social Doctrine of the Church*, which references forty-five articles under the heading "Technology-Technical-Technique."[83] These articles draw upon several Papal encyclicals, letters and addresses, as well as Bishops' statements, documents published by Pontifical Councils, and the Catechism of the Catholic Church. Although technology is not treated in great depth, given that these articles are scattered throughout nine out of a total of twelve chapters, it is clearly considered relevant. Without claiming to adequately summarize or discern the official Catholic view of technology, the following paragraphs will point out several interesting and recurrent themes.

Technological Change Has Come to Define Progress

Many Catholic statements begin by situating the church in the world. Indeed, the first article in the *Compendium* builds upon Pope John Paul II's insistence that "Jesus came to bring integral salvation"[84] by suggesting that the salvation of Christ "permeates this world" in, among other things, our technology (§1). Article 6 in this opening chapter goes on to highlight the growing recognition of the need for "greater moral awareness that will guide [humanity in] its common journey." In fact, it is noted that this sense of shared destiny is "often conditioned and even imposed by technological

---

83. Pontifical Council for Justice and Peace, *Compendium of the Social Doctrine*, 432–33. The Compendium was "drawn up in order to give a concise but complete overview of the Church's social teaching" (ibid., xxi). All subsequent page references for this source will be noted in parentheses in the body of the text. Catholic social teaching is the one place where one might expect Catholic theology to be the most alert to the moral nature of technology, a point that Caldecott makes in "New Sins."

84. Pope John Paul II, *Redemptoris Missio*, 21.

and economic factors." It seems that the "integral and solidary humanism" longed for by Catholics is now within reach thanks to new technologies of communication and a global economy.

What is perhaps the most striking about the discussion of technology in the *Compendium* is the way in which technological change is framed by enthusiastic language even when there is some concern to acknowledge the pain it has caused. For example, in article 6 we read: "Marveling at the many innovations of technology, the men and women of our day strongly desire that progress be directed toward the true good of the humanity, both of today and tomorrow" (§2). Once again, it seems clear that progress is closely connected to, if not defined by innovations of technology. In the chapter on "The 'New Things' of the World of Work," we read that economic systems in more developed countries are in the midst of a transition from relying on industry to being "essentially built on services and technological innovations" (§136). This transition should be welcomed, for even though the workers in the industrial sector are losing ground, "the world of work is being enriched with new professions" that provide alternative employment prospects (§136). And even the chapter on "Safeguarding the Environment" is full of praise for the changes wrought by technology. Article 457 emphasizes that "the results of science and technology are, in themselves, positive":

> The Magisterium has repeatedly emphasized that the Catholic Church is in no way opposed to progress,[85] rather she considers "science and technology are a wonderful product of God-given human creativity, since they have provided us with wonderful possibilities, and we all gratefully benefit from them." (§199)[86]

In the words of the Second Vatican Council: "Although we must be careful to distinguish earthly progress clearly from the increase of the kingdom of Christ, such progress is of vital concern to the kingdom of God insofar as it can contribute to the better ordering of society."[87]

Recent Attempts to Grapple Theologically with Technology Fall Short

If technology in general is enthusiastically associated with progress in official Catholic teaching, this is even more the case when particular technologies such as the Internet are discussed. As the latest in a "line of media" that has

---

85. Pope John Paul II, Address given at Mercy Maternity Hospital, 13.

86. This article quotes Pope John Paul II in a meeting with scientists and representatives of the United Nations University in Hiroshima.

87. Second Vatican Ecumenical Council, *Gaudium et Spes*, 1057.

"progressively eliminated time and space as obstacles to communication," this "marvelous technological instrument" can clearly serve the cause of religion even if "the benefits have not been evenly shared up to now."[88] Perhaps since communication "is of the essence of the Church," the church "has taken a fundamentally positive approach to the media," seeing them as "gifts of God."[89] This providential view of new technological developments reflects the view that the church is "in the very midst of human progress," and reinforces or encourages a posture of openness and adaptation to these developments.[90] Thus it also suggests a rather superficial engagement of this technology—the point of reflecting theologically on the Internet is simply to uncover the way it fulfills God's plan and to make sure its benefits are shared by all.

Attempts to grapple theologically with technology in official Catholic teaching also appear to fall short because connections or distinctions are not clearly drawn between different technologies, a tendency that is shared with the field of bioethics. The most prominent example of this shortcoming is found in discussions of biotechnology. For example, article 477 in the *Compendium* chapter on "Safeguarding the Environment" insists that "scientists and technicians involved in the field of biotechnology are called to work intelligently and with perseverance in seeking the best solutions to the serious and urgent problems of food supply and health care" (208).[91] This endorsement of biotechnology in agriculture is clearly evident in the church's official embrace of genetically modified foods.[92] Yet article 235 in the chapter on "The Family, the Vital Cell of Society" also insists that "The rapid development of research and its technological application in the area of reproduction poses new and delicate questions that involve society and the norms that regulate human social life" (106). Article 236 makes it clear that applying the techniques of genetic manipulation to *human* cells through, for example, cloning, is strictly forbidden because it threatens longstanding

---

88. Pontifical Council for Social Communications, "Working for Solidarity in a Cyberspace World."

89. Pontifical Council for Social Communications, "The Church and the Internet." In the words of Pope John Paul II: "The rapid development of technology in the area of the media is surely one of the signs of progress in today's society." See "Do Not Be Afraid," 184.

90. Pope John Paul II, "The Church Must Learn to Cope."

91. This article draws upon Pope John Paul II's addresses to the National Academy of Sciences on September 21, 1982, and to the Pontifical Academy of the Sciences on October 23, 1982.

92. Pontifical Council for Justice and Peace, Study Seminar: "GMOs: Threat or Hope?" Prior to 2003 there were a variety of perspectives on genetically modified foods within the Catholic church—see, for example, the statement from the Catholic Bishops of South Africa: "Genetically Modified Food: The Impending Disaster."

church teaching related to reproduction. Drawing sharp lines in the sand can seem rather arbitrary when the very same, or at least analogous technologies have already been blessed by the church for use in other realms.

In short, technology is of theological concern in official Catholic teaching because of the ends it is applied to, or the extent to which all have access to its benefits. The ethical evaluation of particular technologies is based on important principles—a concern for the dignity of the human person, and the common good—yet it is too narrowly focused on the realm of choice and application. That technology is put to proper use and leads to the greater good, rather than being put to improper use and leading to harm, is simply a matter of making the right decisions about how it is used.[93]

Technology is Morally Neutral?

The embrace of technological change, and the rather thin theological engagement of technology in official Catholic teaching reflects the problematic assumption that technology itself is morally neutral. As has become clear in the brief survey above, throughout the *Compendium*, technology is talked about in instrumental terms. This pattern continues even when an attempt is made to reign in enthusiasm for technology. For example, article 283 in the chapter on "Human Work," offers the reminder that:

---

93. Moral theologian Mark Graham provides further support for this observation in an unpublished paper: "Catholic Moral Theology, Technology, and the Ethic of Use." Graham argues that discussions about technology in the Catholic tradition tend to get derailed quickly because of the dependence on a form of moral evaluation commonly called "Catholic Act Analysis." When this approach has been applied to technology in recent decades, it has led to what Graham calls an "ethic of use." He writes:

> Any particular technology can usually be used in many different ways, and the specific way in which it is actually used is subject to a moral judgment. So, for instance, personal computers can be used to email, write letters, create spreadsheets and graphs, surf the world wide web, post reading assignments for students, download music, or many other things. According to the Catholic ethic of use, none of these activities carries any inherent moral meaning, so that it would be possible to label them as either right or wrong; they only become subject to moral evaluation when contextual information about specific activities is supplied (ibid., 2).

Graham's concern is that "as an evaluative tool . . . the Catholic ethic of use typically leads moral reflection down a road so narrow and restrictive that it barely scratches the surface of the manifold moral issues involved with technology." By making discrete, individual uses of specific technologies the focus of moral evaluation, we tend to "tether moral analyses to the here-and-now, to the immediate contextual circumstances surrounding the act that render it intelligible" (ibid., 2–3).

> The new discoveries and technologies, thanks to their enormous potential, can make a decisive contribution to the promotion of social progress; but if they remain concentrated in the wealthier countries or in the hands of a small number of powerful groups, they risk becoming sources of unemployment and increasing the gap between developed and underdeveloped areas (125).[94]

Similar cautionary notes can be found in articles 290 and 322 in the same chapter, and in articles 365 and 376 in the chapter on "Economic Life." In each of these cases, however, problems are caused by economic or political factors rather than the technologies themselves.[95] There is no mention of the possibility that some modern technologies might be more (or less) likely to be concentrated in the hands of the powerful given the nature of the systems they depend upon, or the ways of thinking that led to their existence in the first place. Another example is found in the discussion of communications technologies in article 416 in the chapter on "The Political Community":

> Moral values and principles apply also to the media. "The ethical dimension relates not just to the content of communication (the message) and the process of communication (how the communicating is done) but to fundamental structural and systemic issues, often involving large questions of policy bearing upon the distribution of sophisticated technology and product (who shall be information rich and who shall be information poor?)."[96]

Once again, there is a clear concern to point out that technology is of moral concern, although the structural and systemic issues pointed to are political and economic rather than technological.

To be sure, there are other occasions not cited in the *Compendium* where an effort is made to avoid reducing the impact of technology to politics or economics. For example, one lengthy statement on the Catholic view of the Internet opens with the following reminder:

> Today's revolution in social communications involves a fundamental reshaping of the elements by which people comprehend the world about them, and verify and express what they comprehend. The constant availability of images and ideas, and their

94. This article draws upon article 32 of Pope John Paul II's *Centesimus Annus*.

95. Perhaps the difficulty of viewing technology in more systematic or structural terms should not be surprising given that structural evil is downplayed in much of Catholic thought—see Baum, "Structures of Sin."

96. This article quotes the Pontifical Council for Social Communications in "Ethics in the Media of Social Communications," 347.

rapid transmission even from continent to continent, have profound consequences, both positive and negative, for the psychological, moral and social development of persons, the structure and functioning of societies, intercultural communications, and the perception and transmission of values, world views, ideologies, and religious beliefs.[97]

This statement goes on to talk about the "cultural dimensions" of the "digital divide," noting that "the new information technology and the Internet transmit and help instill a set of cultural values—ways of thinking about social relationships, family, religion, the human condition—whose novelty and glamor can challenge and overwhelm traditional cultures."[98] The authors of this statement even point out that "the technological configuration underlying the Internet has a considerable bearing on its ethical aspects."[99] It seems, however, that this statement is the exception that proves the rule.

The presumed neutrality of technology becomes most clear in the chapter on "Safeguarding the Environment." Article 458 states that technology "could be a priceless tool in solving many serious problems," before going on to note the importance of repeating "the concept of 'proper application,' for 'we know that this potential is not neutral: it can be used either for [our] progress or for [our] degradation'" (200).[100] Article 465 adds: "Technology that pollutes can also cleanse, production that amasses can also distribute justly" (203).[101]

To be clear, the intent of this overview is not to argue that the Roman Catholic tradition is worse than others—I certainly could have highlighted examples of this kind of thinking in other Christian traditions as well. Furthermore, I am more confident than David Noble that theological resources can be found within the Catholic tradition that will enable Christians to engage technology in a more discerning way. In my view, half of the problem is simply helping theologians see that there is a problem.

---

97. Pontifical Council for Social Communications, "Ethics in Internet," 4. This paragraph was first used in *Aetatis Novae*.

98. Pontifical Council for Social Communications, "Ethics in Internet," 6.

99. Ibid., 5.

100. This article draws upon Pope John Paul II's meeting with scientists and representatives of the United Nations University, Hiroshima in 1981, and his address to the National Academy of Sciences in 1982.

101. This article draws upon Pope John Paul II's address to participants in a convention on "The Environment and Health."

The Amish

This final section will take a closer look at the way the Amish have been raised up by proponents of alternative approaches to technology. It is striking that so many of their fans stress the moral significance of technology while downplaying the role that religious faith and commitment plays in the way the Amish interact with technology.[102] This is just the opposite of what we have seen to be the pattern of official Catholic teaching, which seeks to elevate the role that religious faith and commitment plays in the application of technology, while ignoring the moral significance of technology itself.

The Amish as Luddites

Before getting into the ways the Old Order Amish have been positively appropriated, a few words need to be said about how they have been used as a negative example or foil. Although the Amish are reduced to a caricature by both friend and foe alike, it seems that promoters of technological change cannot resist the urge to invoke the name of the Amish as shorthand for people who reject all technology out of hand. It seems as though the name "Amish" has become synonymous with "modern-day Luddite" in contemporary discourse.[103] Although a case can be made that the Luddites have been given a bad rap by those of us who are ignorant of nineteenth-century British history,[104] when the Amish are used in a similar way the implication

---

102. In what follows I am not writing about the Amish *per se*, but about the appropriation of the Amish by those in their surrounding culture. Thus the Amish are secondary characters, mediated by my primary characters: those who make reference to the Amish in their reflections on the topic of technology. The closest parallel to this kind of treatment is Weaver-Zercher's *Amish in the American Imagination*, although his primary characters are those who write novels, make films, and build tourist enterprises featuring Amish people and their practices. Using Weaver-Zercher's words, I am "transforming those who have made Amish people their subjects into subjects themselves" (ibid., xii).

103. In one informal study, 4 percent of Internet user queries related to the Amish over a one week period included the term "Luddite." This compares quite respectably to the 13 percent share for "furniture" and 9 percent share for "quilts." It is also noteworthy that the Amish are the subject of "more searches than many other religions, including the Methodists, Episcopalians, Lutherans, and Christian Scientists" (Holznagel, "Of Horses, Buggies, and the Web").

104. The original Luddites were inspired by a late eighteenth or early nineteenth-century figure named Ned Ludd, who is thought to have destroyed textile machines that were threatening the livelihood of skilled knitters in England. The movement spread rapidly, and many wool and cotton mills were destroyed until the government harshly suppressed them—"machine breaking" or industrial sabotage was made a capital crime, and 17 men were executed after a trial in York in 1813.

As David F. Noble has pointed out in *Progress Without People*, the Luddites were not

is that they are extreme, that they are confused, and that they are irrelevant. Not only are they out of step with reality, but they too will one day be consigned to the dust-bin of history. The Luddites or Amish are also frequently invoked when people feel compelled to qualify critical comments they have made about a particular technology—it seems as though these comments are lent credence when it is clear that they do not come laden with an excessive agenda. Indeed, some people find the Amish even more useful for these purposes than the Luddites. For example, in his online column for *Wired* magazine—a flashy periodical with its finger on the pulse of current and future trends in technology—Tony Long insists "I am not, strictly speaking, anti-technology. I just don't treat it like a freaking religion." He goes on to add: "I'm a Luddite who nevertheless uses technology (I mean, I'm not Amish, for crying out loud)."[105]

The Amish as Technological Saints

In any case, it is more common to see the Amish portrayed as modern-day saints in literature on technology, and Amish enthusiasts can be found in the most unlikely places. One of these places is in the pages of *Wired* magazine. Unlike his anti-Amish colleague Tony Long, *Wired* contributor Howard Rheingold has gone to great length to point out that the Amish approach to technology is actually quite reasonable. Rheingold respects the fact that the Amish "have long been engaged in a productive debate about the consequences of technology."[106] He goes on to explain the "elaborate system by which [the Amish] evaluate the tools they use," pointing out that

---

opposed to technological progress, since this was an alien ideal that was invented after them (perhaps even to prevent their recurrence). Indeed, they "were not against technology *per se* but rather against the social changes that the new technology reflected and reinforced . . . Machine breakers were not concerned with technical progress in the abstract" (ibid., 4–5). If Noble's view is correct, then it may be quite appropriate to see parallels between the Amish and Luddites. He also helps to explain why a pejorative view of both groups persists: "the idea of machine breaking became more threatening to the ideological edifice than the fact of machine breaking" (ibid., 16).

Although the Amish do not claim any inspiration from the Luddites, others have sought to appropriate insights from this movement for their own initiatives for social change. This includes Mahatma Ghandi and the Indian independence movement in the first half of the twentieth century, as well as contemporary environmentalists—see "Historical Frames of Abstinence," chapter 2 in Mullaney, *Everyone is NOT Doing It*; and "Gandhi Meets the Luddites," chapter 1 in Scarce, *Eco-Warriors*.

105. Long, "Dark Underbelly of Technology."
106. Rheingold, "Look Who's Talking," 128.

"new things are not outright forbidden, nor is there a rush to judgment."[107] Instead of "precise philosophical yardsticks" there is "deliberation," "struggle," and a "long conversation with their tools."[108] Rheingold also affirms the motivation of the Amish for their decidedly rational discernment process—he shares their concern for the way the use of particular technologies comes to shape people,[109] and their suspicion that "you can't design foolproof machines, because fools are so clever."[110] And although he stops short of endorsing the conclusions reached by the Amish, Rheingold hopes to prompt similar conversations about technology, something that both enthusiasts and critics agree is "the most important influence on our lives today."[111]

Another place where it is surprising to find the Amish talked about in positive ways is in the pages of the *MIT Technology Review*, a magazine established in 1899 that, to quote from its web site, is "committed to the belief that technology changes the world; that it's a powerful force for good in humanity; that if we talk about it, it matters."[112] Authors of several articles in past years have pointed out that what appear to be contradictions in the way the Amish use technology actually reflects a sophisticated strategy. One contributor to *Technology Review* who has gone beyond speculating about the lessons the Amish have to teach the rest of society is Eric Brende, a graduate of MIT who spent over a year living in an Old Older community, experiencing their lifestyle first-hand. Brende quickly discovered that "the Amish turn out to be surprisingly enlightened, at least with regard to the material conditions of their life." He writes that "next to them I feel sheltered from the world around me."[113] For Brende, the Amish are far more sophisticated and strategic in their approach to technology than anyone else he has met—they "consciously steer their cultural course in the sea of alternatives opened up by technological advance, accepting only those that enhance their way of life." He goes on to point out that "unlike mainstream technologists, who never test the social impact of their products but unscientifically

---

107. Ibid., 131.

108. Ibid., 162. This echoes the words of Paul Levinson in an earlier *Wired* article: "The Amish have not so much said no to high-tech as developed an ingenious strategy for getting the most out of it." They "struggle with the appeal of technologies . . . agonizing over . . . real and projected social consequences." Thus they "come the closest I have seen to a living embodiment of a philosophy for technology" ("The Amish Get Wired," 124).

109. Rheingold, "Look Who's Talking," 129.

110. Ibid., 160.

111. Ibid., 162.

112. http://www.technologyreview.com/about/.

113. Brende, "Technology Amish Style," 28. Brende provides a much more substantial discussion of his experience in his book *Better Off*.

presume a beneficial effect, the Amish often adopt new technologies only after a trial period in which they assess the effects."[114] The larger point to note is Brende not only portrays the Amish as reasonable and sophisticated, but as relevant for those outside their communities.

The Amish as Followers of Christ?

To what extent then do admirers of the Amish recognize the necessary role that theological convictions play in the Amish engagement of technology? At first glance, it would appear that the theological nature of this witness is abundantly clear. The Amish are clearly identified as a Christian community or sect, and many discussions of the Amish in the literature even include a brief introduction to their origins in the sixteenth-century Anabaptist movement.[115] Indeed, their unique approach to technology may be the reason why the Amish are discussed in the first place, but at times this results in a discussion of some of the unique dimensions of their faith tradition.[116] Moreover, the religious faith of the Amish is also noteworthy due to the central role it plays in the life of the community. As the political scientist Richard Sclove puts it, every dimension of household, farm, and community life is "subordinate, in turn, to an overarching religious purpose."[117] Or, as another admirer said, "the Amish don't have a Sunday only religion but try to closely follow and live by the Scriptures in everything they do."[118] Clearly then, religious faith must play a central role in the Amish engagement of technology, and this is a common explanation for why their approach is properly viewed as considered and complex rather than crazy and confused. It is much more than an authoritarian decree or a knee-jerk reaction.

A few authors not only highlight the centrality of religious faith and practice for the Amish, but they imply that if this theological perspective is jettisoned then so too is the ability to engage technology as the Amish do. For example, the farmer and writer Wendell Berry is convinced that "technology joins us to energy, to life . . . By it we enact our religion, or our lack of

---

114. Brende, "Technology Amish Style," 28.

115. See, for example, Rheingold, "Look Who's Talking."

116. Although adult or believer's baptism is now commonplace in North American, and the separation of church and state is taken for granted, the practices of excommunication and mutual aid, along with the refusal to bear arms and swear oaths remain novelties that are sometimes noted.

117. Sclove, *Democracy and Technology*, 95.

118. Stone, "Amish Answer," 2.

it."¹¹⁹ Unlike the admirers of the Amish discussed above, Berry makes more than a passing reference to the Amish emphasis on *Gelassenheit*, or yieldedness.¹²⁰ It may seem obvious that there are strong connections between the Amish posture of yielding themselves to higher authority—to God's will and to the will of the community—and their theological or doctrinal distinctives such as nonresistance and the ban. And yet Berry helpfully highlights the connection with more practical distinctives, including the profoundly counter-cultural implications of this posture for technology. Berry writes that the Amish "have mastered one of the fundamental paradoxes of our condition: we can make ourselves whole only by accepting our partiality, by living within our limits, by being human—not by trying to be gods. By restraint they make themselves whole."¹²¹ The very thing that enables Amish communities to make different choices—or even to make choices at all—when it comes to technology, strikes those of us living in an individualistic and consumeristic society as rather strange.

In contrast to Berry, however, most of the authors encountered prefer to stress the possibility of engaging technology as the Amish do while leaving their religious baggage behind. Most are confident that little—or at least little that is of use in engaging technology—will be lost by losing the religious faith of the Amish. Rather than *Gelassenheit*, in this case the key distinctive that is highlighted as making the Amish approach to technology work is *Ordnung*—the largely unwritten rules that order or regulate the life of the community. The goal of the *Ordnung* is to preserve the Amish community, and a crucial element in this is the maintenance of a strict barrier between the Amish and non-Amish.¹²² Thus most admirers emphasize

---

119. Berry, *Unsettling of America*, 82.

120. In the words of Donald B. Kraybill, the authority cited on this concept by virtually every author mentioned above, "The culture of Older Order groups rests on the bedrock of *Gelassenheit*—a German word that roughly means yielding and surrendering to a higher authority. However *Gelassenheit* is layered with many meanings—self-surrender and self denial, resignation to God's will, yielding to others, gentleness, a calm and contented spirit, and a quiet acceptance of whatever comes . . . It reflects the most fundamental difference between Old Order culture and modern values." See "Plain Reservations," 102.

121. Berry, *Unsettling of America*, 95.

122. As Kraybill writes: "Old Order groups are what sociologists sometimes call sectarian groups because they draw sharp lines of separation between themselves and the larger society. Mainstream cultural values are viewed as a threat to their religious faith and practice. Separation from the world is based on biblical phrases such as 'Be not conformed to the world' [Romans 12:2], 'Love not the world or the things of the world' [1 John 2:15], 'Come out from among them and be ye separate saith the Lord' [2 Corinthians 6:17], and 'Be not unequally yoked together with unbelievers' [2 Corinthians 6:14]" ("Plain Reservations," 101).

that Amish decisions around technology are really more about culture than religious faith. Eric Brende is perhaps the most notable in this regard. He writes: "while religion is inextricably interwoven with Amish practice for the Amish themselves, for the rest of us such issues can be kept more distinct." This perspective led Brende to several attempts at initiating communities that, although "chary of religious codes" or "less enmeshed with dogma," sought to make similar technological choices as the Amish. In fact, while Brende insists that he has not "disavowed religion," he also insists that he does "not wish to make religious belief the basis of technological norms."[123] Despite failures along the way,[124] he continues to try to "enshrine" Old Order principles rather than the Old Order community itself. In particular, this means insisting that "it is better to find a non-technological solution than a technological one, or failing that, a less technological solution than a more technological one," a principle Brende calls "minimization."[125] His underlying assumption is that "a principle is not the prisoner of the particular. It is transportable."[126]

Perhaps Brende and many others like him are correct. Perhaps the wisdom of the Amish will someday be replicated in nonreligious yet technologically sophisticated communities. Perhaps intentional communities of discernment will begin to not only sustain themselves past a single generation, but grow beyond expectation. On the other hand, the fact that this has yet to happen should cause Brende and many others like him to reconsider their

123. Brende, "Technology Amish Style," 33. Brende does "appreciate the need such measures [i.e., religious codes] address: that of conscious boundary setting, backed by some kind of clout . . . For our part, we are trying to translate the Amish religious codes into deed restrictions, aiming for a kind of low-technology zoning . . . In other words, we hope for the best of both worlds: a reliable structure for neighborly solidarity without the pincers of theological sanction" (ibid., 33). Brende also recognizes that for Old Order groups it is "only by first yielding power to one another and to what they regarded as the spirit of their unity, a spirit from above" that "members wield it over machines." And he demonstrates a grudging admiration for this spirituality: "Here were members of an obscure sect in a prayerful meeting—rationally evaluating the implications of a technology that the rest of us accept on faith" (*Better Off*, 132, 134).

124. Brende notes that he subsequently "learned that in its early stages, a fledgling community is very fragile and requires the right blend of many ingredients, including personal outlooks. It presumes a certain level of psychological stability. If any ingredient is missing, the whole thing can quickly cave in—and thus, like a failed soufflé, did this one" (*Better Off*, 220).

125. Ibid., 229.

126. Ibid., 135. The theologian George De Vries makes a similarly idealistic argument about the transportability of insights from the Amish: "The model of the Amish community is not one that the larger society can hope to imitate; but the Amish culture can be studies with interest for certain principles, views, and practices which may well have a broader application" ("Lessons From an Alternative Culture," 219).

appropriation of the Amish. It seems to me that something crucial—something irreplaceable—is missing when admirers of the Amish seek to filter out their theology while promoting, adopting, or translating their technological practices.[127] As will become clear in the coming chapters, I disagree with the assumption that principles can be de-particularized or disembodied, and thus be transported or generalized in a straightforward fashion.

CONCLUSION

This chapter has surveyed a diversity of disciplinary perspectives in order to establish the viability—if not the urgency—of a sustained theological exploration of the topic of technology. The bottom line is that philosophers, historians, and social critics have argued persuasively that technological artifacts, systems, and ways of thinking are not morally neutral, but rather that they embody and encourage particular moral vision. Technologies not only reflect a particular way of viewing the world, but they train us to see the world in particular ways. However, the point of this book is not simply that a philosophical or historical or sociological examination of technology raises theological issues that theologians need to respond to, but that a theological consideration of technology provides us with insights into technology that would not be otherwise possible. Thus the focus in subsequent chapters will be more explicitly theological.

---

127. Perhaps the Amish should also bear some of the burden for this disconnect. I do agree with Donald Kraybill and Marc Olshan when they insist that "a pluralist society on the brink of the twenty-first century cannot call on a small group of Christian fundamentalists to provide moral leadership. The value of the Amish lies instead in their struggle to define for themselves the shape of their lives" (*Amish Struggle With Modernity*, 236). However, the Amish do clearly recognize that their struggle is now taking place before a watching—and interested—world.

2

Using the Work of John Howard Yoder as a Resource for Engaging Technology

THE PREVIOUS CHAPTER ATTEMPTED to build a case for the theological significance of technology. It also suggested that, even though there are shortcomings with some of the more obvious pathways to addressing this topic, there *are* resources available in the Christian tradition that make theological reflection on technology possible. Certainly the way in which official Catholic teaching often seems to assume that technology is morally neutral is cause for concern, as are attempts to appropriate an Amish approach to technology while jettisoning the theological roots of this approach. Nonetheless, the rest of this book will be utilizing the work of one theologian in order to propose one possible way to engage technology theologically. Since this amounts to a constructive proposal more than a restatement of a clearly articulated theology of technology, I intend to not only focus attention on the work of this one theologian, but to spark attempts to appropriate insights from other thinkers and traditions.

The thesis of this chapter is that John Howard Yoder (1927–1997), one of the most prominent Mennonite theologians of the twentieth century, provides significant theological resources for grappling with technology. In building the case for this argument, I hope to answer the question: granted that we need to think theologically about technology, why should we utilize Yoder? This is an understandable question, for while Yoder made a wide variety of contributions to fields ranging from peace studies to church history, missiology, biblical theology, and Christian ethics, he did not publish an essay much less a monograph devoted to the topic of technology. At times he did make passing comments on the theme of progress in his writing,[1] and on occasion he did make conference presentations that touched on issues in religion and science[2] and bioethics,[3] but he did not reflect explicitly on the moral implications of technology.[4] Nonetheless, by the end of this chapter it should be clear that much of what Yoder wrote has significant technological implications. Indeed, subsequent chapters will draw upon the resources Yoder offers for engaging technology, and will also make it clear that this application of his thought to this realm has ramifications for how we understand his work.

Having said this, hints of the relevance of Yoder for the topic of technology are not hard to find. Most obviously, he was a Mennonite, and for many people, the name "Mennonite" is synonymous with "Old Order Mennonite" or "Amish." It connotes a group of people who maintain a unique religiosity and lifestyle, most notable for their plain dress and rejection of modern conveniences; at the very least, it might bring to mind a postcard image of a horse and buggy. Thus, even though many who are familiar with Yoder's work are also aware that Yoder was a different kind of Mennonite—that he, like most Mennonites in North America, could not be distinguished from mainstream society merely on the basis of the technologies he utilized—they might wonder at the reasons for these divergent paths in the Anabaptist-Mennonite tradition. They might think it somewhat ironic, in fact, that so-called "modern" Mennonite theological and ethical reflections have not directly addressed the topic of technology.[5]

---

1. For example: "In an age marked by the idea of progress as both fact of history and transcendent validation, it has become easy to juxtapose hope for the cumulative results of human achievement with hope in Yahweh" (Yoder, "Discerning the Kingdom of God," 366). Or: "Historically, collapse, catastrophe, and decay are as important as progress" (Yoder, "Theological Revision," 74).

2. Yoder, "On Generating Alternative Paradigms."

3. Yoder, "From Basic Orientation to Concrete Discernment."

4. It could be argued that one exception is when Yoder challenged the assumptions of the nuclear pacifist movement, suggesting that it is problematic for the church to revise its stance toward war based on developments in military technology: "We should . . . ask about the 'technological turn' the conversation [about war] has taken. Now that bishops are taking testimony from arms experts and diplomats, what authority have the informed technical judgments to which they come with regard to the likelihood of escalation, the possibility of 'prevailing' in a nuclear war, or the other technical data (including politics as a kind of technique) which the experts they consulted told them should be decisive? Can moral theology say anything while the experts differ?" (Yoder, "Armaments and Eschatology," 44). See also "Nuclear Arms in Christian Pacifist Perspective."

5. The word "technology" is sprinkled throughout a number of essays by the Canadian Mennonite theologian A. James Reimer as a result of his interaction with philosophers such as Hans Jonas and George Grant. Like Grant, however, for Reimer the topic of

Although the abundance of secondary literature that engages Yoder's work tends to focus on his primary interests, another clue to the relevance of Yoder for the topic of technology can be found in an article on bioethics and the church by the Canadian Mennonite theologian Chris K. Huebner.[6] Like Gerald McKenny, Huebner attempts to "draw attention to the fact that technology is central to contemporary bioethics" and suggests "that we need a better appreciation of the way our many technological investments in medicine imply deeply held moral convictions that often go unrecognized."[7] These convictions include the importance of mastery, possession, and control in order to escape from luck, finitude, and vulnerability, and serve to highlight once again that technology is not a morally neutral tool. Although Huebner does not cite Yoder in this article, he is one of the most prominent of several scholars who see themselves as advancing Yoder's project. Indeed, he is relying on Yoderian categories when he talks about the basic moral thrust of technology.[8]

The sections of this chapter that follow will move beyond hints to directly engage Yoder's work. After noting some of the challenges involved in reading Yoder, I will first address the common charge that Yoder was sectarian. Many people assume that, as evident in Old Order Mennonite and Amish communities, those concerned with separating themselves from society would have little to say that is helpful to those beyond their communities about politics, economics, or (especially) technology. Far from being sectarian, Yoder exemplified what I have termed the "conscientious engagement" of issues at the fore of his cultural context. Another common charge against Yoder that might lead some to wonder how much of a *theological* resource he could provide for any topic is that he reduced theology to ethics. Thus the next section will summarize Yoder's understanding of the relationship between theology and ethics, arguing that his discussion of Christian practices is a worthy theological contribution. Indeed, a Yoderian approach to technology, like a Yoderian approach to politics, peace,

---

technology is only raised as a symptom of an underlying intellectual problem. See Reimer, "Theological Method, Modernity, and the Role of Tradition," and "Transcendence, Social Justice, and Pluralism: Three Competing Agendas in Contemporary Theology," chapters 1 and 4 in *Mennonites and Classical Theology*. The approach of another Mennonite theologian, Gordon D. Kaufman, is clearly motivated by his concern over the human capacity to destroy life on earth, a capacity made possible by recent weapons technology and widespread industrialization. For Kaufman the solution to this problem is found in the radical reconstruction of our understanding of God in light of our contemporary situation. See Kaufman, *Theology for a Nuclear Age*; and *In Face of Mystery*.

6. See Huebner, "Bioethics and the Church."

7. Ibid., 74.

8. See also Huebner, *Precarious Peace*.

or mission is given its fundamental shape by his ecclesiology. After moving past these roadblocks, the final section of the chapter will follow up on the most obvious connection with technology that can be found in Yoder's work—his references to Jacques Ellul. As with Ellul, it will become clear that Yoder's discussion of the biblical concept of the principalities and powers can be fruitfully applied to technology.

PREAMBLE: NOTES ON READING YODER[9]

Many have pointed out the fundamental coherence of Yoder's work.[10] This coherence is made all the more impressive by the fact that Yoder conversed with historians, church leaders in his own denomination and beyond, biblical scholars, missiologists, ethicists, and systematic theologians. One would suspect that someone whose thinking was so rigorous and consistent would have attempted a more systematic project, but Yoder repeatedly disavowed "starting from scratch." He concluded his only book dedicated to formal theology, *Preface to Theology*, with an explanation of why he avoided the issues normally dealt with in the prolegomena of systematic theologies: "we do not begin with the fiction of starting from scratch with a blank mind that needs to be convinced. There are no blank minds."[11] And he introduced his last collection of essays with a similar comment: "One reason I do not start from scratch to do a book on just one subject is that there is no scratch from which to start. Every theme is already awash in debate."[12] Yoder rejected the foundationalist assumptions so common in modern scholarship—that all knowledge should be built upon universally accepted categories such

---

9. A much more substantial preamble on reading Yoder would be required to do justice to the complexities of not only his scholarly but his personal legacy. Indeed, new insights into Yoder's abusive behaviour toward women and the ensuing church discipline process that concluded shortly before his death may end up recasting my discussion of Yoder and the practices of the church in important ways. As this book went to press, a discernment group has been established by Mennonite Church USA and the Anabaptist Mennonite Biblical Seminary in order to work toward the restoration of those directly harmed by Yoder, and the prevention of similar kinds of abuse in the future. For more background, see: http://www.ambs.edu/about/documents/AMBS-statement-on-JHY.pdf.

10. For example, Reimer, "Mennonites, Christ, and Culture." My summary of Yoder in this section resonates with Harry Huebner's extended treatment in "The Christian Life as Gift and Patience." For a guide to Yoder's published and unpublished work, see Nation, "A Comprehensive Bibliography"; and "Supplement to 'A Comprehensive Bibliography.'"

11. Yoder, *Preface to Theology*, 401.

12. Yoder, *For the Nations*, 10. This was the last collection of essays that were published prior to Yoder's death—he died unexpectedly on December 30, 1997, the day after his 70th birthday.

as reason or experience; instead, he argued there was no neutral or non-particular place from which to begin.

Yet to characterize Yoder as "anti-foundationalist" would be misleading. While there are resonances between things he said and anti-foundationalist movements such as narrative theology, postliberal theology, and other currents in postmodern theology, he refused to embrace any of these labels. He was skeptical not just of foundationalist methodology, but of what he called "methodologism"—of all attempts to uncover the "first principles" that supposedly lie "before" or "beneath" a discussion:

> The worst form of idolatry is not carving an image; it is the presumption that one has—or that a society has, or a culture has—the right to set the terms under which God can be recognized.[13]

Yoder's writing was clearly consistent with his attitude toward methodology. Rather than constructing a timeless systematic theology, he assembled (or allowed others to assemble) anthologies—collections of essays organized around particular themes.[14] For Yoder, like his sixteenth-century Anabaptist forebears, system building was "a rare privilege." He argued that a theologian "is always 'on the way' because his or her first duty is always to a present crisis of disobedience or opportunity."[15] Thus Yoder wrote essays when he was asked to respond to or clarify a particular issue in a particular context—he once told a colleague that he "was lost without an assignment."[16] Furthermore, he was certain that whatever overall coherence there was to be found in his work had less to do with his own intellectual might than to the working of God's spirit through the various communities that had commissioned it.[17]

---

13. Yoder, "Walk and Word," 77. In a note Yoder cautioned that "to make rejecting foundationalism a *basic* defining statement is itself a foundationalist move" (ibid., 313n6).

14. Gerald Schlabach has highlighted this point in "Anthology in Lieu of System."

Since Yoder's death the publication of his essays has continued. These include: collections that he had already begun to give shape to—see *To Hear the Word* and *Jewish-Christian Schism Revisited*; lecture notes that had already been circulated in photocopied form—see *Preface to Theology*, *Christian Attitudes to War, Peace, and Revolution*, and *Revolutionary Christianity*; and collections of previously published essays arranged thematically by editors—for instance, see *War of the Lamb*, *Nonviolence: A Brief History*, and *End of Sacrifice*.

15. Yoder, "Why Ecclesiology is Social Ethics," 121.

16. Hauerwas and Huebner, "History, Theory, and Anabaptism," 404.

17. Whatever Yoder might have said about methodologism, even he did not dispute the virtue of being methodical in exploring the topic under consideration. Indeed, his logical rigor was widely regarded, and he had no time for other critics of system-building such as deconstructivists. See Yoder, "Can One Be Methodical without Methodologism?"

Yoder's essays, pamphlets, and unpublished memos provide a variety of examples of how his theological "stance" could be applied by churches in specific cases.[18] Indeed, he proposed that Christians accept a plurality of approaches, a general grammar of faith, rather than restricting themselves to one approach or another. Yoder wrote that "there is no obligation to reason in the same way on all subjects . . . Instead of making the case for the priority of one style what I have argued is thus that all of them are needed, precisely because none of them may be dominant."[19] He advocated proceeding in an "ad-hoc" or even "fragmentary" way, one issue at a time,[20] and thus was content to propose "rules of thumb, proverbs, and not a broad programmatic yardstick or a single key theory."[21] This stance also has much in common with the biblical narrative and its "multiplicity of styles," a "mixing and matching" of praise and blame rather than concern for one proper mode of discourse.[22]

Yoder's comments have not dissuaded a number of attempts to discern an underlying structure to his work, or to find the hermeneutical key that ties it all together. For example, the Canadian Baptist theologian Craig A. Carter laments the fact that "Yoder wrote no major systematic treatise in which the comprehensiveness, logical rigor, and originality of his theology could be readily ascertained."[23] Carter is clear that he intends to provide "a guided tour"[24] of Yoder's thought rather than turn it into a system, yet he structures his book around classic Christian doctrines (Christology, eschatology, and ecclesiology) in a way that suggests that Yoder did indeed operate with an implicit systematic theology.[25] And he concludes with a list of "eight characteristics as keys to the proper interpretation of his thought."[26] Certainly Yoder himself frequently made use of lists in his writing, and he probably would not object to being associated with any of the labels Carter assigns to these characteristics, but in my view Yoder would have discouraged the

---

18. Yoder recommended the use of the word "stance" rather than "system" to describe the coherence of his writing. See *For the Nations*, 10.

19. Yoder, "Walk and Word," 84, 86.

20. Yoder, *Royal Priesthood*, 250, 256.

21. Yoder, "Discerning the Kingdom of God," 367.

22. Yoder, "Walk and Word," 88.

23. Carter, *Politics of the Cross*, 18.

24. Ibid., 19.

25. The way Carter depicts Yoder's theology as providing the source, context, and shape of his social ethics also reinforces the idea that theology can be somehow separated or distinguished from ethics. I will discuss this point in greater detail below when I address the charge that Yoder reduced theology to ethics.

26. Ibid., 226–34.

spirit of this kind of venture.²⁷ Strikingly, the Mennonite theologian Earl Zimmerman is also well-acquainted with Yoder's perspective on system-building and methodology, and yet his book can also be characterized as an attempt to reconstruct Yoder's constructive theology.²⁸ Not to be outdone by Carter, in his concluding chapter Zimmerman spells out the ten "basic principles" of Yoder's "Politics of Jesus."²⁹

Both Carter and Zimmerman's books have their origins as doctoral dissertations, and perhaps the urge to uncover Yoder's underlying methodology reflects the standard practice for dissertations in theology.³⁰ No doubt they both provide helpful orientations for newcomers to Yoder's wide-ranging work, and so if nothing else, are of pedagogical value. Yet something crucial is also lost along the way. This is evident most clearly in Nancey Murphy's attempt to show how Yoder's theology "fits the form of a scientific research program."³¹ Indeed, Murphy claims to be able "to isolate a core theory—a central thesis from which all the rest of the theoretical structure follows."³² While it is not directly testable, a core theory is surrounded by "auxiliary hypotheses" which explain and are confirmed by data (scripture and historical evidence, in the case of theology). Murphy recognizes that Yoder would have denied having any plans to interpret Christian doctrine according to some central vision, but she argues that such a "positive heuristic" can be implicit. She thinks that Yoder's core theory can be summed up as follows: "The moral character of God is revealed in Jesus' vulnerable

---

27. In an unpublished memo Yoder wrote: "It might well be that there is some set of common assumptions or constructive implications which would tie together all of the things I have been discussing in the various fields dealt with above: but it has never been my task to operate on that level of abstraction and synthesis. Therefore those who read a systematic structure into what they take me to be saying are going beyond what I have spoken to, and doing so in the authority of their logic, not mine" ("Apologia pro imagine sua," a memo "to whom it may interest").

28. Zimmerman, *Practicing the Politics of Jesus*.

29. Ibid., 216–20.

30. Of the dozens of dissertations that have been written on Yoder, this tendency is especially apparent in more comparative works. See, for example, Collier-Freed, "Building a Case for the Communicability of Christian Experience"; Parham, "An Ethical Analysis of Christian Social Strategies"; and Reames, "Histories of Reason and Revelation." I should also note that several dissertations not only avoid, but seek to argue against this tendency. See, for example, Cartwright, *Practices, Politics, and Performance*; and Huebner's "Unhandling History."

31. Murphy, "Yoder's Systematic Defense of Christian Pacifism," 45. Elsewhere Murphy has used the work of contemporary philosophers of science (in particular, Imre Lakatos) to demonstrate the similarity between scientific and theological reasoning—see *Theology in the Age of Scientific Reasoning*.

32. Murphy, "Yoder's Systematic Defense of Christian Pacifism," 47.

enemy love and renunciation of dominion. Imitation of Jesus in this regard constitutes a *social* ethic."[33] It seems to me that the underlying thrust of this kind of effort is to demonstrate the rationality, the reasonableness, and the general applicability of Yoder's work, rather than recognizing the prophetic challenge it posed to very particular questions.

To be sure, each of these interpreters demonstrates a keen understanding of Yoder, and provides helpful introductions to his thought. From my perspective, however, they also provide a helpful reminder of the difficulty of making sweeping claims about how Yoder thought. Thus, even though I will be providing my own portrayal of Yoder in this chapter, my aim is to avoid imposing a rigid interpretive grid on his work. The point of this chapter is simply to explain why, of all possible theologians, I chose to use Yoder as a resource for thinking about technology.

YODER WAS NOT SECTARIAN

John Howard Yoder's understanding of the relationship between the church and broader society presents a clear challenge to Catholic and mainline Protestant understandings. However, the characterization of Yoder as a sectarian, a label that has been applied both pejoratively and as a kind of backhanded compliment, is inappropriate.[34] Rather than encouraging separation or disengagement from society, the following paragraphs will attempt to demonstrate that Yoder provides motivation for the church to conscientiously engage its surrounding society. Rather than being socially irresponsible, I will argue that Yoder preached and modeled a particular kind of responsibility.

International and Ecumenical Experiences

Sustained attempts to refute the charge that Yoder was sectarian, and was thus socially irresponsible, can be found in recent books by leading scholars on Yoder such as Mark Thiessen Nation.[35] Indeed, Nation devotes an entire chapter to this task, and argues that this is the most substantial challenge to Yoder's legacy *within* rather than beyond his Mennonite tradition.[36] While

---

33. Ibid., 48.

34. In fact, Yoder often accepted the label "sectarian" for himself. As he put it in the Introduction to *For the Nations*, however, he did so only because he had "no choice but to play by other people's rules," and he recognized that this "routinely has led to misunderstanding and misrepresentation" (see ibid., 4).

35. Nation, *John Howard Yoder*.

36. See chapter 5, "'Social Responsibility' or the Offense of the Cross? Yoder on

I will, as Nation does, provide an argument that is grounded in Yoder's thought, perhaps the most profound argument for why Yoder is relevant for a discussion of social issues is provided by his life.

As Nation has pointed out, "we err if we imagine that John Yoder was born into some backwater, rural ethnic Mennonite world." Born in 1927, Yoder grew up in Oak Grove Mennonite Church in northern Ohio. Not only was Oak Grove "one of the most liberal and acculturated Mennonite communities," while attending public schools in Wooster, Ohio, Yoder was the only Mennonite in his classes.[37] He reluctantly attended Goshen College, a small Mennonite liberal arts college in Indiana, out of respect for his parents' wishes. And although Yoder would end up spending most of his professional life in northern Indiana, he was formed by significant experiences far beyond this Mennonite enclave.

While at Goshen College, Yoder studied under Harold S. Bender and Guy F. Hershberger, two of the most significant American Mennonite church leaders of the twentieth century, yet he completed his degree requirements in just two years. A couple of years later, in 1949, he was off to post-war Europe to begin an assignment with Mennonite Central Committee as a youth worker in France. Over the next decade he also earned a doctorate in theology from the University of Basel (awarded in 1962)[38] and became involved in a wide variety of conversations about pacifism in ecumenical circles.[39] When Yoder

---

Christian Responsibility." I disagree with Nation's assessment of Yoder's legacy in this regard. As discussed in the following section of this chapter, I think the biggest stumbling block in the Mennonite church is related to the starting place, not the impact of, his social ethics. In short, Yoder's view of the church has been characterized as either reductionist or perfectionist. In my view both of these critiques emerge out of a misreading of the proper relationship between theology and ethics.

37. Nation, "John H. Yoder, Ecumenical Neo-Anabaptist," 10–11. See also chapter 2: "John Howard Yoder, a Particular Mennonite, a Catholic Vision: A Biographical Sketch," in *John Howard Yoder*.

38. Much has been written about the influence of Yoder's high profile teachers at the University of Basel, figures such as Karl Barth and Oscar Cullmann—See, for example, Zimmerman, "Doctoral Studies with Barth and Cullmann," chapter 4 in *Practicing the Politics of Jesus*, and Nation, *John Howard Yoder*, 18. Between 1950 and 1957 Yoder enrolled in 63(!) courses and five colloquiums at Basel, which covered topics in historical theology, dogmatics, theological ethics, philosophy, comparative religion, linguistics, Old Testament, and New Testament. He took five courses and five colloquiums with Barth, and nine courses with Cullmann, although he took more courses in Old Testament (fourteen) than in any other area, and his dissertation was in historical theology. Yoder's dissertation was published in 2004 as *Anabaptism and Reformation in Switzerland*.

39. Earl Zimmerman has been the most helpful in expanding on the significance of these involvements for Yoder—see "European Experience and the Debate About War," chapter 3 in *Practicing the Politics of Jesus*. While Yoder worked for the renewal of diverse Mennonite communities throughout Europe who were coming to grips with

returned to the U.S., it was not to a teaching post but as an administrator with the Mennonite Board of Missions, which allowed him to maintain contact with Mennonite churches in Europe and elsewhere around the globe. By 1965, he had agreed to teach full-time at the Goshen Biblical Seminary (now the Anabaptist Mennonite Biblical Seminary), although apparently with some reluctance. Soon after this he also began teaching courses at the nearby University of Notre Dame on an adjunct basis, and in 1977 he accepted a full-time appointment in the Department of Theology there. Finally, Yoder's myriad of involvements in scholarly societies[40] and ecumenical peace and social justice groups,[41] not to mention teaching and lecture assignments at schools and churches in Latin America, Africa, Asia, and Australia, suggests a perspective that was anything but provincial. In short, while Yoder was clearly grounded in the American Mennonite church tradition, as Nation and others have pointed out, he cannot be understood apart from his ecumenical and catholic commitments. He always sought to direct the gaze of his church community outward.

Starting with the Church

Having said all this, one obvious reason why Yoder has been criticized as having nothing to contribute to discussions of broader societal issues is that he insisted time and time again that Christian ethics are for Christians.[42] The basic reason for this insistence was Yoder's conviction that "Christian ethics calls for behavior that is impossible except by the miracles of the Holy Spirit."[43] Thus he was convinced that the starting place and primary audience for the Christian ethicist should be the place where those miracles are most evident. He was convinced that the "church precedes the world

---

their actions during WWII, he also represented the historic peace churches in World Council of Churches debates about the morality of war throughout the 1950s, and represented Mennonites in dialogue with European Protestant Churches, for example, at the Puidoux Theological Conference in Switzerland in 1955. Key conversation partners for Yoder included French Reformed church leaders such as Jean Lasserre and André Trocmé. Finally, Yoder's European experience prompted him, along with several other young Mennonites serving and studying in Europe, to publish critical reflections on the Mennonite church in the U.S.—see Vogt, ed., *Roots of Concern*.

40. For example, Yoder served a term as president of the Society of Christian Ethics in 1987/88.

41. For example, on several occasions Yoder served as a resource person for the *Sojourners* community in Washington, DC.

42. This refrain can be found in *Christian Witness to the State*, 28; *Priestly Kingdom*, 96; *Royal Priesthood*, 62; and *For the Nations*, 108.

43. Yoder, *Royal Priesthood*, 174.

epistemologically and axiologically."[44] Indeed, as a Mennonite, Yoder had a high view of the church as the visible body of Christ, and as God's primary agent for the transformation of society: "biblically the meaning of history is carried first of all, and on behalf of others, by the believing community."[45] It follows then that the relationship between the church and society is framed inadequately when we ask what the church can contribute to society; for Yoder, society "functions for the sake of the church, not vice versa."[46]

It is with Yoder's use of the word "church" that many encounter their first stumbling block, for despite the rich theological language used in every tradition to describe the multi-faceted nature of the church, what usually comes to mind is an institution. What comes to mind are buildings and vestments, pastors and priests, offices and bylaws, all of which exist for the purpose of facilitating the ongoing life of a worshiping community. When Yoder uses the term "church" he has something that is both much broader and more particular in mind. In the first place, as an advocate of the Free-church tradition, for Yoder the primary manifestation of the church is the local congregation, not a conference, denomination, or global institution. Furthermore, this congregation is much more than a group that worships together—in Yoder's words, it is more like "an assembly, a parliament, [or a] town meeting." It is "a gathering in which serious business can be done in the name of the Kingdom."[47] Thus when he talks about the church Yoder has much more in mind than traditional sacramental practices. In addition to these, he is talking about all the other things that church communities do, including holding each other accountable, sharing resources with those in need, reaching out to welcome neighbors into the community, affirming gifts for the work of the kingdom, and discerning God's call together. This obviously includes a broad spectrum of activity in the life of a local congregation, but it also includes activities beyond the local congregation such as education, social work, health care, international relief and development, missions, and conflict resolution. Perhaps with this view of the church in mind, it does not seem like quite so small a place to start.

Coupled with Yoder's high view of the church is what appears to be a low view of the world. Once again, however, a definitional misstep is often made here that leads to confusion or misunderstanding. In this case, it needs to be emphasized that Yoder's definition of the "world" is narrower, not broader than it is usually taken to be. By "world" Yoder means "structured

44. Yoder, *Priestly Kingdom*, 11.
45. Yoder, *Royal Priesthood*, 118.
46. Yoder, *Christian Witness to the State*, 13.
47. Yoder, *For the Nations*, 177.

unbelief," or that which is directly opposed to the Kingdom of God. It is "a rebellion taking with it a fragment of what should have been the Order of the Kingdom."[48] By its very definition then the world must be opposed to the church (and vice versa), and yet when Yoder insists that the church is opposed to the world he is *not* rejecting all of society, humanity, or nature that falls outside the church. Indeed, Yoder objected to H.Richard Niebuhr's *Christ and Culture* typology precisely because of the way that Niebuhr treated culture as a monolithic entity—in reality there is no such thing as a "culture-in-general," and even the most pervasive cultures are only particular cultures writ large.[49] Thus Yoder thought it was nonsensical to suggest that an individual or group, much less the church, could either reject or accept a culture in its entirety. Likewise then for Yoder it was nonsensical to speak of a sectarian church—certainly some churches are more discriminating than others when it comes to particular dimensions of a culture or society, but complete separation is never possible. Even the Amish pick and choose which aspects of their surrounding culture they will embrace and which they will reject. A key point to understanding Yoder's perspective on the relationship between the church and society is that it actually involves many different relationships.

Yoder's definitions of the church and world highlight his conviction that it is possible—not necessarily easy, but possible—to distinguish between the church on one hand, and that which is not the church on the other. Ultimately the church is a visible, concrete reality, and so too are the forces and institutions that oppose the church. In his words: "To say the church must be visible demands an existence, a structure, a sociology of its own, independent of the other structures of society."[50]

Implications Beyond the Church

As already indicated, Yoder's high view of the church does not mean he thought there were no implications for the ethic of the church beyond the church. In fact there were lots of implications, and the tone of these implications (i.e., more critical or more supportive) differed depending on which dimension of society or culture or the world (broadly speaking) was in play at a given time. Indeed, Yoder argued that Christ was Lord not only over the church, but over all of reality, and that his grace was at work in the world as well as the church: "both in the order of knowing and in the order of

---

48. Yoder, *Royal Priesthood*, 62.
49. Yoder, "How H. Richard Niebuhr Reasoned."
50. Yoder, *Royal Priesthood*, 170.

valuing, the priority of the faith does not exclude or deny everything else."[51] However, Yoder also insisted that the church was called to be today what the world was called to be tomorrow. This trajectory is reinforced by the many evocative images Yoder used to describe the church—for example, it is "God's beachhead in the world as it is; the downpayment, the prototype, the herald, the midwife of the new world on the way."[52] Put another way, "the very shape of the people of God in the world is a public witness, is good news for the world rather than first of all rejection or withdrawal."[53] Clearly, even though Yoder focused his attention primarily on the practices of the church, he was convinced there were broader implications to these practices.[54] Even though these practices "are formally rooted in the order of redemption . . . that by no means makes them less public." What it does do, in Yoder's eyes, is "make them more realistic about sin and more hopeful about reconciliation that those approaches that trust the reason/nature/creation complex to derive our knowledge of what should be from what is."[55]

Mission

How then does this prototype of the kingdom witness to its surrounding society? Yoder insisted not only that ethics were for Christians, but that ethics were by definition missional. To do ethics is to do mission.[56] In Yoder's view *every* Christian had the obligation—not the option, the obligation—to share their ethical convictions in whatever setting they found themselves. "If Christian ethics are different from non-Christian ethics then Christians have a duty to bring their contribution to bear on society, for they are doing something that no one else can!"[57] Furthermore, he argued that a community must embrace the challenge of public witness if it wants to be able to justify its existence not only to its neighbors but to its own children.[58]

To be clear then, starting with the church does not mean that Yoder refused to extend the boundaries of the church to include the concerns of

---

51. Yoder, *Priestly Kingdom*, 11.
52. Yoder, *For the Nations*, 218.
53. Ibid., 6.
54. The subtitle of one of Yoder's books puts this well: *Body Politics: Five Practices of the Christian Church Before the Watching World*.
55. Yoder, *Royal Priesthood*, 371.
56. Ibid., 81.
57. Yoder, *Priestly Kingdom*, 82.
58. Yoder, *For the Nations*, 42.

other communities.[59] Far from advocating sectarian withdrawal, Yoder argued that the church, by focusing first on being the church, was capable of affecting the authentic transformation of elements of its surrounding culture. Some interpreters of Yoder insist that this transformation is not about re-building society as much as it is about building the church; it is not about the witness of the church leading to social transformation in the world at large as much as it is about the transformation of the world *into* the church. The implication of this posture for Christian ethics is that the church should be less concerned about translating its worldview into non-theological terms, and more concerned about extending its borders by teaching others its particular theological language.[60]

This perspective is grounded in Yoder's notion of the church as a "hermeneutic community."[61] He affirms that "the validity of what we [in the church] believe is founded on grounds more solid than a whim,"[62] that it is not only true for ourselves, even though "all such belief has been arrived at historically, in one's own setting and language."[63] The very strength of that

---

59. Yoder has repeatedly pointed to examples where so-called sectarian groups did not choose isolation but were excluded by the so-called establishment who "walled off the ghetto." See Yoder, "On Not Being Ashamed of the Gospel," 291; and *Ecumenical Movement and the Faithful Church*.

60. Interpreters of Yoder seem to agree that the presence of Christ in the church is the agent that God uses to affect authentic transformation. Chris K. Huebner and others influenced by Stanley Hauerwas downplay the possibility of social transformation and emphasize the transformation of the world into the church. See "Patience, Witness, and the Scattered Body of Christ." Duane K. Friesen is a good representative of those who draw upon Yoder in order to emphasize the possibilities of social transformation. See *Artists, Citizens, Philosophers*; and *At Peace And Unafraid*.

As will become apparent in the following section, my own reading of Yoder is that he did not find it necessary to make distinctions about the way transformation happens. Certainly, from an eschatological perspective, all will one day be enveloped within the body of Christ. In the meantime, however, it is still possible that the church will effect real change in elements of its surrounding culture that continue to exist apart from the church.

61. Parallels have been drawn between Yoder and the hermeneutic theory advocating by literary critic Stanley Fish—see Nation, "Theology as Witness"; and Hauerwas, "Stanley Fish, the Pope, and the Bible," chapter 2 in *Unleashing the Scripture*. Fish's notion of the primacy of the "interpretive community" for determining the meaning of a text as discussed in *Is There a Text in This Class?* is foreshadowed by Yoder's explication of the "hermeneutic community" of the Anabaptists. As Yoder put it in an early essay, "It is a basic novelty in the discussion of hermeneutics to say that a text is best understood in a congregation" ("The Hermeneutics of the Anabaptists," 301). At the same time, Yoder did not think highly of the use of Fish by Hauerwas, or of Fish himself—see Yoder, "Responding to Stanley Fish."

62. Yoder, "On Not Being Ashamed of the Gospel," 290.

63. Ibid., 289–90.

conviction is what allows us to relax and take the "low road" in reaching out to others.⁶⁴ "Instead of seeking to escape particular identity, what we need, then, is a better way to restate the meaning of a truth claim from within particular identity."⁶⁵ Yoder continued to advocate for a particular truth while recognizing that he could never offer a final reading: "The key to the obedience of God's people" as one of Yoder's best known quotations puts it, "is not their effectiveness but their patience."⁶⁶

While this vision of a Spirit-filled church turned outward may strike some as more acceptable than the caricature of Yoder as a naval-gazing sectarian, it may strike others as a recipe for a new Christendom. Eventually, if the mission of the church is successful, it would appear that all dimensions of society will be swallowed up and transformed within it. This is where Yoder's non-Constantinian perspective needs to be inserted in order to clarify the nature of the church's mission.⁶⁷ For Yoder, the downfall of the church, for which Constantine is the chief symbol, came when Christians started to make "generalizability" the criteria for ethics. Instead of asking what would be faithful to the gospel, the question became: What would happen if everyone acted this way? As a member of a minority church tradition, Yoder never had any illusions that all would follow a Christian ethic any time soon; nor did he have any illusions that he could get close enough to the reigns of political power to seize control and make history come out right.

Even if one could maintain these illusions, from Yoder's perspective such an approach must be rejected because it fails to cohere with the model of Jesus, and it diminishes his victory over the powers of evil. The success, therefore, of the church's mission is measured against the incarnation, not church growth or societal power.

Conscientious Engagement

If this is where Yoder stopped, then his critics may be right in saying that he was more concerned with the purity of the church than with justice or suffering or salvation. However, in addition to this basic posture of starting with the church, embodying practices in the church, and welcoming others into the church, Yoder also advocated that Christians become actively

---

64. Yoder, *Priestly Kingdom*, 62.
65. Yoder, "On Not Being Ashamed of the Gospel," 290.
66. Yoder, *Politics of Jesus*, 232. See also "'Patience' as Method in Moral Reasoning."
67. Yoder's reading of Constantinianism has been put under the microscope in recent times. See Schlabach, "Deuteronomic or Constantinian"; Heilke, "Yoder's Idea of Constantinianism"; and Sider, "Constantinianism Before and After Nicea."

involved in the dimensions of society that they found themselves in. Indeed, this is a current of Yoder's thought that runs from the beginning to the end of his writing, although his language evolves over time. For example, in comments first published in 1964, Yoder uses the concept of "middle axioms" to explain how the gospel message and the practices of the church can be translated into practices that lead to the betterment of those outside the church. He pointed to many crucial societal institutions such as education systems and hospitals as examples of Christian practices that had been successfully mimicked by governments. Thus, in addition to the necessary option of conscientious objection, he argued that it can "be no less appropriate to speak of 'conscientious participation' in the life of society."[68]

Yoder's understanding of how the church relates to elements of its surrounding society throughout his corpus is thus properly situated between the extremes of careful, considered rejection on the one hand, and careful, considered participation. As he put it in a paper presented in 1980: "Neither the position of conscientious objection nor that of conscientious involvement can be adequate if taken as a sweeping recipe. Only the insistence that both are open options, needing to be chosen situationally, can permit either to have integrity."[69] Thus for Yoder, the proper stance of the church cannot be characterized as either the blind adherence to the counter-cultural positions of a particular tradition, or as the blind acquiescence to whatever is dictated by a particular culture. The church's stance must, in the first place, be *conscientiously* adopted. Second, for Yoder, the proper stance of the church cannot be characterized as passive—both objecting to and participating in something are examples of an active posture. I think the term *engagement* provides a helpful handle for the full spectrum of actions that the church may well be called to embark upon. Indeed, I think the expression "conscientiously engaged" provides the most adequate summary of Yoder's vision for the church's relationship with its surrounding society.

Nonetheless, Yoder went on to provide other helpful ways to picture the stance of the church that flesh out his early writings on this topic. For example, in Yoder's last book, *For the Nations*, he urged Christians to develop a "third language" to relate to their society in a similar way that the Jews did during the Babylonian exile. Indeed, envisioning Christians as living in the diaspora is a key image for Yoder. In a post-modern, post-Constantinian era, this is an image that now has wide resonance among both Protestants and Catholics.

68. Yoder, *Christian Witness to the State*, 20.

69. Yoder, "Behold My Servant Shall Prosper," in *Karl Barth and the Problem of War*, 159. This essay was originally the third of five "Stone Lectures" presented at Princeton Theological Seminary in February, 1980.

Yoder suggested that the experience of the Jews in Babylon challenges the false dichotomy that is often set up between withdrawing from, or assuming responsibility for, the direction of a society. Instead of fearing pluralism, Yoder welcomes it, refusing to concede that it is impossible to pursue value-laden communication across community boundaries without resorting to supposedly universal, general, or neutral terms. As an alternative to developing a grand vision for their society or withdrawing completely from it, Jews engaged it on an issue-by-issue basis, working for relative improvement by eliminating one evil at a time. At times this posture led to suffering and to further displacement, but at times it also led to the creative transformation of particular aspects of Babylonian society. Indeed, Yoder wondered whether challenging the rules of engagement may be a more basic ethical task than struggling to find the most acceptable option as they are presented by society. And he wondered whether this alternative might not lead to less despair and more hope than the "management model" that has been tried, tested, and proven to fail.[70]

The parallel Yoder draws between contemporary Christians and ancient Jews living in the diaspora also points to the fact that the church is not immune to influence or even correction by anything beyond itself. Yoder's perspective is certainly not intended to legitimate the status quo within the community, and perhaps this is why he spent so much time dwelling on the possibility of overlap between communities. Indeed, he was convinced that the impossibility of escaping a particular or "provincial" standing place was actually "a more optimistic and more fruitful affirmation of the marketplace of ideas" because without a "nonprovincial general community with clear language . . . we must converse at every border".[71] Yoder argued that the way to address differences between communities was "not to imagine or proclaim or seek or discover some 'neutral' or 'common' or 'higher' ground, but rather to work realistically at every concrete experience of overlap and conflict." By overlap Yoder meant areas in which the people of two (or more) communities shared "common enterprises"—in his mind an inevitable occurrence.[72] Technology is clearly one such realm in which overlap is inevitable.

THEOLOGY AND ETHICS ARE INSEPARABLE

If John Howard Yoder was frequently dismissed by those outside the Mennonite tradition as sectarian, the charge most commonly made against him

---

70. Yoder, *For the Nations*, 150.
71. Yoder, *Priestly Kingdom*, 41.
72. Ibid., 44.

by Mennonites is that he reduced theology to ethics. The concern is that Yoder, like sixteenth-century Anabaptists and Old Order Amish and Mennonites, is so focused on discipleship, on following the way of Jesus in every dimension of life, that he verges on works-righteousness. It seems to some that he has written much about what we should do (e.g., love our enemies), and even more about what we shouldn't do (e.g., kill our enemies), but very little about the theological basis for this behavior. It would seem that Yoder is not a promising place to start then if we are looking for *theological* resources for grappling with technology.

Mennonite Critiques

There are several variations of this critique, but they all draw upon a sense of discomfort within contemporary Mennonite theology that was articulated most pointedly by Stephen Dintamen in his article "The Spiritual Poverty of the Anabaptist Vision." Dintamen argues that the Mennonite focus on discipleship, something that was eloquently and passionately encouraged by Harold S. Bender's self-described "recovery" of a vision rooted in sixteenth-century Anabaptist sources,[73] lacked the spiritual vitality necessary to enable people to live up to its high demands. For Dintamen, the solution is to emphasize that discipleship is the outgrowth of grace—that it is made possible by God's grace, rather than simply being the human response to grace.

The Canadian Mennonite theologian A. James Reimer has taken this general assessment of Mennonite faith and practice and honed in on what he sees as its theological manifestation in the work of John Howard Yoder. Reimer recognizes that "a commitment to 'Jesus as Lord' was the heart of [Yoder's] intellectual and ethical project,"[74] and yet he argues that Yoder's work reduced theology to "moral-ethical categories," paying scant attention to theological and philosophical issues or areas of human existence that were not "exclusively or even primarily ethical in nature."[75] In short, Yoder viewed "every event, text and theory" through "sharply focused ethical glasses."[76] In this regard Reimer considers Yoder to be emblematic of a larger problem in recent Mennonite theological reflection: Yoder shares a

---

73. See Bender, "Anabaptist Vision." This article was based on Bender's 1943 presidential address to the American Society of Church History.

74. Reimer, "Theological Orthodoxy and Jewish Christianity," 432.

75. Ibid., 433. Examples that Reimer mentions include "existential meaning in the face of personal suffering and death," "numerous issues raised by science and cosmology," and "music and the arts."

76. Reimer, *Mennonites and Classical Theology*, 296.

common "suspicion of metaphysical-ontological thought in favor of historical-ethical categories."[77] Thus, in Reimer's view, he buys into modern historicism and continues to advance the modern Enlightenment project.

Although Reimer is still motivated by the central Mennonite concern with ethics, he is convinced that this motivation is best served by paying greater attention to the theology that is needed to undergird our ethics. He agrees that Mennonites "have perceived their distinctiveness not to be in the area of doctrinal questions but in the consistent application of belief and faith to life."[78] And he also agrees that (like Catholics) Mennonites have had a high view of the church: "moral and ethical issues need to be addressed not on the basis of individual hermeneutics, reason or experience but corporately in the context of the church."[79] Yet he goes on to argue that contemporary Mennonites have failed to recognize the way in which their tradition saw doctrinal statements as the necessary theological framework for ethics: "Mennonites have in the past taken 'right belief (orthodoxy)' as being the basis and theological framework for 'right action (orthopraxis).'"[80] Thus, far from diminishing the importance of Mennonite ethics, Reimer has tried to strengthen Mennonite ethics:

> I sought not to compromise the Mennonite peace witness but searched for ways to ground it theologically. I remain convinced that ethics devoid of metaphysical-theological foundations is like building a house upon the sand.[81]

Indeed, he insists that "We need doctrine because of ethics! Doctrine can never be a substitute for ethics or an escape from an upright moral life."[82]

Reimer's critique is echoed by another Mennonite systematic theologian, Thomas Finger.[83] While Finger argues that Yoder had a greater sense of appreciation for early Christian creeds than Reimer acknowledges, and that Yoder did not endorse historicism or any other *ism*, he agrees that Yoder's work lacks the kind of discussion of transcendence that theology requires.[84]

---

77. Reimer, "Theological Orthodoxy and Jewish Christianity," 435. Reimer first made this argument in: "Nature and Possibility of a Mennonite Theology."

78. Reimer, *Mennonites and Classical Theology*, 184.

79. Ibid., 514.

80. Ibid., 239.

81. Ibid., 248

82. Ibid., 367.

83. Finger, "Did Yoder Reduce Theology to Ethics?"

84. Finger's assessment of Yoder may be skewed by his own, rather narrow definition of a "theologian" as someone who pursues systematic or constructive theology, and thus excludes "biblical scholars, historians, ethicists, and missiologists" (see Finger,

For example, Finger writes: "I have discovered no clear affirmation of, or even strong implication concerning, any transcendent dimension of Christology—that is, any reference specific enough that it cannot be sufficiently expressed in terms of human (and/or subhuman) realities."[85] To be sure, Finger immediately qualifies this charge by acknowledging that Yoder never denied the possibility of the transcendent. He also points to (but fails to discuss) another place in Yoder's work where he does make transcendent affirmations—his frequent references to the guiding role that the Holy Spirit plays in the life of the church.

Clarifying Yoder's Posture

In my view these readings of Yoder are mistaken, primarily because they share a common misunderstanding about the way theology and ethics are related. Reimer's insistence that Yoder needs to balance his attention to the ethical realm with greater attention to theology reflects the underlying conviction that "one's moral stance within the world surely follows logically from one's presuppositions in theological method."[86] In short, in order to get our actions right we need to get our thinking right. While he acknowledges the "thorny question" of whether ideas or social-historical forces hold more sway in the movement of history, as a systematic theologian Reimer feels compelled to focus on ideas, on the "normative questions arising out of any study of historical events."[87] He is convinced theological developments "cannot be explained comprehensively with reference solely to the sociopolitical milieu in which [they] occurred."[88] Practice should not be severed

---

"Did Yoder Reduce Theology to Ethics?," 318). Interestingly, although Yoder apparently liked to describe himself as "a dilettante having no real field," his academic competencies covered each of the fields that Finger marginalizes, as well as those that he elevates. And Earl Zimmerman's archival work demonstrates that Yoder's ambition in pursuing graduate studies was to develop a "contemporary, updated theology from an Anabaptist perspective (a theological *Vergegenwärtigung*), rather than the historical work being done by most other American Mennonites studying in Europe." It was only because he could not find a theologian in a European university who would allow him to work from an Anabaptist perspective that he turned to historical research for his dissertation. See Zimmerman, *Practicing the Politics of Jesus*, 102, 140–41

85. Finger, "Did Yoder Reduce Theology to Ethics?," 333.
86. Reimer, *Mennonites and Classical Theology*, 32.
87. Ibid., 212–13.
88. Ibid., 269. Elsewhere Reimer states that "my own systematic theological reflections generally emerge out of the history of ideas" (ibid., 443). In addition to his bias as a systematic theologian, I think this reflects Reimer's engagement with the Frankfurt school of Critical Theory—see his "Introduction" in *Influence of the Frankfurt School*; and "Doctrinal Renewal and the 'Dialiectic of Enlightenment,'" chapter 3 in *Mennonites*

from theory, but to counter the Mennonite overemphasis on practice, Reimer's contribution is to stress the importance of theory. In fact, he goes so far as to say that "theory always in some sense is prior to and even separate from practice."[89]

John Howard Yoder refused to make a clear distinction between theory and practice, or between theology and ethics, in the way that Reimer does. Indeed, this is the crux of the problem for those who argue that he reduced theology to ethics, just as it is for those who argue that he was socially irresponsible or sectarian for insisting that Christian ethics are for Christians. For Yoder theology and ethics were two sides of the same coin, and in my view, by refusing to prioritize one over the other he enriches our understanding of how they relate.

One place where this perspective is most clear is in Yoder's essays on Karl Barth. There he points out that for Barth, "ethics is part of dogmatics."[90] Unlike many commentators, for Yoder this certainly does not mean the marginalization of the discipline of ethics, for:

> Instead of being a branch of empirical anthropology, describing how men *do* behave, or of philosophy, describing how they *think* they *should* behave, ethics becomes a part of the science which interprets the Word of God as to how man *must* or *shall* or *may* behave in free response to God's sovereign grace.[91]

Ethics can thus be seen to participate fully in "the bindingness and the objectivity" of theology, "for it deals not simply with man as he is, but with Jesus Christ, perfect Man, God's first and last Word to man."[92] The implication for Yoder is that theologians should be prepared to make the same kinds of claims for ethical issues as they do for doctrinal issues. If Christian ethics are truly part of dogmatics, then, just as we test our doctrinal formulations, we must test our actions by asking whether they are consistent with "the general line of Christian revelation."[93] Put another way, "we must claim,

---

and Classical Theology. Reimer also comments favorably on the neo-Marxist historian Ernst Bloch's analysis of Thomas Müntzer in chapter 28 of *Mennonites and Classical Theology*: "Dreams, emotions, enthusiasm, and inspiration are clothed by more than pure necessity and suffering, and are never only hollow ideologies . . . economic conditions and means of production depend upon higher simultaneous mental constructs for reinforcements" (ibid., 454–55).

89. Reimer, *Mennonites and Classical Theology*, 585.
90. Yoder, *Karl Barth and the Problem of War*, 39.
91. Ibid.
92. Ibid.
93. Ibid., 43.

within the limits of present understanding and subject to correction, the same degree of certainty and universality for ethics as we are accustomed to claiming in Christology."[94]

In addition to these parallels between ethical and theological reasoning, the clearest indication of the theological nature of Yoder's ethics is found in the starting place for all his work—the church. In place of theoretical foundations or a general methodology, he grappled with each issue he faced by clearly situating himself within a particular group of people. As he put it in the conclusion to *Preface to Theology*: "We have not found that we needed for our purposes to set up any particular rules about logic. We just went ahead with the discussion in the community in which we found ourselves."[95] Yoder's ad-hoc or fragmentary approach to theology wasn't bound together by a philosophy or methodology, but by his commitment to the church—to persons of every tribe and tongue, people and nation, who confess that Jesus is Lord. Putting this in more traditional doctrinal terms, for Yoder, ecclesiology is the starting place for theological and ethical reflection.

More importantly, starting with the church makes the indivisibility of theory and practice, and of theology and ethics, readily apparent. In Yoder's mind it makes no sense to talk about our understanding of God as revealed in Christ without reference to the embodiment of that knowledge in the life of the body of Christ. And it makes no sense to talk about what the church does apart from the divine power that makes that action possible:

> Ethics is more than ethics . . . actions proclaim . . . the medium and the message are inseparable . . . *How* God is doing it is indistinguishable from *what* God is doing, and *how the world can know* about it is again the same thing . . . therefore the new humanity is a pulpit.[96]

To put this another way, the church is both infused with and embodies God's grace; it is both impossible without grace and gives shape to it. In one interview Yoder insisted that "we must recognize that the reciprocal interlocking of behavior patterns and thought patterns must be a two-way street."[97] At the same time he tried to make it clear that he had no interest in coming across as "antitheological," pointing out that "giving lifestyle the priority to the exclusion of care for doctrinal formulation" is unhelpful.

---

94. Ibid., 48.
95. Yoder, *Preface to Theology*, 401.
96. Yoder, *For the Nations*, 41.
97. Yoder, "Jesus and Lifestyle," 3.

Christians have been called to "reestablish the integrity of the total witness with both ideational and behavioral dimensions."[98]

Christian Practices

Yoder is certainly not alone in his understanding that theology and ethics, not to mention theory and practice, need to be seen as indivisible. Indeed, most everyone would agree that our theories or beliefs *should* shape our practices, but the reality is that often they don't. Our actions do not always cohere with what we think is right or believe to be true. Why is this? The approach of many systematic theologians such as Reimer is to suggest that this is because we choose to ignore what we believe, we have forgotten what we believe, or we have allowed our beliefs to be twisted in order to justify our actions. Their solution to this problem is to recover and re-state beliefs that are true to the Christian tradition. However, this still begs the question: why do we ignore or forget what we believe, or allow our beliefs to be twisted in the first place? Contemporary philosophers such as Alasdair MacIntyre, Charles Taylor, and Albert Borgmann have argued that this disconnect is not just an intellectual challenge, it is also a practical challenge.[99] Not only do our thoughts shape our practices, but our practices shape our thoughts.

In my view, Yoder's perspective on the indivisibility of theology and ethics resonates with these philosophical insights, and has been affirmed by recent theological reflection on practices. For example, in introducing her second collection of essays on religious practices, Dorothy Bass notes:

> Contemporary academic and popular culture tends to subordinate beliefs to practices to the point of completely functionalizing beliefs. At the same time, other academic and popular voices, claiming the mantle of tradition, resist this approach by insisting that the influence goes only in the other direction, from beliefs to practices, with practices being mere enactments of beliefs. The essays in this volume offer a more complex response.[100]

---

98. Ibid., 4.

99. MacIntyre, *After Virtue*; Taylor, *Modern Social Imaginaries*; and Borgmann, *Technology and the Character of Contemporary Life*. I will be discussing MacIntyre, Taylor, and Borgmann's perspective on practices in greater detail in chapter 4.

100. Volf and Bass, *Practicing Theology*, 3–4. Additional contributions to this discussion include: Bass, *Practicing Our Faith*, and *On Our Way*; Murphy, Kallenberg, and Nation, *Virtues and Practices in the Christian Tradition*; Dykstra, *Growing in the Life of Faith*; Hütter, *Suffering Divine Things*; Miller, *Consuming Religion*; Pinches, *Theology and Action*; and Smith, *Desiring the Kingdom*.

Contributors repeatedly highlight the complex relationship between belief and practice, noting that even when there are gaps or "slippage" between the two, it makes no sense to speak of one without the other. Indeed, Miroslav Volf wraps up this collection with two complementary assertions:

> Christian beliefs are indispensable for the creation of the Christian moral space in which alone engagement in Christian practices makes sense.[101]

> In most cases, Christian practices come first and Christian beliefs follow—or rather, beliefs are already entailed in practices, so that their explicit espousing becomes a matter of bringing to consciousness what is implicit in the engagement in practices themselves.[102]

Yoder's perspective has also been affirmed by widespread interest in the church as the starting place for theology and ethics. In addition to the zeal of prominent theologians such as Stanley Hauerwas, the revival of interest in Karl Barth, and the work of John Milbank and others in the Radical Orthodoxy movement have all contributed to what has been called the "ecclesial turn" in contemporary theology. However, Yoder's work continues to makes a significant contribution because of his emphasis on the broader implications for the practices of the church—as indicated in the previous section, he is able to bind together not only ethics and theology, but *social* ethics and ecclesiology. For example, in his essay "Why Ecclesiology is Social Ethics" Yoder points out that he is simply trying to overcome the way Christian ethicists have "dichotomized ethics from gospel, or at least social ethics from the Good News."[103] And in the essay "Sacrament as Social Process" Yoder insisted that "what New Testament believers were doing in their social practices can be spoken of in social process terms easily translatable into nonreligious terms."[104] Thus when Yoder spoke of Christian "social practices" he was clear that these are grounded in the power of the Holy Spirit. At the same time he was also clear that these practices are empirically accessible; they are observed and can be understood and even appropriated in an approximate way by nonbelievers.[105] This insight is worked out most

---

101. Volf, "Theology for a Way of Life," 251.
102. Ibid., 256.
103. Yoder, *Royal Priesthood*, 103–4.
104. Ibid., 364.
105. Tanner makes a similar point when she argues that "Christian practices seem to be constituted in great part by a slippery give-and-take with non-Christian practices; indeed, they are mostly non-Christian practices—eating, meeting, greeting—done differently, born again, to unpredictable effect." Thus she concludes her essay by asking:

fully in his book *Body Politics*, a text that I will be drawing on in greater detail in the fourth chapter of this book.

Finally, I think Yoder's refusal to reduce theology to ethics or to prioritize theology over ethics is precisely what allowed him to grapple theologically with the kinds of things that many theologians have tended to hold at arms-length. When he was asked, he made theologically informed statements about not only war, but about things such as time, power, taxes, economic growth, and the environment, without articulating a theological prolegomena or referencing a tightly constructed system.[106] There was no question in his mind that all moral issues required a theological response, and that all theological reflection had moral implications. Subsequent chapters of this book will attempt to demonstrate how a Yoderian approach to technology is grounded in this perspective.

TECHNOLOGY IS A POWER

If John Howard Yoder's work, far from being sectarian, actually called Christians to conscientiously engage all aspects of the societies in which they live, and if, far from reducing theology to ethics, it demonstrates the indivisibility of theology and ethics, then perhaps it is becoming plausible that Yoder's work could be a fruitful resource for grappling theologically with technology. In this final section I will attempt to demonstrate that the thesis of this chapter is not only plausible based on the general contours of Yoder's work, but based on specific connections with the work of Jacques Ellul, the prominent critic of technology discussed in the previous chapter.

Connections with Ellul

Readers familiar with Ellul will no doubt see several points of connection based upon the above discussion of Yoder's theological stance. For example, like Yoder, Ellul was a prolific writer who refused to be confined to one field. Like Yoder, Ellul's writing was always related to a specific setting—he was

---

"One need to look . . . away from the Christian practice itself to its relations with similar practices in the wider society. How does a Christian practice of welcome differ from other practices of welcome current in the wider society? That, to a great extent, is the clue to its Christian point" (see "Theological Reflection and Christian Practices," 230, 242).

106. See Yoder, "Time and the Christian"; "Jesus and Power"; "Why I Don't Pay All My Income Tax"; "Theological Perspectives on 'Growth with Equity'"; and "On Generating Alternative Paradigms."

clearly "at grips" with his surroundings.[107] Furthermore, despite the overall coherence of their writing, they both disavowed system-building. As we have already seen, Yoder's theological stance went beyond anti-foundationalism to reject methodologism. For Ellul, a similar concern is evident in the dialectical way he tried to relate his sociological analysis on the one hand, with his biblical and theological analysis on the other. Yet he went even further:

> I have refused, you might say systematically, to produce a system . . . I think that from the beginning of Christianity there has been a sort of passion for unity—bringing everything under a single principle or else carrying out manipulations to obtain a unified system. Every time a contradiction appears, we try to reduce it to the ideal *one*, the unique, the explanation of everything that moves, the reduction to a single dimension, and so on. Now, I believe this is intellectually impossible, spiritually wrong, and concretely dangerous. All the great massacres were done in the name of unity. I am viscerally opposed to all unity.[108]

From Ellul's perspective, system-building can be seen as evidence of the impact of technological ways of thinking on theology. The pursuit of "unity" is equivalent to the pursuit of absolute efficiency and is apparent throughout the history of theology, from the rationality of Scholasticism, to the presumed universality of Enlightenment thinking, to the self-directedness and autonomy of theology in the modern academy. Indeed, each of these nouns—rationality, universality, self-directedness, and autonomy—have been used pejoratively by Ellul to depict *la technique*. When Ellul reflects on technology he is grappling with the dominant characteristic of contemporary life, with the tyranny that separates us from God.[109]

Of greater significance, however, is the fact that Ellul shares Yoder's penchant for exposing the fallacy of modern myths that have too often gone unquestioned. Perhaps because of the influence of Barth, instead of demythologizing the biblical world view they both chose instead to use the Bible

---

107. Dawn, "Introduction," 5.

108. Ellul, *In Season, Out of Season*, 203. Yoder actually took issue with the way Ellul "sweepingly condemned 'system' or 'casuistry,'" and argued that "rather than denying systematic discipline" it is better to be "committed to several systems." See Yoder, "Creation and Gospel," 9; and "The Casuistry of Violence."

109. In addition to the search for "unity," Ellul also associates technology with the moral relativism that is typical in a post-modern context (see Dawn, *Sources and Trajectories*, 85). Since technology remains a constant—or has become even more dominant—it would appear that Ellul emphasizes the continuity between modern and post-modern thought.

to demythologize the contemporary world.[110] Ellul characterized his approach as "Christian realism,"[111] while Yoder pointed to the influence of "the mood of 'biblical realism.'"[112] This perspective is crucial for understanding Ellul's response to the autonomy of technology—hope is only possible when we see things not as they are depicted by the social sciences, but when we see things as they really are, when we begin with "the spiritual plane."[113]

As revealed in his early writings, the biblical concept of "the principalities and powers" is central to Ellul's understanding of the spiritual plane, and thus provides a way to relate his sociology and theology:

> We must first use the revelation that is given us to have a deeper, truer view of the phenomena than that which our experience, our senses, our reason alone can give us . . . it teaches us that the phenomena are never anything but the signs of another reality, of another existence.[114]

Ellul goes on to describe this other reality as one of "the powers," which he defines in a number of his books. Power, first of all, "is something that acts by itself," "is autonomous," and "presents itself as an active agent." Secondly, power "has a spiritual value. It is not only of the material world, although this is where it acts." And thirdly, power "is more or less personal"—it has "a reality of its own."[115] When we understand that when Ellul describes *la technique* he has this notion of the powers in mind, that technology is the "expression of the might of Satan,"[116] his use of the term "autonomous" is seen in a dramatically different light. Technological systems and ways of thinking are beyond human control, but ultimately they are overcome by the power of Christ.[117]

---

110. Ellul has frequently written about the impact that reading Karl Barth had on his thought. For example: "Obviously, once I began reading Karl Barth, I stopped being a Calvinist—in my understanding of the world and politics as well as, theologically, in my understanding of predestination, original sin, and the question of universal salvation" (see *Perspectives on Our Age*, 17).

111. Ellul, "Political Realism (Problems of Civilization III)," in *Sources and Trajectories*, 32.

112. Yoder, *Politics of Jesus*, 157.

113. Ellul, *Presence of the Kingdom*, 25.

114. Ellul, *Sources and Trajectories*, 76.

115. Ellul, *Money and Power*, 75–76. See also Ellul, *Ethics of Freedom*, 151–52.

116. Ellul, *Ethics of Freedom*, 55.

117. It is the concern that so-called technological determinists are willing to turn their backs on the world and thus are socially irresponsible that seems to get Ellul's critics the most worked up. See, for example, Stahl, *God and the Chip*, 162. There are parallels here with the concern of those who accuse Yoder of being sectarian.

In Ellul's discussion of the powers we find yet another, and perhaps the most important point of connection between Yoder and Ellul. Both are drawn to the principalities and powers language from the Pauline literature that has often been explained away as part of an antiquated worldview.[118] The reality of the powers and Christ's Lordship over them was a "declaration of the nature of the cosmos," to use Yoder's words,[119] or "the true situation of the world" to use Ellul's.[120]

This essay is not the first that highlights Yoder and Ellul's common interest in the powers. On more than one occasion Yoder himself commends Ellul for his use of this concept,[121] and one of Yoder's former students, Marva Dawn, has written that it was Yoder's interest in the powers that pointed her to Ellul.[122] In my case, however, it was Ellul's analysis of technology that pointed me back toward Yoder in my search for a theological approach to technology. What, I wondered, would Yoder's discussion of the principalities and powers have to say to Christians about the power of technology, of technological systems, and of technological ways of thinking as they seek to live faithfully within contemporary society?

---

118. See Rom 8:38–39, Eph 6:10–17, and Col 1:15–17.

119. Yoder, *Politics of Jesus*, 157.

120. Ellul, *Presence of the Kingdom*, 25.

121. Yoder, *Politics of Jesus*, 157, and *For the Nations*, 35.

Yoder also interacted with a number of key American interpreters of Ellul such as David W. Gill. See Gill's discussion of parallels and differences between Yoder and Ellul in *Word of God*, 85, 152; and *Doing Right*, 9. As the long-time editor of *The Ellul Forum*, Gill was responsible for soliciting a contribution in which Yoder indicates that he is "a lifetime admirer of Ellul" (Yoder, "Casuistry of Violence," 6).

Yoder's interest in Ellul is also evident in his correspondence. For example, he wrote several letters to Gill encouraging him to videotape an interview with Ellul after plans fell through for Ellul to visit the U.S. Gill did subsequently interview Ellul at his home in Bordeaux in 1982; excerpts were published as: "Interview with Jacques Ellul" and "Jacques Ellul." And on one occasion Yoder wrote to Ellul to ask him about the roots of his interest in the powers, to which Ellul responded by noting the influence of Yoder's teachers at Basel, Barth and Oscar Cullmann.

Aside from Ellul, the only other prominent philosopher of technology that Yoder appeared to be familiar with was Hannah Arendt—see his comments on her significant book *The Human Condition* in *For the Nations*, 30–31.

122. "Biblical Concept of 'the Principalities and Powers,'" 168–86. Yoder supervised Dawn's dissertation, and played a significant role in the translation of *Sources and Trajectories*. Dawn has continued to write about the principalities and powers—see, for example, *Powers, Weakness, and the Tabernacling of God*.

To my knowledge, the only other doctoral dissertation that brings together Yoder and Ellul is Parham's "An Ethical Analysis of Christian Social Strategies," although Parham does not discuss the concept of the powers.

Yoder's Analysis of the Powers

Yoder's fullest discussion of the powers is found in chapter eight ("Christ and Power") of *The Politics of Jesus*.[123] He begins by reviewing the variety of ways the word "structure" is used in contemporary discourse, suggesting that this provides an analogy to the biblical concept of the powers. "Structure" can refer to a physical artifact such as a bridge, to the grammar and syntax of language, or to a network of persons and agencies. Yet it also points to "the patterns or regularities that transcend or precede or condition the individual phenomena we can immediately perceive."[124] "Structure" reminds us that a bridge is more than the sum of the cables and girders that are used to build it, a language is more than the sum of the words and rules that are used to compose it, and an institution is more than the sum of the individual persons who participate in it. In the same way the biblical concept of the powers enables us to perceive this "more than the sum of" factor that, despite its profound significance, has often remained nameless. Of course, while the biblical authors' use of principalities and powers language often referred to social realities, for example, to the political realm ("thrones or dominions"), at times they also referred to the cosmic realm ("angels and archangels"). Thus "structure" is only partially similar to the biblical concept of the powers, but it highlights the aspect of this concept that Yoder believes is most translatable in modern times.[125]

The extent to which the Apostle Paul's discussion of principalities and powers was intended to refer to the political or to the cosmic realm has been a subject of great debate.[126] In the comment above it appears as though Yo-

---

123. References to the principalities and powers abound in Yoder's published and unpublished writing. I agree with Earl Zimmerman that the significance of Yoder's interaction with the Dutch theologian Hendrikus Berkhof during and after his time in Europe has not been appreciated, especially in comparison to the attention paid to Barth and Cullmann. See *Practicing the Politics of Jesus*, 132–33.

Perhaps Yoder's most significant contribution to North American scholarship in this area is his English translation of Berkhof's 1952 book *Christus en de Machten*. This text has been important for the work of, among others, Walter Wink. See *Naming the Powers*; *Unmasking the Powers*; and *Engaging the Powers*. Interestingly, a number of Mennonite theologians have been attracted to Wink's thought in recent years—see, for example, Gingerich and Grimsrud, *Transforming the Powers*.

Prior to Yoder's work in the 1970s, discussion of the principalities and powers are harder to find, but two sources include Stewart's "On a Neglected Emphasis in New Testament Theology"; and Caird's *Principalities and Powers*.

124. Yoder, *Politics of Jesus*, 138.

125. Ibid., 138–40.

126. In Evangelical circles, for example, the latter is stressed. Yoder was accused by some Evangelicals of ignoring the cosmic dimension of the powers, a criticism he

der is siding with those who stress the political at the expense of the cosmic, or at least choose to highlight this aspect of Paul's writings because it is the only one that makes sense for a post-biblical cosmology. On a number of occasions, however, Yoder sought to clarify his perspective on this question. For example, in a subsequent essay he stressed that the principalities and powers are clearly "cosmic authorities": "They are not human persons. Yet they influence human events and structures."[127] And he took issue with Walter Wink's preoccupation with trying to explain how the human and the superhuman, or the political and the cosmic dimensions of the powers can be related.[128] In particular, he was unsatisfied with Wink's depiction of the "spiritual" as not having an existence of its own, but as the "inward aspect of outward realities."[129] Yoder did not have a better explanation, but he doubted that there needed to be or could be a better explanation. He thought that trying to find a way to resolve the either/or way that the material and spiritual, the visible and invisible, or the institutional and personal dimensions of the powers have been related was to focus on the wrong problem.[130] Indeed, in an unpublished memo Yoder emphasizes that there is no ecumenical consensus on how to interpret Paul on this point—not that "a count of commentaries" is the way we should determine the best approach. Yoder says he is content, as was Oscar Cullman, to simply maintain that the powers have both human and "super human" dimensions and leave it at that.[131] These debates got in the way of his larger objective to make the New Testament message understandable by emphasizing that the powers are undeniably real.

Yoder reminds us that these powers were created by God and remain under God's sovereignty even though they have fallen. Indeed, society would not be possible without order and structure, and so we "*cannot live without them.*"[132] Thus Yoder stresses the positive role of the powers in human existence to a greater extent than Ellul, valuing the order and regularity that they, as part of the good creation of God, enable.[133] On another occasion he insisted

---

addressed head on in three letters to John R. Stott between 1976 and 1978.

127. Yoder, *He Came Preaching Peace*, 114.

128. Yoder, "Review of Walter Wink's *Naming the Powers*," 25.

129. Wink, *Naming the Powers*, 5.

130. Yoder, "Review of Walter Wink's *Naming the Powers*," 25. See also Yoder's letter to Wink dated April 26, 1985.

131. Yoder, "Footnote on The 'Powers' Debate," 2.

132. Yoder, *Politics of Jesus*, 143.

133. In another setting Yoder wrote: "It is said about these 'entities' at the same time that they are good creatures of God and that they are fallen, evil, oppressive . . . Everything we call "culture" is both in some way created and creative and positive, and in

that "the same cosmic perception" that enables us to recognize runaway powers can also "illuminate . . . our best visions."[134] Furthermore, even in their fallen state the powers perform necessary functions—Yoder goes so far as to say that "tyranny is still better than chaos."[135] To be sure, however, he also makes it clear that instead of enabling freedom and love, these powers demand our loyalty and enslave us, and so we *"cannot live with them."*[136] Bridges make travel easier, but they also favor particular modes of transportation and particular destinations over others. Languages enable the communication of knowledge and the formation of relationships, but they also exclude ways of thinking and groups of people from our conversations.[137] Institutions make it possible for people to accomplish far more than they ever could on their own, but they also perpetuate evils such as racism and warfare that individuals would otherwise find unfathomable. Yoder himself does not go any further in discussing the manifestations of these powers:

> It cannot be the task of this chapter to spell out at length samples of the relevance of this kind of approach for concrete social and ethical thought . . . Probably Jacques Ellul, in his writing on money, the law, violence, and technology, thinks the most consistently within the framework of this approach.[138]

This endorsement of Ellul suggests that in Yoder's discussion of how the powers are overcome we will find his suggestion for how the church should approach particular manifestations of the powers such as technology.

Yoder's Response to the Powers

Like Ellul, Yoder doesn't believe that humans can simply get rid of the powers; after all, our subordination to the powers is what makes us human:

> If then God is going to save his creatures *in their humanity*, the Powers cannot simply be destroyed or set aside or ignored. Their

---

other ways rebellious and oppressive" (see Yoder, "How H. Richard Niebuhr Reasoned," 85).

134. Yoder, "From Basic Orientation to Concrete Discernment," 2.

135. Yoder, *Politics of Jesus*, 151. In contrast, while Ellul recognized that society could not exist without some organization or authority, he was attracted to political anarchism. See Ellul, *Anarchy and Christianity*.

136. Yoder, *Politics of Jesus*, 143.

137. Yoder helpfully expands on this point by discussing the reification of language in: "Moral Theology Miscellany #19."

138. Yoder, *Politics of Jesus*, 157.

sovereignty must be broken. This is what Jesus did, concretely and historically, by living a genuinely free and human existence.[139]

Jesus, like all people, was subject to the powers, but he refused "to support them in their self-glorification" and thus refused the temptation of idolatry. His willingness to give up his life to the powers manifest in the Roman government and Jewish religious elites is a sign of this refusal: "Not even to save his own life [would] he let himself be made a slave of these Powers."[140] Jesus' death was a victory over the powers, disarming and making a public example of them by revealing their true nature. It is this victory over the powers that the church proclaims by confessing that Jesus Christ is Lord. In Yoder's words: "It is precisely this attitude toward the structures of this world, this freedom from needing to smash them since they are about to crumble anyway, which Jesus had been the first to teach and in his suffering to concretize."[141] In the words of Ellul, the victory of Jesus over the powers "reveals another direction for life, another choice, namely, of non-power."[142]

Yoder stresses that the church itself does not break the sovereignty of the powers, but "concentrates on not being seduced by them"—it is not a matter of fighting the battle that Christ has already won.[143] Yoder's primary concern with particular powers such as technology would thus appear to be that the church needs to avoid being seduced by them. And the seduction of technological systems and ways of thinking lies in their ability to blind us to their real power, to make us think we are doing the "responsible" thing, or solving worthy problems when we are actually placing our faith in something other than the power of God. The "real power" or the "greater than the sum of" factor of our pursuit of technology is not readily apparent to us. Ellul's work suggests that, even more than the power afforded by political involvement and intellectual respectability, embracing technological ways of thinking represents the greatest temptation for the church today.[144]

How can the church avoid this seduction? In Ellul's writing one is left wondering if it can. While technology ultimately remains subordinate to Christ, in Ellul's view it is clearly autonomous from human control, and so any efforts to redirect or transform technology will ultimately be futile. As a power, technology is fallen, and so it can only be overcome or transcended,

---

139. Ibid., 144–45.
140. Ibid., 145.
141. Ibid., 187.
142. Ellul, "Technology and the Gospel," 114.
143. Yoder, *Politics of Jesus*, 150.
144. Albert Borgmann contrasts the "seductiveness" of technology with "the good news of Christ" in "Contingency and Grace," 18.

it cannot be redirected or transformed. In this regard I think Yoder would part ways with Ellul, and argue that instead of focusing on the possibility that individuals might avoid the seduction of technology through spiritual heroics, we should focus on the possibility that a community might avoid the seduction of technology through concrete practices. While Ellul's later writing did shift away from describing the powers as "the might of Satan,"[145] Yoder more closely links the powers with human and social realities:

> The Powers have been defeated not by some cosmic hocus-pocus but by the concreteness of the cross; the impact of the cross upon them is not the working of magical words nor the fulfillment of a legal contract calling for the shedding of innocent blood, but the sovereign presence, within the structures of creaturely orderliness, of Jesus the kingly claimant and of the church who herself is a structure and a power in society.[146]

Thus, not only does Yoder emphasize the positive role of the powers in human existence, he stresses that Jesus' overcoming of their sovereignty was a human and social act, not just a spiritual one.

It should therefore be clear that Yoder not only rejects the withdrawal option, he also rejects the idea that we can spiritually transcend culture in the manner that Ellul suggests. In my view, Yoder would agree with Ellul that efforts to take responsibility for the direction of technology in general are futile, and this is why it would be going too far to draw parallels between Yoder and those who stress the possibility of taking "responsibility" for the direction of technology,[147] or, even stronger, "redeeming" the power of technology.[148] And although Yoder might have been sympathetic to Albert Borgmann's proposal that efforts to reform the paradigm of technology should be focused on the "recognition" and the "restraint" of this paradigm, the principle context for these efforts at restraint would be the church rather than the public realm.[149] Furthermore, within the context of the church, Yoder's perspective would be more optimistic than both Ellul and Borgmann. Indeed, I think that being pessimistic about efforts to take responsibility in general does not preclude the possibility that a community might end up transforming particular technologies by following the way

---

145. Marva Dawn makes this point in "Biblical Concept of 'the Principalities and Powers,'" 183–84.

146. Yoder, *Politics of Jesus*, 158. David Gill points out Ellul's inadequate portrayal of the church in *Word of God*.

147. See, for example, Monsma's *Responsible Technology*.

148. See, for example, Franklin's *Real World of Technology*.

149. Borgmann, *Technology and the Character of Contemporary Life*, 220.

of Jesus. For in the presence of an alternative power it becomes possible to resist the seduction of the fallen powers. Thus I think Yoder would say that the authentic transformation of a particular technology *is* possible when it is subordinated to the power of Christ and embodied in the church. The effect this witness has beyond the church may be difficult to measure, but should not be underestimated.

Yoder's approach contrasts with, at the one extreme, modern theologians who are preoccupied with the search for the "right 'handle' by which one can 'get a hold on' the course of history and move it in the right direction."[150] These theologians often end up at least appearing to be rather instrumental, or, better yet, technological—they know that their theology is right when history is moving in the right direction. In my view Yoder would argue that it isn't human complacency or ignorance that has led to problems associated with technology, but the very imperative to act, to take control, and to construct that modern (and post-modern) approaches to theology urge us to pursue with greater gusto. Indeed, despite their awareness of the destructive potential of the material manifestations of our technology, many theologians seem to embrace the thinking that makes these manifestations possible.[151] From Yoder's perspective, this kind of theological project demonstrates the same hubris we find in contemporary society's technological project.

At the other extreme, Yoder's approach contrasts with Christian millennialists or spiritualists who, to an even greater extent than Ellul, are preoccupied with getting out of the way as God steers the course of history to completion. By confining faith to other-worldly concerns, spiritualists often end up baptizing as God-ordained whatever the status quo happens to be in human history. As Yoder has argued, the alternative power of Christ is not merely "cosmic hocus-pocus," but is a human and social reality that is evident in the "concreteness of the cross" and subsequently in the concrete practices of the church.

CONCLUSION

The majority of this chapter attempted to address objections that could be made to my assertion that John Howard Yoder's work is relevant to the topic of technology. The final section then went beyond responding to critiques to show that, following the example of Jacques Ellul, a fruitful way to think theologically about technology is to consider Yoder's understanding of the principalities and powers. This also provides a further explanation for the

---

150. Yoder, *Politics of Jesus*, 228.
151. See, for example, Kaufman's *In Face of Mystery*.

way that the church is understood by Yoder to engage its surrounding society, and for the way in which his ethics depend upon theological commitments even as they are firmly grounded in social practices. Unlike Ellul, not only does Yoder also emphasize the positive role of the powers in human existence, but he stresses that Jesus' overcoming of their sovereignty was a human and social act, an act that the church, through its very existence, proclaims. Thus I think Yoder's work suggests that the authentic transformation of technology *is* possible when it is subordinated to the power of Christ and embodied in the church.

The obvious challenge to the above suggestion is *not* that it fails to endorse the efforts of Christians to take responsibility for the direction of technology in the world, or that it is not theologically grounded, but that Christians do not seem to be able to avoid the seduction of technological systems and ways of thinking in the church.[152] Indeed, it would seem that our interaction with modern technological systems even as a church is at best ambiguous. For example, the countless benefits of cheap and available transportation, food, and communication options often fail to be weighed against environmental, economic, and social costs. These systems make new educational and worship experiences possible even as they contribute to the break-down of traditional communities; they provide for our health and well-being even as they jeopardize the possibility that future generations will enjoy the same privileges; and they make it possible to relate as a global church even as they contribute to growing gaps within that same church. Does Yoder leave us with no option but to join his Old-Order Mennonite and Amish cousins in traditional church communities that would make the strict regulation of the use of technologies such as automobiles, tractors, and computers possible? Indeed, the topic of technology poses a challenge not only for the church, but for theologians seeking to engage the work of John Howard Yoder.

I think that Yoder's theological stance *does* provide helpful resources for the church as it seeks to resist the seduction of technology, and I intend to make this clear in the following chapters as I put Yoder to the test.

---

152. Ted Koontz makes a similar point in addressing J. Lawrence Burkholder's challenge to the claim of Mennonites such as Yoder that the gospel offers a social ethic. See "Goshen College not China," 110–14.

3

The Moral Vision Embodied and Encouraged by Three Particular Technologies

THE PREVIOUS TWO CHAPTERS have attempted to build a case for the validity of the general contours of this book. By this point it should be clear that technology is of theological significance, and that John Howard Yoder might have something helpful to say about this topic. Without minimizing the significance of the arguments made thus far, the next two chapters will make the most important contribution of this project, drawing upon Yoder's work in order to demonstrate how technology can be conscientiously engaged through the practices of the church. I am convinced that theological reflection on technology needs to move beyond theoretical analysis—that we should not only describe the nature of technology, or critique the impact of technology, but propose theologically informed ways of engaging technology. As noted in the previous chapter, I am also convinced that Yoder's work is a good resource for this kind of endeavor even though he did not address the topic of technology directly.

In Yoderian fashion, I think that the primary responsibility of theologians is to nurture those practices that make it possible for a community of faith—rather than society at large—to conscientiously engage the dimensions of culture that they come into contact with, including technology. In short, I am convinced that the most significant gap in theological discourse on the topic of technology is a discussion of the kinds of practices that Christian communities can embrace in order to live faithfully in a technological age.

This chapter begins this more constructive task by going beyond talking about technology in general to focus on the way particular manifestations of technology embody and encourage a particular kind of moral vision. In one sense then it provides further evidence for the argument made in chapter 1, demonstrating that, far from being morally neutral, technology has moral implications. However, the intent here is not to make a general argument as much as it is to provide background information on three particular examples of technology: the automobile, genetically modified food, and the Internet. This background work sets up the next chapter, which will argue that these technologies can be understood in a new way when viewed through the lens of Yoder's theological ethics.

PREAMBLE: ENGAGING TECHNOLOGY IN THE PARTICULAR

Before proceeding it needs to be emphasized that this project is not attempting to suggest that a full-blown theology of technology is implicit in Yoder's work. It does not claim that he could have provided all the answers about technology without addressing a particular question about a particular technology. Indeed, just as Yoder refused to "start from scratch" with his theological reflections, so too should we resist the urge to begin with sweeping claims about technology in general. Rather than developing a general or theoretical position and then applying it to specific technological artifacts, systems, and ways of thinking, if we are to think like Yoder we need to begin with the specific.

One indication of the importance of starting small can be found in Yoder's discussion of H. Richard Niebuhr's well-known typology for relating Christ and culture.[1] Since Yoder rejects the way Niebuhr sets up the categories, he does not feel obligated to argue for any of the five paradigms that Niebuhr proposes. Yet, as he repeatedly demonstrated, Yoder is not afraid to enter into a conversation even if it is under terms he disagrees with. Thus he takes issue with Niebuhr's critique of the oppositionalist or radical position, especially the way pacifism is discounted at the same time as it is acknowledged as being the clearest reflection of the teachings of Jesus.[2] While defending the oppositionalist position is not the same as advocating it, Yoder seems to be trying to shift the burden of proof from those who oppose, to those who propose the acceptance of an element of culture. He is more sympathetic to the minority, marginalized perspective than he is to

---

1. Yoder, "How H. Richard Niebuhr Reasoned." Niebuhr's typology was developed in *Christ and Culture*.

2. Yoder, "How H. Richard Niebuhr Reasoned," 61–65.

the mainstream, dominant perspective. For this reason it could be argued that the basic posture of a theology of technology that is consistent with Yoder's thought would err on the side of opposing rather than providing spiritual sanction for technological artifacts and systems.

However, the more important insight from Yoder's discussion of Niebuhr is found (as mentioned in chapter 2) in his concern with the way Niebuhr defines culture, treating individual cultures in a monolithic fashion:

> Each position was measured by Niebuhr according to the *consistency* with which a thinker responds to the entire realm of values called "the world" or "culture" . . . you must either withdraw from it *all*, transform it *all*, or keep in *all* in paradox.³

According to Yoder, Christians have always discriminated among the variety of elements that make up a culture. Some elements may be rejected (e.g., pornography), some may be embraced (e.g., agriculture), some may be accepted with certain limits (e.g., economic production), some may be transformed (e.g., music), and some may even be created (e.g., hospitals).⁴ As we have seen, Yoder values a plurality of approaches rather than consistency. Thus Mennonites and others that Niebuhr characterizes as "radicals" should not be depicted as being categorically against culture just because they oppose a particular element of culture such as the military. As Yoder put it in another essay:

> It is not fitting to assume a far-reaching symmetry so as to deal with all of the different orders or powers in just the same way . . . A monolithic view would seek for logical symmetry saying that if we want to be affirmative about the family we must be equally affirming about the arts. If agriculture, then commerce, if education then engineering, if social sciences then the arts, if transportation then war, and so on.⁵

Thus, I would argue that if, following Ellul, Yoder thought it proper to think of technological artifacts, systems, and ways of thinking as a principality or power in the Pauline sense, then he would also have been discriminating in how he thought about the variety of manifestations of this power. Indeed, Yoder can be seen to part ways with Ellul not only because of his more nuanced evaluation of the nature of the powers, but because of his desire to avoid all tendencies toward "monolithic," "univocal," or "globalizing" analysis. Precisely because we can think of any given power as both

---

3. Ibid., 54.
4. Ibid., 69. All of the examples noted are Yoder's.
5. Yoder, *Karl Barth and the Problem of War*, 165.

good and necessary and at the same time evil and dangerous, it is possible to make distinctions between the many elements that can be seen to belong to that power. It would seem then that Yoder's theology could be used to advocate a variety of approaches to technology rather than just one. "No," one could easily imagine him saying, "I neither accept nor reject technology in general, but I *do* reject the use of technology to create and distribute pornography. I *do* embrace efforts to beat swords into plowshares. I *do* believe in limiting technologies that harm the environment. And I *do* encourage the development of life-saving medical technologies." In Yoder's own words, it is "an advantage, rather than a handicap, that social ethics must be worked out piecemeal rather than derived from a general slogan."[6] Once again, what is crucial for the purposes of this chapter is that Yoder would have been more inclined to comment on particular examples of technology rather than technology in general.[7]

Yoder's preference for the particular is actually crucial not only for this chapter, but for the approach of this book as a whole. Rather than focusing on the effort to develop a theoretical approach to technology that is then tested with examples as a way to wrap things up, the focus will be on the examination of examples. Not that this is a straightforward shift from a deductive to an inductive approach, for although patterns will emerge, the point is not to find another way to make general claims about technology, but to demonstrate a variety of ways to go about making claims about particular technologies. The methodological contribution of this project lies in the process for conscientiously engaging technology suggested by Yoder's work—as Yoder put it: "A methodological debate which makes a difference for concrete choices [is] more illuminating than one whose argument can be carried out without reference to cases."[8]

One parallel to the approach of this book can be found in Samuel Wells' book *Improvisation*. Wells argues that Christian ethics is best thought of not as acting out or performing a script that has already been

---

6. Ibid., 167.

7. In this regard Yoder would have allies among philosophers such as Joseph Pitt who take issue with the tendency of colleagues to "assume that there is some one thing out there called Technology," which is then reflected on from the "Olympian heights" of "an intellectually global perspective." See Pitt, "In Search of a New Prometheus."

Pitt (not to mention Paul Durbin) is interested in contributing to interdisciplinary inquiry into the details of particular technologies rather than creating a new academic discipline called the philosophy of technology—i.e., he advocates a broad rather than narrow definition of the field. See Pitt, *New Directions in the Philosophy of Technology*; and Kroes and Meijers, *Empirical Turn in the Philosophy of Technology*.

8. Yoder, "Walk and Word," 84.

written, as much as it is "faithfully improvising on the Christian tradition."[9] Thus the Bible is best thought of as a "training school" that teaches us how we can face the unknown rather than a book with predetermined answers to every possible question.[10] Wells fills out this metaphor with a helpful discussion of the practice of improvisation in drama, including the importance of being committed to accepting rather than blocking anything offered by a fellow actor. Every word, gesture, or action must be treated as an invitation to respond if the drama is to move forward. In a similar way, Christians must make choices in the drama of life, and, Wells suggests, must never block the offers of the world. This does not mean, however, that everything the world offers, including that which is evil, must be accepted. Instead, he suggests that the church should "overaccept" all offers by refusing to see ethics as the clash of givens. The larger story of Scripture teaches us that we have more options than simply saying "yes" or "no," more options than simply accepting or blocking an offer. We can also receive what is being offered in an active way, retaining the initiative to transform what is being offered by reincorporating elements of the larger salvation story that we see ourselves a part of, and thus anticipating the fulfillment of that story. In the words of Wells:

> The interpretation of all human action and gesture in terms of accepting and blocking introduces the practice of overaccepting, in which the church receives the world's offers by placing them in a far larger story than the world ever imagined, and thus comes to see challenges and demands as gifts rather than givens.[11]

John Howard Yoder worked in a similar way. All assignments were accepted on their own terms, and he always took great care to acquaint himself with, and to situate his response relative to the range of discourse on any topic he was called on to address. After rigorously depicting and often complexifying this discourse, Yoder would usually end up asking a different question, to which he would then end up providing an insightful response. To use Wells' term, he "overaccepted" his assignments, moving beyond polarizing discourse by reframing the discussion in the light of the biblical narrative. The remainder of this chapter will attempt to follow this example as it examines the state of current debates over three particular manifestations of the power of technology.

---

9. Wells, *Improvisation*, 11.
10. Ibid., 12.
11. Ibid., 152.

Deciding to focus on particular examples of technology does present challenges, however, including deciding how many examples to consider, and choosing which examples to consider. I decided to focus on three examples because I was interested in exploring a range of issues, and yet I also wanted to be able to provide a relatively thorough examination of each example. Explaining why automobiles, genetically modified food, and the Internet were chosen as the three examples is a little more difficult. It may be helpful to note that I was looking for three examples that are fairly representative of, or central to life in contemporary Western societies, and that I was looking for examples that were both more mature and more recently developed.[12] While the main argument in chapter 4 will be that each of these technologies needs to be understood in a new way, this chapter seeks to demonstrate that the examples chosen are ripe for theological consideration. Finally, although I have no illusions that these examples will permit a comprehensive assessment of technology in general, each of them does raise issues that have broader applicability.

REFLECTING ON THE AUTOMOBILE

Background

Over the past century the automobile has become a significant force in the economy, environment, and culture of industrialized nations. In the words of Jacques Ellul, the automobile is "the most perfect symbol of the technical society."[13] Nonetheless, because the development and use of this particular manifestation of technology is now pervasive and routine, it may not seem to be the most enthralling entry point into a discussion of the *theological* significance of technology. Indeed, the historian Wesley Swanson has suggested that the study of "common cultural artifacts" such as the automobile is "often clouded by over-familiarity and a lack of perspective."[14] Yet this is precisely why the automobile makes such a good case study. It is *because* the automobile is now mundane, because the arguments extolling both its virtues and pitfalls are now mature, that an ex-

---

12. In the concluding section of *Ethics in an Age of Technology*, Ian Barbour provides a similar rationale for considering the "critical" technologies found in agriculture, energy, and computers. Thomas Homer-Dixon would seem to agree with my particular choices when he argues in *The Ingenuity Gap* that advances in transportation, agricultural, communication, and military technology over the past couple of centuries provide the most compelling markers for the pace of technological change.

13. Jacques Ellul, *Technological Bluff*, 372.

14. Swanson, "Cult of the Automobile," 98.

amination of the issues involved can benefit greatly from the perspective offered by theological discourse.[15] In addition, our intimate knowledge of a familiar or mature technology has the potential to enrich further reflection on unfamiliar or new technologies.[16]

Extremes

A significant problem with any mature argument is that positions become polarized and entrenched. The possibility of finding common ground in the middle diminishes as arguments are reduced to points lofted back and forth by those minding the extremes. Thus, not surprisingly, clarity is *not* what one finds when searching for an overarching assessment of the automobile in contemporary culture.[17] On one side, authors in the fields of environmental science and political philosophy such as Julia Meaton and David Morrice provide helpful summaries of the litany of social and technical problems that we are all aware of, ranging from unsightly urban sprawl and the pain caused by accidents, to the unpleasant delays of traffic congestion and the unbelievable scale at which nonrenewable resources are being converted into dangerous pollutants.[18] While many are sympathetic toward those who argue that the use of automobiles should be restricted or at least reduced, in general we continue to drive more and more.[19] In the words of the Austrian philosopher Ivan Illich, "Many more

---

15. Of course, automotive technology has also evolved quite significantly over the past century. My focus in this section is on the automobile itself rather than one of the key technologies that made the automobile possible, the internal combustion engine, because the same issues are raised regardless of whether cars are powered by gasoline, electric batteries, or hydrogen fuel cells.

16. This is a point that historians of technology stress over and over, although it is rarely noted in contemporary debates. One exception is the sociologist Carl D. Bowman's "Emerging Biotechnologies."

17. The polarization I will be describing is evident in the essays collected for the "Opposing Viewpoints" series by Andrea C. Nakaya in *Cars in America*.

18. Meaton and Morrice, "Ethics and Politics of Private Automobile Use." Numerous books have been published on each of the problems discussed by Meaton and Morrice—examples include Kay, *Asphalt Nation*; Conover, *Routes of Man*; Brottman, *Car Crash Culture*; Vanderbilt, *Traffic*; Porter, *Economics at the Wheel*; and Hart and Spivak, *Automobile Dependence and Denial*.

19. The total number of vehicle miles traveled annually in the United States has increased dramatically since records started being kept. While the total has dipped slightly in recent years, the total increased from 1,120 billion vehicle miles in 1970 to a peak of 3,003 billion vehicle miles in 2007. This translates into almost 4,000 additional miles traveled per year on average for every person in the U.S. (after adjusting for the change in population over the same period of time). U.S. traffic volume trends and month-by-month data

people are against cars than are against driving them."[20] We are, according to critics of the automobile, not being rational.

On the other side of the argument, those who defend the automobile agree that its status has declined and that drivers are often seen to be a public nuisance. Columnist John Tierney, echoing Illich, notes that "Americans still love to own their cars, but they're sick of everyone else's."[21] However, in contrast to the suggestion of critics that a conspiracy of corporate interests is responsible for foisting automobiles on us all, benefactors such as Tierney suggest that liberal intellectual elites are responsible for turning people against the automobile.[22] To be sure, no advocate of driving more will deny the reality of the environmental problems caused by driving. However, they are convinced that these costs will continue to decrease with the development of new technology,[23] and that the benefits of the automobile have been under-appreciated. Critics of the automobile, according to its benefactors, are not being rational.

The result of all this irrationality is that car enthusiasts and car critics end up shouting at a crowd that cannot hear them, a crowd that, to use historian Howard P. Segal's apt term, has found a way to *accommodate* the automobile.[24] For the most part, North Americans have accepted this particular type of technology, whether they do so happily or grudgingly. The word I would choose to use is that we have been *seduced* by the automobile. Whether we know it, and resent being manipulated, or whether we don't know it, and feel nothing but love, automobiles have seductively found their way into our lives.

In my view, the key for moving beyond this impasse toward a more helpful overarching assessment of the automobile is to recognize that it is more than a scientific, economic, or political debate. In the words of Swanson: "To understand the appeal and vital symbolic power of the automobile

---

are available on the U.S. Department of Transportation Federal Highway Administration's Policy Information website: http://www.fhwa.dot.gov/policyinformation/travel_monitoring/tvt.cfm. Comparable data is harder to find for Canada.

20. Illich, *Tools for Conviviality*, 55.

21. Tierney, "The Way We Drive Now," 60. Of course, there are many more books that glorify rather than demonize cars—a few examples include Flink, *Automobile Age*; Finch, *Highways to Heaven*; Dunn, *Driving Forces*; and O'Rourke, *Driving Like Crazy*.

22. Tierney, "The Way We Drive Now," 65.

23. Evidence of the expectation of a technical fix to the environmental problems of the automobile abound. See, for example, Vaitheeswaran and Carson, *Zoom*; and Sperling and Gordon, *Two Billion Cars*.

24. Segal, "Automobile and the Prospect of an American Technological Plateau," 83; italics added.

it is essential *not* to view it as a transportation device."[25] Drivers will not necessarily give up their wheels on the basis of a more compelling cost-benefit analysis, or even when they are encouraged to by political policy. Nor will car critics endorse new highway construction even if everyone drove hybrid vehicles. At its core, this impasse relates to disagreements that cannot be separated from differences in moral reasoning.

One study of the automobile that refuses to reduce everything to science, economics, or politics, or better put, refuses to neatly distinguish science, economics, politics, and morality, is *For the Love of the Automobile*, written by Wolfgang Sachs. Sachs, who has studied both sociology and theology, is a German professor currently working in the areas of globalization and sustainable development. He begins his book with the same question that other critics of the automobile find so vexing:

> The problem with the automobile today consists precisely in the fact that the automobile is *not* a problem. Why, I asked myself, does the loyalty to automobiles remain so unassailable, even though everyone knows that cars already have their future behind them?"[26]

Sachs' reading of the development of the automobile in Germany is one attempt to show that it is a "morality play."[27] He demonstrates this alternative view by discussing the motivation of the first drivers, all of whom were elites and enthusiasts more concerned with social status and the mastery of their environment than with mobility. Thus the "automobile sank its roots into society from the top down."[28] The rest of the book is a portrait of just how deep these roots go—of how the automobile itself became dependent on complex technological systems, and, more importantly, came to embody specific moral ideals. Citing the often quoted phrase from Roland Barthes that the automobile is "the Gothic cathedral of modern times," Sachs argues that just as "the cathedral is not merely a shelter, so the automobile is more than a means of transport; automobiles are, indeed, the material representations of a culture."[29] The following paragraphs will discuss three of the key ideals of this culture: autonomy, speed, and comfort.[30]

25. Swanson, "Cult of the Automobile," 99.
26. Sachs, *For the Love of the Automobile*, vii.
27. Ibid., viii.
28. Ibid., 36.
29. Ibid., 91.

30. Sachs also includes chapters on the desire for novelty ("A Flood of Novelties and the Hunger for Improvement"); consumption ("Travel and the Tourist's Gaze"); and instantaneousness ("Space and Time as Resources").

Ideals Embodied and Encouraged by the Automobile

Autonomy

Sachs's discussion of the moral thrust of the automobile comes in a section of chapters called "Desires." The first of these he titles "Independent as a Lord," a desire that points to the ideal of autonomy. In contrast to the railroad, which leaves us "condemned to passivity," according to one critic, the automobile requires our active involvement.[31] It requires that *we* choose when to depart and which route to take. Perhaps the centrality of individual choice is why, in the words of the engineer Jack Swearengen: "The most cherished American freedoms have come to be identified with privately owned vehicles, almost as if prior to the twentieth century Americans were not free."[32] Philosopher Loren Lomasky has expanded on this point in his essay "Autonomy and Automobility," arguing that self-directedness or autonomy is a distinctively human trait, and thus any technology which enhances this trait is inherently good. In short "automobile transport is good for people in virtue of its intrinsic features."[33] Lomasky is convinced that the ability of the automobile to enhance autonomy is rivaled only by the printing press and possibly the computer.

Lomasky's essay helps explain what was described earlier as the irrational behavior of drivers. People prefer driving cars to riding the bus, streetcar or train; they "vote with their tires"[34] because the costs of driving do not outweigh the importance they ascribe to autonomy, an ideal that the automobile's critics have not fully considered. The depth of this desire can be seen in the fact that drivers are willing to put up with such high economic and social costs. For example, if cars were valued strictly for their mobility, why do so many people endure spending so much time sitting in traffic jams during their daily commute? The desire for autonomy is not met by mobility alone, but also includes the exertion of control over our immediate environment.

Jack Clayton Swearengen attempts to come up with a similar kind of summary after discussing the needs that automobile advertisements claim to address in *Beyond Paradise*, 246–47. A more enthusiastic take on the benefits of the automobile can be found in the "Automobile in American Life" exhibit at the Henry Ford Museum in Dearborn, Michigan. For a discussion of the ideological underpinnings of this museum, see Staudenmaier and Schlereth's review of the exhibition "Made in America."

31. Sachs, *For the Love of the Automobile*, 93.
32. Swearengen, *Beyond Paradise*, 245.
33. Lomasky, "Autonomy and Automobility," 6.
34. Ibid.

Nonetheless, there are some significant problems with Lomasky's essay. Although autonomy was desired long before the car came along, Sachs wonders to what extent this particular technology allowed this particular desire to increase in importance:

> Technology does not simply fall from the sky; rather, the aspirations of a society (or a class) combine with technical possibility to inject a bit of culture into the design like a genetic code. Yet neither do lifestyle and desires emerge from the thin air of culture; instead they coalesce around a given technology. A technological invention is often accompanied by cultural creativity.[35]

Thus the desire for autonomy has "coalesced" around the automobile, and the automobile has allowed it to appear as though it was "natural."[36] To what extent then has the premium Lomasky places on autonomy as an ideal been influenced by the very technology he endorses because it complements this ideal? To what extent has the automobile contributed to a wave of "cultural creativity" characterized by the marks of autonomy and the flourishing of individualism? Sachs goes on to suggest that independence or autonomy is embodied not only in automobiles, but in all modern technology: "Technology fulfills the desire to leave behind burdensome social, spatial, or temporal ties and become one's own master."[37] What began as a desire, as an ideal to strive toward, has become a moral imperative.

For Sachs the irony of this emphasis on the desire for autonomy is that the more prevalent automobiles became, the less autonomous the drivers became. This autonomy is not lost simply because of traffic jams, but because of our dependence on the vast technological systems that make driving possible: "Ultimately all these 'independence machines' depend on streets and power lines, pipelines and radio waves, which in turn bind the individual with multiple ties to industries, power plants, drilling rigs, and broadcast stations." Every "increment of freedom in our private lives" comes at the cost of greater dependence on others. Thus "we have metamorphosed once again from drivers into passengers, even if self-propelled."[38] Put another way: "The desires of yesterday rain down on us as the compulsions of today."[39]

---

35. Sachs, *For the Love of the Automobile*, 92.
36. Ibid., 98.
37. Ibid., 100.
38. Ibid., 101.
39. Ibid., 208. Jacques Ellul's discussion of the automobile stresses this point, noting that "technological discourse tells us that the car is only an instrument of freedom," all the while ignoring the way in which cars actually undermine freedom by confining our choices to the options presented by one particular transportation

Speed

The second ideal embodied by the automobile that Sachs discusses is something he calls "Victorious Speed." Once again, this is a desire that was absorbed in the early days of the automobile, when the new invention was promoted through competitive races. Sachs suggests that the spectacle of car racing and the corresponding thrill of high-speed driving resulted in "nothing less than a new perception of reality":

> The drawing of pleasure and superiority in the role of driver, by teasing the limits of both the automobile and one's own fate, so that the world, the tired, old world, flew by and an admiring gaze looked after.[40]

The Czech novelist Milan Kundera describes this reality in terms the enthusiast understands best: "Speed is the form of ecstasy the technical revolution has bestowed on [humanity]."[41]

It is not difficult to see how, as with autonomy, speed is embodied in numerous other examples of modern technology. Indeed, the French philosopher Paul Virilio coined the term "dromology" to highlight the logic of speed that is integral to military and media technologies, and has come to permeate all dimensions of contemporary life.[42] Technology is better when it is faster, whether it is the computer used to design the car, the assembly line used to build the car, the car itself when it accelerates to pass a truck on a country road, or the pay-at-the-pump service station used to replenish the car with fuel. Speed, it turns out, is not only pleasurable because it is exciting or even risky, it is pleasurable because it appears to be efficient. In the words of the esteemed historian of technology Lewis Mumford, "There is only one efficient speed: *faster*."[43]

Just as our desire for autonomy is both embodied and encouraged by the automobile, so too is our desire for speed. The transformation of the tired, old world into the blur of a new world that makes our eyes water as it goes rushing by contributes to our assumption that history too is rushing

---

system. Quoting his good friend Bernard Charbonneau, Ellul points out that "the vehicle that was going to take us out of the crowds puts us back in them." Thus "vaunted autonomy quickly turns into increasing dependence relative to the car's demands." See Ellul, *Technological Bluff*, 373–74.

40. Ibid., 111. Compelling portrayals of the way motorsports continues to link the automobile with the desire for speed include: Post, *High Performance*; and Hughes, *Speed Addicts*.

41. Kundera, *Slowness*, 2.

42. Virilio, *Speed and Politics*. See also *Art of the Motor* and *Information Bomb*.

43. Quoted in Sachs, *For the Love of the Automobile*, 120.

forward, that it is progressing in a straight line toward ever greater accomplishments. Not simply progress, but the rate of progress—speed—is an ideal that has become a moral imperative.

Once again, there is a certain irony here. As Kundera reminds us, often speed is more about what we are rushing away from than what we are rushing to: "the degree of slowness is directly proportional to the intensity of memory; the degree of speed is directly proportional to the intensity of forgetting."[44] Furthermore, the seduction of speed is evident in the way more time is lost than gained as the speed of travel increases. As Sachs points out, instead of saving time, the automobile encourages us to travel farther: "its powers of speed are cashed in not for less time on the road, but for longer routes."[45] Ivan Illich goes so far as to make the claim that once a society breaks "the barrier of bicycle velocity" there is a demonstrable increase in "the total per capita monthly time spent at the service of the travel industry."[46] Thus, in the poetic words of Sachs, "The masters of space and time awaken to find themselves slaves of distance and haste."[47]

Comfort

The third ideal embodied and encouraged by the automobile that Sachs discusses is comfort. This is one desire that continues to increase with no end in sight, even as speed limits and traffic congestion, along with safety and economic costs, make alternatives to the automobile more attractive in regards to our desire for speed and autonomy. Indeed, an entry level car today includes features that were typically found only on high-end luxury cars

---

44. Kundera, *Slowness*, 39.

45. Sachs, *For the Love of the Automobile*, 185.

46. Illich, *Tools for Conviviality*, 79. Illich goes on to say that "addicts of any kind are willing to pay increasing amounts for declining satisfactions . . . Minds accustomed to thinking that transportation ought to provide speedy motion rather than reduction of the time and effort spent moving are boggled by this contrary hypothesis" (ibid., 82). Not only does Illich critique an obsession with speed because it leads to inefficient travel, but also because it separates people: "When a society commits itself to higher speeds, the speedometer becomes an indicator of social class" (ibid., 37).

It needs to be noted that Illich's critique of the ideal of speed is motivated by his interest in the value of autonomy. Indeed, his notion of conviviality—"autonomous and creative intercourse among persons, and the intercourse of person with their environment" (ibid., 11)—reflects a longing for individual freedom in the face of "industrial productivity" and the "radical monopoly" of technology that has "frozen not only the shape of the physical world but also the range of behavior and imagination" (ibid., 55).

47. Sachs, *For the Love of the Automobile*, 187.

just a few years ago. As Sachs puts it, "The tamer of the gasoline monster has become the pampered inhabitant of a comfort machine."[48] The problem he sees with this is that, as our cars become our castles and not simply our means of transportation, they serve to distance us from our environment in another significant way. Sachs' accusations seem excessive at first glance—for example: "Once sensation and gestures have been stilled, the comfort technology boasts that it will do away with thinking."[49] However, when we reflect on the introduction not only of new comfort features such as active noise reduction systems which provide a quieter ride, but on new safety features such as anti-lock brakes, stability control systems, and air bags, not to mention sonar technology to detect objects behind a vehicle, and navigation systems to plot the easiest route from point A to point B, it seems as though he may have a point. Comfort involves reducing the demands on drivers, including the demand to think.

Aside from the safety risks this poses, Sachs argues that

> When the supply of comfort has exceeded a certain limit, the probability rises that what once was welcomed as shelter comes to be experienced as a disabling prison. Not as a prison of oppression, but as one of understimulation—for it is inherent in the essence of the comfort technology that human senses, capacities, and responsibilities lay fallow.[50]

Thus comfort poses a risk to contrary desires for things like adventure, effort, and challenge. Yet Sachs thinks that the larger impact of technologies of comfort such as the automobile may be even more significant:

> Perhaps, indeed, we are all the more defenseless today in that technological development, rather than saving us, has in fact caused our moral-cultural capacity to deal cheerfully and easily with our limitations—to be able "to suffer" them well, as the old expression paradoxically puts it—to atrophy.[51]

The desire for comfort, as with speed and autonomy, is thus of considerable moral import. Not only has it become a moral imperative as well as a technical specification, but something significant has been lost along the way.

48. Ibid., 134.
49. Ibid., 131.
50. Ibid., 135.
51. Ibid., 130.

REFLECTING ON GENETICALLY MODIFIED FOOD

Background

The automobile has undoubtedly led to a revolution in the way many people travel, although it is far from the only revolution in transportation technology in human history. Societies have been dramatically reshaped by horses, sea-faring ships, and trains long before cars came along, and by the advent of air travel, not to mention bicycles, after cars became commonplace. In a similar way, it is possible to pinpoint several dramatic revolutions in agriculture throughout human history, although most do not come to mind quite so easily. For example, following the dramatic decline of the population of England in the fourteenth and fifteenth centuries due to the plague known as Black Death, that country's agricultural practices were dramatically altered. Instead of continuing to grow grains that were no longer needed for human consumption, farmers put land to grass and began raising more sheep for wool and cattle for dairy, and in the process they transformed the English economy and diet.[52] A better-known revolution occurred in the decades following World War II, when agricultural practices in the Western world were transformed by the application of scientific research and modern technology. This led to a "Green Revolution"—to an exponential increase in crop harvests that managed to keep pace with the exponential increase in the world's human population.[53] While some people talk today about the need for another Green Revolution to overcome hunger and famine through the transformation of the farm economies of Africa and Asia, one of the most commonly discussed and contentious issues in agriculture in recent years is the revolutionary impact of genetic engineering. Insights from the new scientific field of molecular biology have, in relatively short order, led to an explosion of experimental research and to the commercialization of genetically modified organisms.

Before going any further, this section will provide some background on the basic discovery that led to the field of molecular biology in the first

---

52. Thirsk, *Alternative Agriculture*, 7–10.

53. This expression was coined by William S. Gaud, the director of USAID in 1968. After noting the myriad of new technologies that were being applied to farming, he said: "These and other developments in the field of agriculture contain the makings of a new revolution. It is not a violent Red Revolution like that of the Soviets, nor is it a White Revolution like that of the Shah of Iran. I call it the Green Revolution." See Gaud's address to the Society for International Development: "The Green Revolution: Accomplishments and Apprehensions." This label now seems ironic, given that the widespread use of mechanized equipment and application of fertilizers, herbicides, and pesticides has led to significant environmental problems.

place: Deoxyribonucleic acid or DNA. It is often said that this complex molecule provides us with the blueprints of life, since it is found in the cells of all living things. DNA is what links humans not simply to their own species or to chimpanzees, but to trees and amoebas as well. Every DNA molecule is composed of a double helix structure of sugars bound together by sets of genes, the segments of the molecule that carry information by being paired up in different combinations. While individual pairs of genes control certain cell processes and characteristics, the sequence or relative arrangement of these pairs along the DNA strand is also significant. Furthermore, genes are also organized into sections or chromosomes in order to facilitate the process of cell replication—DNA are located in the nucleus of the cell,[54] and must themselves be replicated in order for cells to divide. A human DNA molecule is composed of between 20,000 and 25,000 different genes that are combined in a chain of 3 billion pairs that can be divided into 23 pairs of chromosomes.[55]

James D. Watson and Francis Crick are the scientists most commonly associated with the discovery of DNA, after publishing what is accepted to be the first accurate model of its structure in the journal *Nature* in 1953,[56] and receiving the Noble Prize in Medicine in 1962. Nonetheless, their model would not have been possible had scientists not already isolated this particular molecule and confirmed the significant role it played in the function and replication of cells.[57] And even before this discovery, the basic principles of genetic science had been articulated by the Austrian monk Gregor Johann Mendel (1822–1884).[58] By systematically breeding hybrid peas in his monastery garden, and, most importantly, carefully documenting the results, Mendel made two revolutionary discoveries. First, since particular characteristics of hybrid offspring tended to resemble either one parent or the other instead

---

54. Exceptions are prokaryotes such as bacteria, where DNA is found in the cell's cytoplasm.

55. Typically more complex organisms have longer DNA molecules with more base pairs of genes, however, there are exceptions. For example, the DNA of the single-celled amoeba *Amoeba dubia* is over 200 times larger than the DNA of a human cell. Furthermore, although fruit flies and round worms have shorter DNA chains than humans, they have twice as many unique genes. See Cavalier-Smith, *Evolution of Genome Size*.

56. Watson and Crick, "Molecular Structure of Nucleic Acids."

57. DNA was first isolated by the Swiss physician Friedrich Miescher in 1869, although he called it "nuclein." And Watson and Crick's model was only developed when they made use of X-ray diffraction images taken by the English biophysicist Rosalind Franklin.

58. Henig, *Monk in the Garden*. The story of Mendel has led some to argue that the field of genetic engineering owes its existence to the Roman Catholic church, or at least to the abbot who encouraged his work. See, for example, Perry, *Food for Thought*, 17.

of being a blend of the two, he conceived of the idea of a hereditary unit or a determining factor that could either be dominant or recessive. He hypothesized that these units or factors normally occurred in pairs in the cells of an organism, but were segregated in the formation of sex cells. Thus when the egg and sperm of an organism unite to form a new pair of hereditary units, the dominant unit masks the recessive unit.[59] Mendel further hypothesized that these units or factors only impacted particular characteristics of the organism. Thus, since the recessive unit is still present even when its impact is masked, it can re-emerge in subsequent offspring.[60] Indeed, Mendel was able to accurately predict the probability that a given pea plant would produce peas of a certain color based on his knowledge of its parentage.

Molecular biology is obviously a much more complicated picture than the basic introduction provided here—there is much more to the story of life than the information contained in genes. For example, it is now known that there is a complex relationship between DNA, ribonucleic acid (RNA), and proteins within the nucleus of a cell. Nonetheless, knowledge of the sequence of genes in the human genome has already led to dramatic insights into the role that particular genes play in dozens of illnesses. Furthermore, this basic picture helps explain the process of genetic engineering— "recombinant" DNA are created by assembling a new DNA molecule from segments of other DNA molecules, and then transferring this new molecule into a cell in order to be replicated, and thus to grow into a new organism.[61]

Many of the developments in genetic engineering that have grabbed the headlines—for example, genetic cloning of animals as an alternative to natural or assisted reproduction, or the insertion of human genes into the DNA of animals—have remained confined to the laboratory. Nonetheless, as mentioned in chapter 1, these are the kinds of topics that seem most prominent in the field of bioethics. While I do not want to downplay other important issues such as the advances in medical knowledge that have resulted from genetic testing, or the significant impact of gene therapy on diseases experienced by many people, this section will only be discussing one

---

59. Mendel's first principle is known as the law of segregation.

60. Mendel's second principle is known as the law of independent assortment.

61. Aside from the complexity of cutting and splicing the DNA itself, inserting the new molecule into the nucleus of a cell represents a significant technical challenge. Successful approaches include the use of enzymes, chemicals and electric charges to break down the cell wall, the use of fine metal particles coated with DNA that are shot at the cell with pressurized helium gas from a "biolistic gun," and "agrobacterium-mediated transformation" which relies on an invasive bacteria to deliver the DNA. This is another case where growth in scientific knowledge depends upon technology at least as much as it leads to new technology. See Liang and Skinner, *Genetically Modified Crops*, 3–7.

small aspect of the genetic revolution: the application of genetic engineering to the plants that produce much of the food we eat.[62]

Extremes

There has certainly been no shortage of headlines related to the topic of genetically modified food.[63] Indeed, in contrast to a search for reflections on the automobile, it is easy to be overwhelmed by the vast amount of literature that has been published on genetically modified food in recent decades. Furthermore, to a greater extent than the automobile, this remains a technology in flux—a technology that is still being developed, that is still be applied in new ways, and, perhaps most importantly, a technology that has still not been fully accepted and integrated globally. Although the acreage of fields sown with genetically modified seeds has grown dramatically in the Americas, in Europe a moratorium on growing genetically modified crops for human consumption was put in place in 1997, and it has only been since 2004 that exemptions to this moratorium have become more common.

Like the literature on the automobile, reflections on genetically modified foods also tend to be polarized. A quick survey of recent book titles makes this clear: on the one side we read about *Fields of Plenty*[64] and a *High Tech Harvest*,[65] and on the other side we read about *Seeds of Deception*[66] and the *Stolen Harvest*.[67] On the one side we read about *Designer Food*,[68] *Food for*

---

62. In this section I will be referring to *genetically modified food*, although some of my sources prefer other terms for the same thing. Genetically modified foods are a specific family of genetically modified organisms that are created using genetic engineering, or, more precisely, recombinant DNA technology. The following explanation by Nancy Harris helps to clarify the use of these terms: "*Genetic engineering* (GE) is the standard U.S. term for this new technology, also called recombinant DNA (rDNA) technology. In Europe, *genetically modified* (GM) is more commonly used to describe the technology, because this term translates more easily between different languages. The organism that is created through genetic engineering is called a *genetically modified organism* (GMO). The terms used to describe the foods produced from genetic engineering include *biotech foods*, *gene foods*, *bioengineered foods*, *gene-altered foods*, and *transgenetic foods*" (Harris, Genetically Engineered Foods, 5).

63. One bibliography published in 2000 included 608 items—see Nordquist, *Biotechnology and Our Food*.

64. By Michael Ableman.

65. By Paul F. Lurquin.

66. By Jeffrey M. Smith.

67. By Vandana Shiva.

68. By Gregory E. Pence.

Thought,[69] and *The Frankenfood Myth*,[70] and on the other we read about *Eat Your Genes*,[71] *Dinner at the New Gene Café*,[72] and *Vexing Nature*.[73] Indeed, it has not taken long at all for positions to become entrenched. Since in many ways this remains a live debate not just among academics but within and between societies, published reflections are a pale reflection of just how conflict-ridden the issue of genetically modified food is.[74] This is a political struggle as well as an intellectual struggle, and as such there are grassroots organizations as well as corporations, professional associations as well as government regulators, and street protests as well as magazine advertisements that all seek to frame the debate.[75] Not surprisingly then, a person's response to a question about genetically modified foods can often be predicted based upon their association with one of these myriad of advocates.

In many cases the dispute over this technology revolves around just how radical or groundbreaking it really is. One regulatory expert insists that genetic engineering "is probably one of the most technologically powerful developments the world has ever seen. It's the biological equivalent of splitting the atom."[76] Proponents are certainly quick to underline the brilliant science and hard work that has unlocked the enormous potential of genetic engineering, but they also stress that humans have manipulated the genes of plants for thousands of years through selective and cross breeding. Sometimes hybrid species emerge when two or three different species with different genetic structures combine without human intervention. By the early twentieth century, however, careful intervention in the plant pollination process led to hybrid species that were incapable of reproducing and thus could never have emerged naturally. Even though they could no longer save and replant seeds, farmers embraced this technology because of

69. By John Perry.
70. By Henry I. Miller and Gregory Conko.
71. By Stephen Nottingham.
72. By Bill Lambrecht.
73. By Gary L. Comstock.

74. John Perry suggests that people respond at a visceral level to issues related to food because it "has both mythic or . . . theological symbolism, as well as a more prosaic meaning" (*Food for Thought*, 12).

75. Key players include organizations such as the Center for Global Food Issues, the Council for Agricultural Science and Technology (CAST), and the Council for Biotechnology Information on the one side, and the Institute for Food & Development Policy/Food First, Physicians and Scientists for Responsible Application of Science and Technology (PSRAST), and the Rural Advancement Foundation International (RAFI) on the other.

76. Suzanne Wuerthele, quoted in the introduction to Harris, *Genetically Engineered Foods*, 5.

the dramatically higher yields it produced. Furthermore, over the past fifty years, nuclear radiation and chemicals have been used to accelerate genetic mutations, providing a much more diverse sample of organisms for breeders to use in selecting desirable characteristics. In fact, this process of "mutagenesis" has been used to produce over two thousand varieties of crops such as barley and wheat that are now grown in more than seventy countries.[77] Thus proponents insist what is new about recent techniques is that genetic manipulation is now much more precise, and can be implemented much faster, since we no longer need to manipulate plant species or hybrids over many generations, or use cumbersome techniques in order to isolate a desired characteristic. Genetic engineering is thus seen by many to be the most recent of numerous approaches along a technological continuum, and its critics are accused of being ignorant, irrational, or deceitful.

Opponents of genetic engineering argue that those who promote this technology are refusing to acknowledge their own ignorance. They stress that it is more than another development along a continuum of manipulation techniques; instead, it represents a qualitative shift of great magnitude. They point out that conventional techniques mimic natural developments in that they manipulate different forms of the same gene already present in a given plant species' gene pool, or, in some cases, a closely related species. The latest techniques, however, transfer genes from completely different species. Bacteria genes are most commonly utilized, but examples have also included inserting Brazilian nut genes into soybeans, daffodil genes into rice, cauliflower genes into potatoes, and firefly genes into tomatoes.[78] It is impossible for these kinds of genetic transformations to happen naturally, or even with the help of conventional techniques, and thus they represent an entirely new frontier with uncertain potential for harm as well as good.[79]

Opponents also point out that our knowledge of molecular biology has not kept pace with our ability to engineer new organisms. The process of genetic engineering remains filled with ambiguity and uncertainty—the precision with which we can transfer particular genes is not matched by a precise understanding of the consequences. We do not know exactly what will happen when we add a new gene to the mix. Thus opponents have

77. Degregori, "Genetically Modified Foods," 836.

78. Many of the genes utilized from foreign species are used as "marker" genes—their purpose is to provide a way to determine whether a section of DNA has been successfully inserted into an organism, rather than to change the fundamental characteristics of the organism itself.

79. The debate over what is "natural," and whether humans should do things that are unnatural is a key front in the debate over genetic engineering, especially among bioethicists. See, for example, Brooke, "Detracting from Divine Power?"; and Scott, "Nature, Technology and the Rule of God."

advocated guidelines based upon what has been termed the "precautionary principle"—it is better to be safe than sorry.[80] They have argued that it is downright irrational not to do more testing on the health effects of consuming genetically modified foods, and the potential for these new transgenetic species to mutate or cross with other species once released into the environment.[81] In the absence of regulatory oversight, opponents insist that at the very least consumers should be informed of the presence of genetically modified organisms in the food they buy. To do anything less is deceitful.

Thus, once again, we find sharply divided perspectives on a particular technology, each accusing the other of the same shortcomings. The debate about the health and environmental risks presented by genetic modification is a significant one, and both proponents and opponents have struggled to muster whatever scientific evidence they can find to make their case. However, another crucial piece of this debate is the extent to which the potential benefits of genetically modified foods mitigate against these risks. For example, to what extent can herbicide, pesticide, and/or fertilizer use be reduced as a result of this technology? Does this measurable, immediate environmental benefit justify the health and environmental risks, which so far appear to be hypothetical costs? Perhaps because the data on whether there is a measurable benefit in this regard is unclear at this point in time, the more common trade-off that is offered is the extent to which farmers can increase their yields as a result of this technology, and thus make more food available to feed a growing global population.[82] Or the potential for

80. The precautionary principle provided the backbone for European agricultural regulations that erred on the side of safety when it comes to genetically modified food, although it is a concept applied in many other realms of risk assessment, including, for example, the pharmaceutical industry in the U.S. The philosophical grounding for this principle can be found in the work of Hans Jonas. As noted in chapter 1, Jonas argued for a "heuristics of fear" that would consider worst-case scenarios before undertaking any technological project. See *Imperative of Responsibility*, x.

81. In high profile cases in the U.S., this testing has been carried out after the fact, partly because the U.S. Food and Drug Administration (FDA) agreed with industry advocates that genetically modified foods such as tomatoes were "substantially similar" to unmodified tomatoes. More recently, U.S. companies have started to encourage rather than resist the government regulation of biotechnology, seeing this as their only hope of winning over skeptical consumers and investors. Nonetheless, critics would likely be surprised by just how involved the FDA and other government agencies have been in the development of genetically modified foods, and how complex this process became as a result. See, for example, Martineau, *First Fruit*.

82. This argument is gaining traction in light of the crises caused by shortages and dramatic price increases in the global food market in recent years. Interestingly, the automobile has been blamed for much of the recent rise in corn prices—more specifically, the increase is blamed on rising demand for biofuels due to changes in government policy designed to reduce dependence on fossil fuels.

cheaply delivering desperately needed vitamins and even medicines to people in poor countries through their food is touted as a worthy spin-off of this technology. It seems as though economic and humanitarian benefits need to be added to the equation if we are going to offer an assessment of genetic engineering.

In fact, the economic and cultural impact of genetically modified food has divided opponents of this technology more than anything else. It is true that European opposition to genetically modified foods was galvanized and eventually entrenched by safety concerns, but more widespread opposition appears to track the rise of the anti-globalization movement in the late 1990s.[83] Criticism coalesced around genetically modified foods in large part because it was a profound symbol of the rise of corporate power, and the sacrifice of cultural and environmental diversity that was often being made for the sake of global competitiveness. It also seems as though the prominence of debates about genetically modified food has declined along with the strength of public protests against the institutions promoting globalization such as the International Monetary Fund or the Group of Eight leading industrialized nations.

In a similar way to these broad-based concerns, theological commentary on genetically modified food often attempts to raise issues of social justice and the common good.[84] Yet I wonder whether these theologians have gone far enough in re-framing the debate. For the moral calculus that is typically proposed still depends entirely upon supposedly objective data generated by scientists, politicians, and especially economists. It still comes down to the numbers—how much food is produced, how many people benefit from it, how much of a reduction in pesticide use is there, and so on. These approaches seem to confirm that economics, even if broadly understood to include issues of sustainability and justice, should be the driving factor behind the development and implementation of this technology.[85] It seems as though the moral efficacy of genetically modified foods cannot be determined *a priori* by theologians, because moral issues only come into play in the *application* of the technology. In fact, there is a striking pattern in the way that those who seek

---

83. Manifestos of the anti-globalization movement include Korten, *When Corporations Rule the World* and Klein, *No Logo*.

84. See, for example, Perry, *Food for Thought*; and Pontifical Council for Justice and Peace, Study Seminar: "GMOs: Threat or Hope?"

85. Not surprisingly then, churches are not immune to debates over genetically modified foods—as noted toward the end of chapter 1, prior to 2003 a variety of perspectives were being advocated by bishops within the Catholic church. For debates in Mennonite circles, see Siemens, *Harvest in the Balance*.

to find middle ground in debates over genetically modified food also tend to argue that the technology itself is morally neutral.[86]

Ideals Embodied and Encouraged by Genetically Modified Food

Control

As demonstrated by the work of Wolfgang Sachs on the automobile, the most helpful approaches for making sense of the flood of information on genetically modified foods stress that this technology is morally weighted, not morally neutral. Its use leads to the elevation of particular ideals that embody and encourage a particular moral vision. Thus, as with the automobile, the impact of this technology goes far beyond what can be scientifically measured. One example of a more helpful approach is offered by Samuel Wells in his discussion of an improvisational approach to ethics.[87] As I have done in the preceding section, he sets out the commonly offered reasons why genetically modified food should be accepted and why it should be rejected.[88] He then questions some of what is assumed by those making these arguments, for example, the tendency of those promoting genetically modified foods to assume that the problem of hunger in the two-thirds world is due to a lack of food,[89] and that progress is defined by getting more for a lower price. He also points out that those resisting this technology need to be clearer about where the threshold lies between interacting with and interfering with the natural world, that their focus on avoiding ingesting impure food ignores the greater danger posed to the human body from impurities within, and the reality that power is always a problem, regardless of whether or not it is concentrated in the hands

---

86. See, for example, Perry, *Food for Thought*; Pence, *Designer Food*; and Lurquin, *High Tech Food*. Some of these voices also seem to hold out hope that it is possible to stay above the fray or step into some neutral, objective, and nonpartisan space in order to weigh all the available options.

87. See chapter 14: "A Promising Offer: Unlimited Food," in *Improvisation*, 201–12.

88. Reasons Wells lists for accepting genetically modified food include: (1) increased food production and decreased use of pesticides by producers, (2) fresher and healthier food for consumers, and (3) hardier crops that producers in the two-thirds world can grow in more hostile environments. Reasons for blocking include: (1) humanity should not "play God" by "interfering with nature, (2) unforeseen and irreversible consequences to human health (e.g., novel toxins) or the environment (e.g., superweeds), and (3) the concentration of corporate power in controlling our food supply.

89. Robert Song provides a theological critique of this assumption, noting that is also assumes "scarcity and death are the truth of things." Song goes on to say that "the idea that genetically engineered food is the *necessary* means to future food provision assumes that only technological solutions will solve the problems of the world." See "Sharing Communion," 390, 398.

of multinational corporations. Finally, Wells suggests that both sides of this debate have more in common than they recognize—for example, they both believe that this issue is really about power. For one side this is a problem, for the other, it is a solution.

A sign of the moral character of genetically modified food is revealed by this discussion of power—more specifically, with the desire for control. Humans have always been preoccupied with food because our existence depends on it; civilizations have risen and fallen based upon the availability of food, and widespread famines remain commonplace in many parts of the world. Indeed, hundreds of millions of people are one bad harvest away from experiencing hunger, and even in North America farmers are engaged in a daily struggle with the weather, pests, and weeds, not to mention with variable market prices, in order to earn their livelihood. Thus finding ways to exert control over these forces is completely understandable—it is what agricultural workers everywhere have always had to do. Even the opponents of genetically modified food would agree that exerting some degree of control over the natural world is both necessary and good. They would also agree that the more control farmers and consumers can exert in the economic world, the better.

What is most interesting about the technology of genetic engineering is the degree to which it both reflects and amplifies this longing for control. Genetic engineering provides us with a contemporary illustration of the Promethean myth—it is a new form of fire that brings with it both great promise and great peril because of the way it dramatically extends human power. Who can resist the seduction of this possibility for control? Who would want to turn down the opportunities it presents?

Framing control in this way—as a perfectly reasonable or even necessary desire that has morphed into a moral imperative—echoes Gerald McKenny's perspective on biotechnology more generally. As discussed in chapter one, McKenny is convinced that modern technologies are only distinctive because of the "vastly greater scope" of their intervention.[90] The potential for control fuels the quest for control, which further increases the potential for control, and so on.

Mastery

The possibilities for control presented by genetic engineering go so far as to suggest the possibility that we might someday not simply control outcomes, but master contingency itself. Humanity might not simply control

---

90. McKenny, *To Relieve the Human Condition*, 5.

the unforeseen and unpredictable variables that our environment throws at us, but understand these variables to the point where biological life is no longer a process that is necessarily marked by contingency and chance. For advocates of genetically modified food, mastery is the logical consequence of taking responsibility; for critics the drive for mastery is the product of hubris. Both seem to agree that the quest for mastery, not simply control, is the driving force behind this technology.[91]

Regardless of how one evaluates it, the ideal of mastery highlights the moral trajectory of genetic engineering. Indeed, it is clear there are moral implications to genetically modified foods that go beyond the effects that can be measured on the health of humans and the rest of creation. I agree with philosopher Conrad G. Brunk that we need to reflect on the impact that this particular technology has on the way we think, on what we come to value as good. Brunk has repeatedly sought to highlight the fact that technologies pose *moral* risks in addition to the readily apparent environmental, economic, and social risks.[92] McKenny makes a similar point when he insists that "the utopian effort to render our lives free from fate or fortune has impoverished our moral lives and entangles us in new forms of control."[93] Instead of freeing us, our preoccupation with mastery enslaves us: the healthy desire to take responsibility for our well-being has morphed into the expectation that we can and must try to seize complete control of creation, not just partial control. We must move beyond limiting the forces of the natural world to actively intervening in the natural world in order to manipulate these forces for our own benefit. Contingency and chance become things we must overcome, not minimize.

---

91. Theologian Peter Scott wonders if there is actually a substantive difference between critics and advocates of genetic engineering in this regard:

> Is stewardship a sustainable position in the context of the manipulation of nature in genetic engineering? In other words, does not the notion of stewardship in fact connect with, and support, the concept of nature in genetic engineering? The terminus of both is the same: the denial of the agency and genuine otherness of nature. Put differently, genetic modification operates with a notion of nature as mastered; stewardship with the demand for action in the face of nature. Both support a view of nature as inert, without agency. We travel by two different routes to a single destination: the denial of the agency and genuine otherness of nature. ("Response to Chapter 4," 112)

92. See "The Biotechnology Vision"; "Religion, Risk, and the Technological Society"; "Ethical Values, the Technological Mind"; and "Professionalism and Responsibility in the Technological Society." Brunk's focus on risk is problematic to the extent that it still lends itself to a utilitarian approach to the ethics of technology. He has simply enlarged the scope of the cost/benefit analysis.

93. McKenny, *To Relieve the Human Condition*, 4.

A quick survey of high-profile controversies with genetically modified foods suggests that differences often have less to do with a concern for control than with a concern for mastery. For example, "Golden Rice," a variety first developed in 1999 by two German scientists to produce beta-carotene, has been heralded as providing the solution to vitamin A deficiency. The lack of this vitamin is estimated to cause death and blindness in hundreds of thousands of children in Asia every year due to weakened immune systems. Certainly, the fact that Peter Beyer and Ingo Potrykus were able to not only successfully develop this genetic modification, but to convince thirty-two different corporations to grant them the right to infringe on seventy related patents in order to bring their seeds to market without paying licensing fees is truly remarkable.[94] Yet even more remarkable is the way promoters of genetically modified food have used Golden Rice to promote other products. The rhetoric not only from corporate advertisements, but from politicians and journalists suggests that just as genetically modified foods make it possible to end vitamin deficiencies, they will make it possible to end diseases by cheaply delivering mass medications, and even end world hunger.[95] The point does not seem to be that this technology will lead to measurable improvements, but that it will solve problems once and for all. The point is not simply control, but mastery.

A second example from the same time period is the development of what became known as "terminator technology," the genetic modification of seeds that made their subsequent offspring sterile. Pioneered by Delta and Pine Land, a U.S. cotton seed company, this technology was attractive to seed producers who were anxious to develop ways to police the use of their technology other than relying on contracts and laws to prevent farmers from saving seed or competitors from stealing their technology. Once again, the impetus here seems to go beyond a desire for control to the desire for mastery over all stages of the life of an organism. Widespread public outcry, especially from the two-thirds world, led to a global moratorium on the use of this technology.

---

94. Pringle, *Food, Inc.*, 33.

95. The irony is that the dramatic increase in crop yields in recent decades has been accompanied by a little-noticed but dramatic *decrease* in the nutritional content of many crops. This means we need to eat more corn, soybeans, wheat, and rice (not to mention fruits and vegetables) in order to get the same amount of essential nutrients. See Halweil, "Still No Free Lunch."

Conformity

A third ideal that is amplified by the power of genetic engineering is conformity. Throughout our history, humans have relied on an amazing variety of food sources in extremely diverse climates and cultures. Somewhere between 10,000 and 50,000 of the more than 250,000 species of plants alive today are edible, and since agrarian societies emerged from hunter-gatherer societies, at least 7,000 of these species have been cultivated and used for food. The diversity within these species can also be substantial—in Papua New Guinea alone more than 5,000 varieties of sweet potatoes have been grown. Of course, this diversity was bound to decline with increased knowledge and trade, but in the past century the application of modern technology meant that farmers had to become increasingly specialized at a much more rapid rate. In recent years, as the Indian scientist and food activist Vandana Shiva notes: "Just 30 species provide 90 percent of world calorie intake, and only four species—rice, maize, wheat, and soybeans—provide most of the calories and proteins consumed by the world's population through global trade."[96] Journalist Peter Pringle provides even more startling evidence of the extent to which U.S. farmers have specialized over the course of the twentieth century. By 1983, only 3 percent of the seed varieties that had been publicly available at some point since the turn of the twentieth century could be found at commercial seed providers. For example: "Of the 7,089 varieties of apple in use during the same period, 6,211 had been lost, and of 2,683 pears, 2,354 no longer existed." As Pringle put it, "A plant had to have something special to offer to survive to the end of the twentieth century."[97] It is widely acknowledged that genetic engineering accelerates this trend, as seed providers seek to build markets for a single variety of a single species that has been equipped with something extra special that sets it apart from the alternatives.

Not surprisingly, promoters and critics of genetically modified foods have different perspectives on this situation. Some emphasize the significant benefits offered by increased standardization to both farmers and those who process or sell their harvests, and others emphasize well-known dangers that monocultures present such as vulnerability to disease, not to mention

---

96. Shiva, *Stolen Harvest*, 79. Journalist Michael Pollan echoes this point in his recent book *In Defense of Food*: "Today corn contributes 554 calories a day to America's per capita food supply and soy another 257. Add wheat (768 calories) and rice (91) and you can see there isn't a whole lot of room left in the American stomach for any other foods. Today these four crops account for two thirds of the calories we eat" (ibid., 117).

97. Pringle, *Food, Inc.*, 39.

the loss of the untold benefits of biodiversity.[98] Some see genetically modified foods as simply another step along a continuum leading toward greater conformity to universal (and better) standards, while others see genetically modified foods as the culmination of a problematic trend, as the epitome of all that is wrong with modern industrialized agriculture. Once again, the issue has less to do with disputes over the data than it does with the underlying moral framework that shape the way the data is understood.

A quick survey of high-profile controversies involving genetically modified foods confirms that differing assessments of the drive toward conformity is often a significant issue. For example, in the late 1980s, researchers at a California biotech company called Calgene figured out how to manipulate the gene that controls the rotting process in tomatoes. Their new tomato, named the "Flavr Savr," could be vine ripened in order to improve the flavor, yet it was also tough enough to withstand the abuse of being picked mechanically, and it had the shelf life of tomatoes that were picked green.[99] This product became the focus of a debate with U.S. regulators over whether genetically altered organisms were "substantially equivalent" to their unaltered relatives, and thus could be "generally regarded as safe" without burdensome testing.[100] Yet this example is especially interesting because, as with many other genetic modifications, the intent was not to improve the crop yield for farmers, it was not to reduce the use of herbicides or pesticides, and it was not to improve the nutritional value of food. The intent was simply to make the organism conform to the demands of modern harvesting and shipping practices. Thus genetic engineering enables a striking reversal of priorities—instead of adapting farming practices to the needs of particular plants, we can simply adapt our plants to the needs of increasingly standardized farming practices.

Another example of how conformity plays a central role in debates comes from a controversy in the late 1990s, when the Canadian farmer Perry Schmeiser was sued by Monsanto after they discovered genetically modified canola plants growing in his fields even though he did not have a license to do so. Schmeiser counter-sued, insisting that these plants were the unwanted consequence of "genetic pollution" from neighboring fields, and he quickly became a global figurehead in the movement to resist genetically modified foods. However, Schmeiser's criticism of Monsanto was not centered on the safety or risks of genetically modified seeds, but on the way their product had

---

98. See the essays collected by Kimbrell in *Fatal Harvest*.

99. Most tomatoes are picked green and immature and then ripened with ethylene gas. See Martineau, *First Fruit*.

100. Pringle, *Food, Inc.*, 61–68.

contaminated his carefully bred varieties of canola, and on the way genetic engineering was enabling them to force all canola farmers to conform to a common practice.[101] From the perspective of advocates of genetically modified foods, questioning the ideal of conformity was unfathomable—yet again, a technological ideal had morphed into a moral imperative.

REFLECTING ON THE INTERNET

Background

The third and final example of technology that will be examined in this chapter is both as recent as genetically modified food and as revolutionary as the automobile. While the long-term acceptance and impact of genetically modified food in contemporary agriculture may still be up in the air, the Internet has clearly revolutionized the way information is communicated to an extent that parallels the way the automobile revolutionized the way people travel. Even more impressive, however, is that this communications revolution has happened so quickly—it wasn't long ago that few people had even heard of the Internet, much less possessed their own e-mail or website address. Who would have fathomed the possibility of phenomena such as eBay, Google, iTunes, Facebook, Twitter, or YouTube? Today the World Wide Web has become the media of choice for consumers of not only information, but of entertainment and goods of all types.

For all the talk of corporate power in agriculture, the companies that have emerged to rival automotive-related businesses in value are those that have led the way in this communications revolution. Oil and gas companies still dominate the list of the most valuable global corporations based on market value, but technology companies such as Apple, Microsoft, and IBM are also in the mix. The market capitalization of Monsanto, the corporation that has dominated the genetically modified seed business, is a small fraction of the largest oil and gas companies. And the application of genetic engineering to agriculture is typically a relatively small part of the business of large pharmaceutical or chemical companies. Clearly the Internet has had a significant economic impact on the structure of the global economy, as well as on the way we communicate.[102]

101. The Supreme Court of Canada eventually ruled against Schmeiser in 2001, although the victory was a hollow one for Monsanto since they were not awarded any damages.

102. Indeed, the very possibility of a global economy is predicated on the kind of flow of information made possible by the Internet. At the same time, the very possibility of organized resistance to globalization in general, and genetically modified foods

As with the above discussion of the automobile, when the Internet is referred to in this book it points to more than one technological artifact. Yet the Internet is a more obvious example of a technological system. It is not simply *part* of a larger system because of the way it is developed and delivered to end users, or because of the way it relies on a larger infrastructure in order to perform as designed, it *is* a system; it is itself an infrastructure. As the expression that was commonly used to refer to the precursor of the Internet suggests, it is an "information super-highway."

The Internet is, in short, a network of computer networks. While computers within local networks have long been able to communicate with each other, the Internet made it possible for computers from different networks, or even individual computers, to communicate with one another. The first example of this system of communication was utilized by the U.S. Defense Department starting in late 1969 to facilitate the sharing of information and computer resources between four universities.[103] The key technological development that made this possible was a shared communications protocol, now known as the Internet Protocol (IP), which relies on "packet switching" rather than circuit switching to transmit data. Simply put, this means that data is broken up into packets or discrete blocks before it is transmitted from one computer, and these packets are then routed between nodes in a network along links that are shared with other traffic. This turned out to be a dramatically more efficient and reliable way to transmit data than circuit switching, which requires the dedicated use of one particular link for every transmission.

In just a few years the Internet has become a global network of immense proportions—millions of publicly accessible networks that are used to transmit electronic mail messages, instant messages, video, music, and a host of other types of files, and, of course, to provide access to Web pages and other documents on the World Wide Web. It is important to stress that the World Wide Web is not the same thing as the Internet, but is one of

---

in particular, has also depended upon the Internet. See "In Cyberspace, Technologies Converge," chapter 16 in Lambrecht, *Dinner at the New Gene Café*.

103. This was known as ARPANET, and was developed by the Defense Advanced Research Projects Agency (DARPA). The first "nodes" of this network were located at UCLA, UC Santa Barbara, Stanford, and the University of Utah. By 1971, connections had been made to the East coast of the U.S. and there were twenty-three "hosts" (participating networks, most of which also served as nodes) at universities and government research centers. Satellite links across both the Pacific and Atlantic oceans were established in 1973, making ARPANET truly global. In 1975 the network started to be administered by the Defense Communications Agency, and in 1983 the U.S. military portion was broken off as a separate network (MILNET), which removed 45 of the 113 nodes from the network. See Abbate, *Inventing the Internet*.

many services accessible via the Internet. They are both interconnected networks, but whereas the Web is a virtual network of documents connected by hyperlinks and addresses ("Uniform Resource Locators" or URLs), the Internet is a real network of computers connected to each other via routers and servers, not to mention copper wires, fiber-optic cables, wireless radio signals, and satellites. Cyberspace is only possible because of things that happen in physical space.

Nonetheless, it was the emergence of the World Wide Web and especially the possibility of viewing images in addition to text in the early 1990s that sparked the most explosive period of growth in the use of the Internet.[104] The technological developments that made this possible were "Hypertext Markup Language" (HTML), the means for creating Web pages, and "Hypertext Transfer Protocol" (HTTP), the means for transmitting the content of Web pages (i.e., publishing and retrieving them) over the Internet. Originally developed by the British scientist Tim Berners-Lee, these are further examples of the central technical premise that underlies the success of the Internet—the electronic exchange of information becomes more efficient and widely dispersed as common standards for sharing data are adopted.[105] The Internet is rightly known for being a decentralized network that has been able to grow organically because it is beyond the control of any single participant, but it did not emerge and grow without guidance. Indeed, it only works because participants play by the same rules. They adhere to non-proprietary technical protocols that have been established and are administered by several central organizations, including the Internet Society (ISOC), the Internet Engineering Task Force (IETF), the World Wide Web Consortium (W3C), and the Internet Corporation for Assigned Names and Numbers (ICANN).[106] And, of course, access to the Internet has been commercialized and is thus controlled by agreements with service providers who have, in turn, financed the necessary (and vast) physical infrastructure.

---

104. For data on Internet use in every region of the world, see http://www.internetworldstats.com/stats.htm. Usage has increased by 566 percent since 2000, and as of June, 2012, over 34 percent of the world's population are categorized as users ("penetration" is highest in North America, at over 78 percent).

105. See Berners-Lee, *Weaving the Web*.

106. Now that the Internet is a more established technology, traditional organizations such as the Institute of Electrical and Electronics Engineers (IEEE) and the International Organization for Standardization (ISO) are also involved.

Extremes?

If there was much more literature on genetically modified foods to sift through than on automobiles, it will probably come as no surprise that there is more still on the Internet. One is confronted with a barrage of reflections on the Internet from all directions—from journalists covering business stories or charting social trends, to specialists writing for colleagues in the field of Information Technology, to novelists and screenwriters attempting to create timely works of fiction, to academics in fields ranging from communications to sociology, history, political science, philosophy, and even religious studies. Indeed, there have been a plethora of publications on the Internet from authors with much more than a passing interest in religious faith and practice. Examples of book titles in this genre include *Give Me That Online Religion*,[107] *Exploring Religious Community Online*,[108] *Cybergrace*,[109] *The Net Commandments*,[110] *The Soul in Cyberspace*,[111] *Religion and Cyberspace*,[112] *Virtual Morality*,[113] *Wired for Ministry*,[114] *A New Kind of Conversation*,[115] *The Web of Text and the Web of God*,[116] *The Spectacle of Worship in a Wired World*,[117] *Christians in a .com World*,[118] *From MySpace to Sacred Space*,[119] and *The Soul in Cyberspace*.[120]

One approach to making sense of this flood of information is to narrow our focus to a particular application of the Internet. After all, to speak of the Internet today is to invoke a whole host of related technologies.[121]

---

107. By Brenda E. Brasher.
108. By Heidi Campbell.
109. By Jennifer Cobb.
110. By Norman Fraser.
111. By Douglas Groothuis.
112. Edited by Morten T. Højsgaard and Margit Warburg.
113. By Graham Houston.
114. By John P. Jewel.
115. Edited by Myron Bradley Penner and Hunter Barnes.
116. By Alan C. Purves.
117. By Tex Sample.
118. By Gene Edward Veith Jr. and Christopher L. Stamper.
119. By Christian and Amy Piatt.
120. By Jeff Zaleski.
121. Certainly the automobile can also be seen to be part of a family of related technologies that it depends on and prompted—as mentioned earlier, this includes oil exploration and refining as well as the largest construction projects in human history that have built and re-built: millions of miles of roads and highways. And the automobile also introduced and prompted new applications for technologies such as internal

From humble beginnings, the growth and evolution of Internet applications—computer software programs that make use of the Internet—has been rapid. As mentioned above, examples include e-mail and Web browsers, as well as electronic auctions and search engines, and online music, social networking, and video sharing services. Yet this is only the beginning. Additional Web-based Internet applications include online retailing, streaming media, blogs, and role-playing games (commonly referred to as Multi-User Domains). They also include maps and other vast databases of information such as library catalogs, not to mention the contents of books and other resources that are rapidly being made available. And they include education management programs that enhance classroom learning or make online courses possible, including massive open online courses (MOOCs). A sampling of Internet applications that do not utilize the World Wide Web include Voice over Internet Protocol (VoIP), which provides an alternative to traditional telephone service, Virtual Private Networks (VPNs) that enable users to remotely access programs and files on their computer network, interactive Computer Aided Design (CAD) applications that allow thousands of engineers to contribute to the design of a complex technology such as an automobile, and Electronic Data Interchange (EDI) systems that automate the purchasing process for retailers, allowing new orders to be placed as soon as merchandise is scanned at the cash register. It would seem then that, just as in the previous section I concentrated on the application of genetic engineering to food rather than on entire fields like genetic engineering or biotechnology, there is much to gain by focusing on a particular Internet application.

The problem with picking one application is that Internet applications come and go at a rapid rate. Thus, although this chapter will discuss mature and widespread applications such as e-mail, it will continue to refer to the underlying system that makes all Internet applications possible. My principle concern is to frame the Internet as a kind of communications technology, because whatever other revolutions it may be seen to be ushering in, the Internet has indisputably revolutionized the way people communicate. Of course, rapid developments in Internet applications also serve as a reminder that, in the words of Andrew Feenberg and Marie Bakardjieva, "we

---

combustion engines, manufacturing processes such as the assembly line, and materials such as rubber and high-strength steel. Nonetheless, the impact of the Internet may yet prove to be just as widespread, and the time it has taken for this technology to become deeply entrenched is far less. In the early days of the Internet, the well-known enthusiast John Perry Barlow claimed that "we are in the middle of the most transforming technological event since the capture of fire. I used to think that it was just the biggest thing since Guttenberg, but now I think you have to go back farther." See Tough, "What Are We Doing On-Line?," 36.

are dealing with an unfinished and flexible technology still far from stabilization and maturity."[122]

What is most striking about the flood of literature on the Internet is that, unlike reflections on both the automobile and genetically modified food, it is not sharply divided into two opposing camps. While cautious or concerned voices are to be found alongside enthusiastic ones,[123] there are very few passionate critics.[124] Not only has this technological system been fully accepted and integrated into our society, but it seems that people are, for the most part, pleased with it. The following section will hone in on three technological ideals that are apparent in reflections on the Internet and are apparently shared by both proponents of the Internet and those who are more cautious about its benefits. Once again, each of these ideals are not only embodied by the Internet, but they have been elevated by this technological system to the point that they have now assumed the status of moral imperatives.

Ideals Embodied and Encouraged by the Internet

Efficiency

As discussed in chapter one, for Jacques Ellul, efficiency—the pursuit of the "one best means"—is the defining ideal of all technological artifacts, systems, and ways of thinking. However, of the three technological examples under consideration in this chapter, in my view the Internet is the most obvious embodiment of the quest for efficiency. This is clearest if we narrow our focus to look at an application such as e-mail. For even those who express reservations about online shopping, social networking, or the increasingly virtual nature of relationships admit that they could not imagine going

---

122. Feenberg and Bakardjieva, "Consumers or Citizens?," 3.

123. Examples include Auletta, *Googled*; Carr, *The Shallows*; Manjoo, *True Enough*; Palfrey and Gasser, *Born Digital*; and Small and Vorgan, *iBrain*. Footnotes in the following paragraphs will point to a number of other concerned voices.

124. Two well-known critics are Clifford Stoll—see, for example, *Silicon Snake Oil*; and Ellen Ullman—see, for example, *Close to the Machine*. For every critic, however, there are dozens of Internet boosters to be found on the shelves of bookstores and newsstands. Two well-known examples are Nicholas Negroponte—see, for example, *Being Digital*; and Freeman Dyson—see, for example, *The Sun, the Genome, and the Internet*. Of course, Internet enthusiasts are most often found not in writings about the Internet *per se*, but about the Internet as the—or at least a key—solution to particular social or political problems. See, for example, Gore, *Assault on Reason*; and McKibben, *Deep Economy*. McKibben, interestingly enough, is a passionate critic of automobiles and genetically modified crops.

about their work without e-mail. And without doubt, e-mail is an efficient way to communicate with people.

Originally intended to duplicate the function of traditional letters and memos, electronic communication replaces a cumbersome infrastructure requiring paper, printing devices, and delivery networks such as postal and courier services. This physical infrastructure is replaced with an even more complex infrastructure that is capable of inexpensively transmitting the same information in a matter of seconds. On the one hand, there is nothing new about breaking the connection between communication and transportation—optical telegraphs like smoke signals and beacons have been used since ancient times, and semaphores (systems used to relay information over long distances using visual signals) were used to great effect by Napoleon. Electrical telegraphs were widespread in the nineteenth century, and telephones along with wireless radio telegraphs emerged before the turn of the twentieth century. What is fundamentally different about e-mail is that, with the growing use of personal computers and smartphones, individuals now have access to what is in effect their own sophisticated telegraph machine to communicate to anyone with similar access. Furthermore, since almost all documents in work and educational settings are now created electronically using computer software, the volume of information that can be communicated using e-mail has increased dramatically in the past decade. Even with the investment in computers, software, and the physical infrastructure that makes up the Internet, the cost when measured relative to the amount of information sent is far cheaper than other forms of communication. Perhaps because all of these investment costs are paid for by their institutions, researchers led the way in adopting e-mail as the preferred method of communication. They are now able to correspond with many more people than ever before, including people who share their interests in other parts of the world. And from the perspective of scholarship, anything that makes it possible for more information to be shared between more people is a good thing.

Cautionary notes about e-mail in particular and the Internet in general tend to raise concerns about efficiency, although not to question whether this should be the ideal by which all technologies should be evaluated, but to ask whether this particular technology really does measure up according to this ideal.[125] A whole host of issues fall into this category, including the potentially addictive nature of online activity, and the fact that careers and relationships have been ruined as well as created or nurtured.[126] A less

---

125. See, for example, Freeman, *Tyranny of E-mail*.
126. See, for example, Gardner, "Tangled in the Worst of the Web."

dramatic but potentially more widespread issue is the loss of worker productivity due to the preponderance of personal e-mail correspondence and Web-surfing on company time. The impact of unsolicited e-mail messages, often referred to as junk mail or spam, is another cause for concern, as studies have shown that they make up a significant percentage of e-mail traffic.[127] In some cases these are simply a routine annoyance, and in others, for example, when they introduce a virus, they can cripple a computer network. Economic arguments have also been made about whether the benefits of Internet access provides a sufficient return on the capital costs of computer networks and software, particularly for schools, and particularly when these networks need constant updating.[128] Finally, the efficiency of electronic communication is sometimes questioned with respect to energy use. Once again, cyberspace is only possible because of things that happen in physical space, and even if technologies become more energy efficient, when their use grows exponentially, then overall power consumption rises as well.[129] Furthermore, at one point in time computers were heralded as ushering in the paperless office, however, paper use has actually increased dramatically in recent years. Perhaps because it is so easy to create, share, and also print electronic documents, the environmental impact of the Internet is certainly not entirely positive.[130]

Nonetheless, the widespread embrace of Internet applications such as e-mail throughout workplaces and homes suggests that these concerns about efficiency have, at least for the time being, been resolved. And on the macro level, conventional wisdom suggests that the digital revolution should be credited for a good part of the dramatic productivity gains made by workers in the U.S. over the past two decades. The Internet has been embraced because it is efficient, so the logic goes. Yet it seems just as obvious that the embrace

127. One spam filtering company, MessageLabs, reported that in 2004 spam constituted 73 percent of all e-mail messages, up from 40 percent in 2003. Year-over-year changes can be dramatic in the other direction as well—according to the global security firm Kapersky Lab, from 2011 to 2012 this total dropped from 80 to 67 percent.

128. Given current accounting practices, it is extremely difficult to distill the portion of school board (and university) budgets that are dedicated to capital and ongoing operating costs for information technology. However, it is clearly a significant and growing portion. In light of this trend, Albert Borgmann urges that we "remember that education is too difficult to be turned over to technology" ("Information and Education," 152).

129. For a discussion of the counterintuitive relationship between efficiency improvements in technology and overall energy consumption, see Rubin, "The Efficiency Paradox."

130. For example, paper consumption in Canada increased by 93.6 percent between the years 1983 to 2003. See Sciadas, "Our Lives in Digital Times."

of the Internet has served to elevate the ideal of efficiency. It is this preoccupation with efficiency, or, better, this *imperative* to pursue the most efficient means possible, that seems to go undiscussed. As the political scientist Janice Gross Stein puts it, efficiency has "turned inward" and thus has become "silent about values, neutral about goals, but vocal about means."[131]

Invisibility

A second ideal that is privileged by technological systems such as the Internet is invisibility. Communications technologies in particular have always been best when they do what they are supposed to do without us noticing, when they recede into the background. What is thought to be important is the experience or the end, not the means utilized to create that experience or to reach that end. And the Internet is better at this than most—in fractions of a second we have at our disposal images from across the globe, long before we have time to think about the thousands of individual steps that were taken by a complex system in order to transmit millions of bits of data over dozens of pathways through hundreds of nodes of the Internet. In the midst of our experience surfing the Web, if everything is working properly, we become unaware of the medium and are lost in the content of the message. This is similar to the desire for comfort in travel nurtured by the automobile, and the desire for control in farming nurtured by genetically modified foods. As with traveling and growing, we want the experience of communicating or gathering information to be as unencumbered as possible.

The ideal of invisibility has obvious implications for the way people relate to each other over the Internet. The Internet preserves the kind of freedom that constitutes the paradigmatic form of modern liberty—"freedom as unencumberedness," the freedom not only to initiate obligations but also to terminate them at will.[132]

---

131. Stein, *Cult of Efficiency*, 28. Stein points out that the trend toward increased attention to efficiency in post-industrial public discourse has been accompanied by less attention to moral ideals such as equity and justice.

Another sign that the Internet has latched onto and accelerated the drive toward efficiency is what the communications theorist Quentin J. Schultze (among others) has called "informationism." In short, Schultze argues that informationism emphasizes "the *is* over the *ought*," or "our high-tech penchant for *measurement* over *meaning*." Internet-based "informational practices" thus should be seen as trying to "position us as *impersonal observers* of the world rather than *intimate participants* in the world." The end result is that "we are sharpening our informational practices while dulling the habits of our hearts" (*Habits of the High-Tech Heart*, 20, 27).

132. Albert Borgmann focuses on the dangers of this kind of freedom in "Is the Internet the Solution to the Problem of Community?," 57. In this article Borgmann

Another way of talking about the ideal of invisibility is to frame the Internet as an example of what the psychologist Sherry Turkle calls an "opaque" technology.[133] Technological systems in general seem to become increasingly sophisticated even as they are hidden from sight, and so any concern to understand the way they work disappears from our consciousness. In Turkle's words, "We have learned to take things at interface value."[134] As a result, technology becomes increasingly mysterious, and we are taught to use or consume it with a "black box" mentality. We turn the ignition key in our car and expect it to start; we plant genetically modified seeds and expect them to be immune to a parasite; or we type a message on our computer screen and expect it to be received by a friend thousands of miles away.[135] Indeed, each of the examples of technology discussed in this chapter reflects growing levels of complexity and sophistication, and at the same time their users tend to reflect growing levels of ignorance or obliviousness to the way they work. As technologies advance there is less and less need for the user to understand the way they work in order to use them. To put it even stronger, the most desirable technologies are the ones that demand the least from their users. Sociologist William Stahl suggests that we have moved beyond simply expecting technology to function as a black box to the point of "venerating" the black box, as evident in the "explicitly magical or religious language" that is frequently used "to refer to computers of those who make, program, or use them."[136]

As with efficiency, concerns, and, on occasion, objections, tend to be raised about the Internet when it *fails* to live up to the ideal of invisibility,

---

develops an idea discussed in *Holding On to Reality*, although, as discussed in chapter 1, the tendency for modern technology to shrink or become concealed is something that Borgmann has long noted. Part of the very definition of a device is that it recedes into the background so that the way it mediates our relationships with the world around us goes unnoticed.

133. Turkle, *Life on the Screen*, 23.

134. Ibid.

135. Turkle is primarily interested in demonstrating the impact of this pattern of use on human relationships. The way we relate to technology, she argues, has become more than simply a metaphor for the way we relate to other people—it has led to a superficial reshaping of relationships that reflects the shift "from a culture of calculation toward a culture of simulation." See *Life on the Screen*, 19.

136. Stahl, *God and the Chip*, 80. Sherry Turkle considers two additional metaphors in the course of trying to explain the allure of the Internet: "The computer's holding power is a phenomenon frequently referred to in terms associated with drug addiction. It is striking that the word 'user' is associated mainly with computers and drugs. The trouble with that analogy, however, is that it puts the focus on what is external (the drug). I prefer the metaphor of seduction because it emphasizes the relationship between person and machine" (*Life on the Screen*, 30).

rather than *because* of the way it embodies invisibility. Examples include frustrations with a software interface because it is either too complicated or lacks desired features, or because it is updated either too frequently or not enough. More significantly, privacy concerns loom large in many of the more skeptical reflections on e-mail, social media, and other Web applications. The invisibility and opacity of this technology means many users are oblivious to the way their online activity can be tracked for commercial gain or illicit purposes such as identity theft. However, the same people who are concerned with privacy also tend to applaud the decentralized, democratic nature of the World Wide Web, something that has led to an explosion of information beyond the control of government and corporate interests. They are quick to highlight the phenomenon of "disintermediarisation"— the removal of the traditional gatekeepers who mediated our access to information.[137] Indeed, the Internet has made many significant and highly visible elements of competing technologies expendable, including the use of a physical medium such as paper, as well as lots of people, including editors, publishers, couriers, teachers, and librarians. Thus privacy concerns are usually satisfied by the promotion of technical fixes—for example, we install a spy-ware program rather than change our behavior. We are looking for solutions that can be forgotten as soon as they are installed and running in the background.

Thus the Internet raises invisibility beyond the level of an ideal to the level of a need. Invisibility is more than a goal to strive for; it has become a part of the very definition of what makes something good.

Novelty

A third ideal that is reflected by and encouraged by the Internet is novelty. Once again, this ideal is not unique to electronic communication, but it does seem to be amplified by it to a significant degree. Perhaps this is because the Internet is the latest in a long line of technological innovations that have been accumulating at an increasing rate, innovations that have created not only the expectation for change, but a receptivity to change. Another explanation for why the Internet amplifies the desire for novelty is the virtual nature of information in cyberspace—everything communicated over the Internet does not exist in any real way apart from its digital signature.[138] The only difference between an e-mail message and a photograph is

---

137. Pullinger, *Information Technology and Cyberspace*, 135.

138. Internet technology expert Pullinger has argued that on the world-wide-web "geography is relatively unimportant. In fact, one could almost define cyberspace as

the number of bits, the number of 1's and 0's, that are required to enable any computer to recompose the text or image. A simple message can be a series of less than 10,000 bits, while a low resolution photograph is over 1,000,000. Web pages are likewise nothing more than an even larger collection of bits that are stored in the memory of a computer server somewhere. Thus the technical barriers to changing or manipulating this information in order to create something new have been significantly diminished. We are not only accustomed to immediate access to information, but to instant updates and never-ending upgrades.

For Internet enthusiasts, the concept of virtual reality holds great promise, while Internet skeptics most often point to virtuality as the primary limitation or danger of this technology. In particular, there is some concern with the assumption that virtual reality can be an adequate substitute for embodied, experiential reality. Skeptics insist that virtual encounters need to be grounded in real encounters in order for relationships to truly flourish. Thus they also express concern with the kind of worldview that is built into technologies such as the Internet, a worldview that the Catholic theologian Mary Timothy Prokes has called "boundary-lessness":

> There is a permissive climate, heady, often arrogant, and dismissive of any external measure or control—a cultural climate not confined to [virtual reality] laboratories and simulators. There is an *atmosphere*, an *ambiance* or *aura* of unfettered virtual experience and technical application that has increasingly become a way of life for many. The desire to eliminate all boundaries as an expression of freedom brings resistance to whatever would restrain the *attempting of what is possible*."[139]

In short, novel experiences can be, and are, pursued for the sake of novelty alone. The growing availability of novel experiences on the Internet only exacerbates this desire.

What is most striking, however, is that critics of virtual reality do not seem to take issue with the underlying premise that technology can and should contribute to making human experience richer. Their problem is not with novelty, with new experiences or with change *per se*, but with the nature of the new experiences and changes brought about by the Internet. Nowhere is this clearer than in the wide spectrum of reflections on the nature

---

when the physical location of information, services, programs, and people are unimportant—if it becomes important to know, you are not in cyberspace." See ibid., 25.

139. Prokes, *At the Interface*, 106. As Albert Borgmann puts it, "At the limit, virtual reality takes up with the contingency of the world by avoiding it altogether" (see *Holding on to Reality*, 183).

of virtual communities.¹⁴⁰ The pursuit of novelty is not simply an ideal that is embodied by this technological system, but has become an expectation. As with efficiency and invisibility, novelty is an unquestioned good that has assumed the status of a moral imperative.¹⁴¹

CONCLUSION

This chapter has sought to demonstrate that particular technologies embody particular ideals, and as a result, they are not morally neutral but have moral implications. They shape our moral visions and our characters. This underlying morality is often hidden or not readily apparent in debates between those harboring polarized views over particular technologies, but can be readily elucidated when we take a closer look at each of these technologies. The moral nature of the automobile is evident in the way it elevates autonomy, speed, and comfort; the moral nature of genetically modified food is evident in the way it elevates control, mastery, and conformity; and the moral nature of the Internet is evident in the way it elevates efficiency, invisibility, and novelty. Nonetheless, these ideals themselves are not challenged or questioned in most debates but are either unacknowledged or assumed to be virtues worthy of encouraging by both sides. Thus both the proponents and the opponents of

---

140. See, for example, Rheingold, *Virtual Community*; Feenberg and Barney, *Community in the Digital Age*; and Turkle, *Alone Together*. Examples of reflections on the implications of the Internet for *church* communities include Willimon, "Community & Computers"; Sample, *Spectacle of Worship in a Wired World*; Wind, "Crossing the Digital Divide"; and Hipps, "Community in Electronic Culture," chapter 6 in *The Hidden Power of Electronic Culture*.

141. A more helpful response to the phenomenon of virtuality is to contrast it with the Christian notion of virtue. See Schultze, *Habits of the High-Tech Heart*; and Ward, "Between Virtue and Virtuality." Ward's perspective is especially intriguing, since it is framed as a response to "Christian theologians who use the tradition as the basis for some Luddite critique" of the Internet, and are best viewed as "victims of that melancholic pathology—nostalgia" (ibid., 56). Ward is convinced that "A certain symbiosis is taking place between technology and being human; a new interface is developing" (ibid., 60). And he is not at all uncomfortable redefining concepts such as space, time, memory, and community as a result of changes in communication technology. However, he *is* uncomfortable with the way that technologies not only reshape our ideals, but attempt to mediate "the timeless and universal Ideal" (ibid., 65). Ward's theological worldview provides a "transcendent corrective" that enables him to recognize the ways in which "advanced technology invokes a 'secular religiosity'" (ibid., 68). Thus, although he continues to affirm the new cultural possibilities opened up by the rise of the Internet, in the end then Ward insists that "Christian theology maintains an exteriority to the ubiquity of the cyber-spatial environment." Theology "bears the tradition forward between virtue and virtuality" (ibid., 70). See also Ward's "Cities of the Good," chapter 9 in *Cities of God*.

automobiles, genetically modified food, and the Internet appear to operate as though they share the same moral framework. With the help of the work of John Howard Yoder, in the following chapter I will suggest that the Christian tradition provides an alternative moral vision that presents a stark contrast to the vision that is framed by these technological systems.

4

Conscientiously Engaging Technology Through the Practices of the Church

HAVING SYNTHESIZED A RANGE of reflections on three particular technologies in the previous chapter, the present chapter argues that each can be understood in a new way when viewed through the lens of John Howard Yoder's theological ethics. The first half of this chapter will demonstrate that Yoder's perspective on the Christian tradition highlights marks of the church that pose a stark contrast to technological ideals such as autonomy, speed, comfort, control, mastery, conformity, efficiency, invisibility, and novelty.[1] As striking as this contrast may be, I have been suggesting all along that Yoder's work provides the impetus for Christians to conscientiously engage rather than simply reject or embrace automobiles, genetically modified food, or the Internet. What then does this suggestion really mean? Following Yoder, in my view the first task for Christian reflection on technology is not to decide whether we should approve of, or oppose technology in general, but to position each of our technological activities in their rightful place within the larger narrative of God's relationship to the world. As discussed in chapter 2, as a principality or power, every technological artifact, system, or way of thinking is necessary, fallen, and capable of being transformed by the power of Christ. Instead of blindly accepting or resisting technology, Yoder's work provides clues to how we might "overaccept" it, to use Samuel Well's term.

---

1. A parallel to this approach can be found in John Milbank's contrasting of "marks of morality" with "notes of Christianity"—see "Can Morality Be Christian?," chapter 9 in *Word Made Strange*.

For Yoder this transformative power is most clearly evident in Christ's body in the world, the church, and thus the second half of this chapter will go on to examine the technological implications of Yoder's discussion of the practices of the church. It is through these practices that we can bear witness to the moral vision that Yoder sees as being central to the Christian tradition, and thus put technological ideals in their rightful place. Not only does Yoder *compel* us to conscientiously engage technology, his discussion of the practices of the church makes it clear that by pursuing distinctively Christian practices we *will* conscientiously engage technology. Perhaps then it is better to think of Yoder's theology of technology as more descriptive than prescriptive—rather than proposing a constructive response to new technologies, revising our theological ethics in light of a new situation, he helps us uncover the deeper engagement that is already implicit within the traditional practices of the church. In effect, Yoder helps us turn the usual way of reflecting on technology upside down; our primary task is to re-describe technology in light of the things we do as Christians.

To summarize, the thesis of this chapter is that Yoder's work demonstrates that technology is conscientiously engaged through the practices of the church. The burden of the first half of the chapter is to point out that key traits or marks of the church as portrayed by Yoder contrast sharply with each of the key technological ideals embodied by automobiles, genetically modified food, and the Internet. The aim of the second half of the chapter is to point out how these alternative traits are reflected in the practices of the church. It is in this discussion that the technological implications of church practices will become clear.

PREAMBLE: PATHS NOT TAKEN

The discussion of the morality of technology in the previous chapter focused primarily on "ideals," although it was also peppered with terms such as "desire" and "imperative." I argued that the moral vision of technology, the process by which technologies are deemed right and wrong or good and bad, is framed by these ideals. And yet there is nothing objectively certain or universal about these ideals—they can shift with time and with the particular technology under consideration. In contrast, the discussion of Yoder's moral vision in this chapter will focus on the "marks" of the church. Although I will also use terms such as "trait" and "characteristic," the implication is that each of these marks should be recognized as being grounded in the biblical vision of the body of Christ. They are not occasional spiritual gifts that may or may not be present at any given point in time, or that may evolve over time.[2]

Before moving into a discussion of the way the moral thrust of Yoder's work contrasts with the moral thrust of the particular technologies under consideration, it should be noted that numerous other responses to the analysis of the previous chapter are possible. The marks of the church can be talked about in many helpful ways, and these discussions can in turn raise provocative questions about the ideals embodied and encouraged by cars, crops, and computers. For example, we could look to Jesus' words as recorded in the sermon on the Mount, particularly the Beatitudes, for the gospel message in crystalized form. We could look to the Apostle Paul's discussion of the fruits of the spirit in Galations 5: love, joy, peace, patience, kindness, generosity, faithfulness, gentleness, and self-control.[3] We could look to the theological virtues pointed to by Paul in 1 Corinthians 13:13:

---

2. Thus I am deliberately moving beyond the use of "values" language in order to avoid the pitfalls of what Alasdair MacIntyre refers to as an "emotivist" approach to ethics. More specifically: "Emotivism is the doctrine that all evaluative judgments and more specifically all moral judgments are *nothing but* expressions of preference, expressions of attitude or feeling, insofar as they are moral or evaluative in character" (*After Virtue*, 11–12). This purely subjective view of moral judgments is one of the contributing factors to the sharp distinction that is often made between facts and values.

D. Stephen Long has helpfully explicated MacIntyre's discussion of the modern fact-value distinction, noting that it was articulated most emphatically early in the twentieth century by the German political economist and sociologist Max Weber. "Facts," according to Weber, are established by the social or natural sciences such as economics and biology, and philosophical or theological ethics then articulates the "values" that, in a non-confessional way, are used to respond to this reality. Interestingly, Weber emphasized this distinction not to marginalize philosophers and theologians, but to curtail what he saw as the encroachment of scientific thinking into the realm of morality. In a lecture in Munich in 1919 that came to influence the thinking of Martin Heidegger, Weber used a technological illustration to make this point. In short, traveling through life is not like traveling on a streetcar. We cannot be ignorant of how things function in society and simply trust that everything has been correctly calculated, for no matter how much technology transforms or rationalizes our modern existence, contingencies cannot be eliminated and certainty can never be achieved in the realm of values.

In any case, Weber's approach ends up marginalizing the position of those concerned with morality in two ways: they are dependent upon others to establish the facts, and they are forced to articulate particular, historically defined values in universal, a-historical terms. In contrast, Long urges that, instead of conforming subjective values to an objective reality made known through the sciences, we must conform our lives to the objective reality made known through the teachings of the church. Thus what is normally ascribed to the realm of values is more real than the data that is normally ascribed to the realm of facts. See Long, *Divine Economy*, 10–12; Long, *John Wesley's Moral Theology*, 15–19; and Long and Fox, *Calculated Futures*, 48–61. Weber's 1919 lecture is discussed by Safranski in *Martin Heidegger*, 89–91.

3. All biblical references in this chapter are from the NRSV translation.

faith, hope, and love. We could look to classical Western virtues rooted in ancient philosophy: prudence (or wisdom), justice, temperance (or moderation), and fortitude (or courage). Or we could look to the capital virtues compiled by Thomas Aquinas in medieval times: meekness, humility, generosity, tolerance, chastity, moderation, and zeal.

Indeed, it would seem as though structuring this book around virtue language would be particularly appropriate, setting up a contrast between technological and theological virtues and vices. However, since my approach is to try to think like Yoder, I will be using his terms rather than relying upon language foreign to his work. Certainly there are many ways that Yoder's perspective resonated with virtue ethics. One of Yoder's essays is included in a collection that seeks to apply the insights of Alasdair MacIntyre, the philosopher most often associated with the renewal of interest in virtue in contemporary philosophy, to Christian ethics.[4] In addition, Stanley Hauerwas frequently draws attention to his indebtedness to both MacIntyre and Yoder.[5] Like MacIntyre, Yoder thought that ethics should be concerned with practices as well as rules and ends. Furthermore, just as MacIntyre traces a narrative that seeks to counter modern liberalism, Yoder's discussion of principalities and powers makes it is clear that the church provides an interpretation or description of reality that competes with the description provided by the wisdom of the world.

Nonetheless, on several occasions Yoder expressed concern for the way that virtue, along with other terms he generally viewed with favor such as narrative, community, character, and freedom, was "subject to abuse."[6] Because of his desire to avoid reducing theology to methodological debates, he was suspicious of the way that categories such as narrative and virtue were elevated to a status higher than the gospel message itself. Just as he thought narrative theology was helpful, but should not be the sole approach to scriptural interpretation, Yoder thought virtue ethics was helpful, but should not be the sole approach to moral reasoning.[7] Indeed, in one lecture Yoder lumped virtue theory in with consequentialist and deontological approaches to moral reasoning, accusing them all of being "punctualistic

---

4. See "Practicing the Rule of Christ," chapter 6 in Murphy, Kallenberg, and Nation, *Virtues and Practices in the Christian Tradition.*

5. Hauerwas, "When the Politics of Jesus Makes a Difference"; and Review of Alasdair MacIntyre's *After Virtue.*

6. Yoder, *Royal Priesthood*, 370.

7. Yoder's reaction to virtue ethics is a good example of his general wariness of philosophers, especially when they are drawing upon classical Greek thought. I think it was the tendency to locate Christian ethics via dialogue with philosophical discourse that rubbed against Yoder's sensibilities more than the specifics of virtue ethics.

in their understanding of what is at stake in moral choice." He went on to suggest that if

> Christ's Lordship over the powers is discerned as a more adequate vision, the several modes will not be played off against one another, but intermingled. We shall be asking not how to test the righteousness of specific punctual choices, but how to locate such choices within a multidimensional reading of what is going on in the interplay of the powers.[8]

This may explain why Yoder tended to use a variety of terms in his writing—he was concerned that "virtue" was too specific to encompass the kind of thinking he was engaged in.[9] Regardless of the reason, this book will stick with Yoder's terms.

Finally, I also want to emphasize that my discussion of Yoderian thought is not intended to be comprehensive or systematic, but occasional. To be sure, many of the characteristic marks of Yoder's own work are thrown into relief and become especially striking in light of the discussion of the previous chapter. And while these marks are more central than peripheral to Yoder's thought, others might have emerged if the subject under consideration was different.[10] As the discussion of chapter 2 should have made clear, I certainly don't want to claim that Yoder's thought can be captured by some sort of list.

---

8. Yoder, "God's Good News and the Runaway powers," 6.

9. Joseph J. Kotva Jr., argues that Yoder falls short of "providing the kind of expansive moral vision that could substitute for a virtue framework." See *Christian Case for Virtue Ethics*, 158. While I do not share Kotva's confidence in the sufficiency of virtue ethics, his critique of Yoder does resonate with the discussion in the following chapter of this book.

Perhaps another way of distinguishing Yoder from virtue ethicists such as Hauerwas is to say that Yoder was more interested in talking about particular character traits with respect to particular situations, than he was about the formation of moral character more generally. He thought that virtue theory often remained too theoretical to be really helpful.

10. Strikingly, the mark that is most commonly associated with Yoder's view of the church, nonviolence, will not be discussed in what follows. A case could be made that automobiles, genetically modified food, and the Internet all exhibit violent tendencies—indeed, as noted in chapter 3, Paul Virilio argues that the ideal of speed is inherently violent. Nonetheless, the capacity for violence is not seen as a technological ideal in any of the cases I am examining (in contrast to, for example, military technologies). Other notable marks that I will not be discussing include reverence, trust, hope, compassion, and stability.

THE MARKS OF THE CHURCH CONTRAST SHARPLY WITH TECHNOLOGICAL IDEALS

The Automobile

The discussion of the automobile in the previous chapter was intended to demonstrate that the polarized and entrenched perspectives of enthusiasts and critics can be traced to a conflict over the ideals embodied and encouraged by this particular technology. If this assessment is correct, then the starting place for addressing this conflict needs to be on the level of moral reasoning rather than scientific, economic, or political data. Our scientific research, economic policies, and political action cannot be viewed in isolation from the moral vision they depend upon.

How then could John Howard Yoder's work inform a theological understanding of the automobile? There are several obvious points of connection with the portrayal of the automobile synthesized from the work of Wolfgang Sachs and others in the previous chapter. However, at the outset it is important to note that the automobile can clearly be thought of as a manifestation of the biblical concept of the principalities and powers as they are understood by Yoder. The automobile is itself comprised of numerous particular technologies and depends on numerous others that form a complex technological system. This system, or structure, to use Yoder's word, is clearly more than the sum of its particular technologies, for it embodies the characteristics of the technological way of thinking that created it. Moreover, the automobile itself encourages and extends this way of thinking, and thus we find ourselves being seduced by its power. Like all the powers, the automobile is both evil and fallen on the one hand, and good and necessary on the other—we (and the rest of creation) cannot live with it, and, at least in contemporary Western nations, we often cannot live without it. Thus, in the words of Sachs: "Even when we find ourselves up to our necks in harmful consequences, a kind of structural irresponsibility blocks the necessary change of course."[11]

For Yoder, the way past this blockage is found in the recognition that the powers have already been defeated, that they have been put in their place by the death of Jesus Christ. As we have seen, for Yoder the authentic transformation of the powers, in this case the power of the automobile, *is* possible when it is subordinated to the power of Christ and embodied in the church. Of course, this transformation involves much more than the physical artifact of the automobile itself, as if the church could provide aftermarket kits capable of redeeming the vehicles in its parking lots. Rather, this

---

11. Sachs, *For Love of the Automobile*, 207.

transformation must touch the vast technological system that automobiles are a part of, and, most importantly, it must touch the ideals embodied and encouraged by the automobile. Indeed, the clash between Yoder's theology and the technological way of thinking epitomized by the automobile could not be more stark.

Commitment

The above discussion leads directly to an obvious point of connection between Sachs and Yoder—their assessment of autonomy. Yoder's starting place for theological reflection, as well as his ethical response to the powers—his commitment to the church—would lead him to question the importance that thinkers such as Lomasky place on individual autonomy. In my view, Yoder would concur with Sachs that individual autonomy as it is manifest in the automobile is ultimately illusionary. We are inevitably dependent upon a community, and technological systems both amplify and obscure this dependence; as Sachs puts it, more than ever we are passengers, even if we are "self-propelled" passengers.

The critical point for Yoder would be the nature or character of the community that we depend on. Is it based upon impersonal and distant relationships mediated by technology and motivated by necessity and economic self-interest, or is it based upon personal, face-to-face relationships motivated by love and the interests of others? Yoder's theology clearly values the latter. Going beyond Sachs then, his theology could be used to argue that, because the church, by focusing on being the church, is able to avoid the seduction of the powers, it is therefore able to avoid the seduction of the ideal of autonomy embodied and encouraged by the automobile. Voluntary allegiance to the church does not mean the end of our individuality, rather, it is a sign of our recognition that individualism is both illusionary and destructive.

Patience

A second obvious point of connection between Sachs and Yoder is their assessment of the desire for speed. In my view, Yoder would concur with Sachs and Kundera that speed is risky not only because of the possibility of accidents, but because of the way it makes us forget. By extending the potential range of travel, the increased speed of the automobile makes us forget what ties us to a particular place. Furthermore—going beyond Sachs now—speed makes us forget about the reality of God's presence. Indeed, Yoder's theology reminds us that, despite the impressive scale and scope of technology, it, and we, have limits. His theological stance, and his suggestion for how we can resist the seduction of the powers, is characterized by patience: "The key to the obedience of God's people is not their effectiveness but their patience."[12] And the mark of patience is of obvious relevance for avoiding the seduction of the ideal of speed embodied and encouraged by the automobile.

In short, patience enables us be mindful of the working of God's spirit in the world instead of rushing in to make the world come out right. While cars encourage us to accelerate our efforts, Yoder encourages us to slow down. While cars encourage us to throw caution to the wind, Yoder encourages us to be careful. And while cars encourage us to stick our noses where they do not belong, at times Yoder encourages us to sit still and wait.[13]

Suffering

Finally, Sachs' assessment of the desire for comfort points toward Yoder's affirmation of the meaning of suffering. Yoder has written that the "readiness of the church to face suffering" since the time of Christ has been its most profound witness of Christ's Lordship to political authorities. Indeed, "the political novelty that God brings into the world is a community of those who serve instead of ruling, who suffer instead of inflicting suffering."[14] Yoder emphasized that although Christians seek "not only to identify but to help change unjust social structures," this is something that must be done "in the way of Christ."[15] And the way of Christ is not a comfortable path. In contrast to the automobile's concern to cocoon drivers and passengers

---

12. Yoder, *Politics of Jesus*, 232. Yoder's most explicit articulation of this mark is found in an essay published posthumously: "'Patience' as Method in Moral Reasoning." The importance of patience as a theme in Yoder's work has been highlighted by Nation in *John Howard Yoder*, and Coles in "The Wild Patience of John Howard Yoder."

13. Yoder himself learned much about patience after he was seriously injured in an automobile accident during his daily commute from Elkhart to South Bend, Indiana, in July, 1989. Not only was Yoder hospitalized for seven weeks, but he was never able to walk again without crutches—he reflected on this experience in "From Basic Orientation to Concrete Discernment." Although the focus of this paper was to portray "institutional health care" (rather than the automobile) as "a prime example of a runaway power," it is also noteworthy because it contains far more autobiographical reflection than is typical in Yoder's writing.

14. Yoder, *Royal Priesthood*, 89, 91. Indeed, martyrdom was a significant factor in the persistence and growth of the Anabaptist movement in the sixteenth century, and this heritage has shaped Mennonites and the Amish to this day. See, for example, Thieleman Van Bragt's *Martyrs Mirror*.

15. Yoder, *For the Nations*, 111.

from various discomforts as they travel through the world, the church's concern is to *connect* its members with discomfort, injustice, and suffering as they travel through life. The point here is not that suffering is good in and of itself, but that, as demonstrated most clearly by Jesus, suffering *can* be meaningful when it serves God's purposes. As Yoder put it, "only if their suffering be innocent, and as a result of the evil will of their adversaries, may it be understood as meaningful before God."[16]

Furthermore, in contrast to the technological objective of minimizing physical and mental effort, the objective of Christian discipleship is to direct our physical and mental effort toward the building of God's kingdom. The point is not that comfort is an evil in and of itself, but that, as noted by Sachs, by encouraging a preoccupation with comfort, automobiles also discourage our proclivity for exerting effort and facing challenges, not to mention debilitating our ability to deal with limitations. Certainly Christians are convinced that, at least until the eschaton, limitations will be a fact of life.[17] In Yoder's words: "The identification of God's suffering servanthood is with [people] *in their suffering*; it does not concentrate *first* upon an illusionary vision of ending all suffering."[18]

Finally, even the *readiness* of Christians to suffer garners meaning because it provides a profound witness. In Yoder's words, "the willingness to bear the cross . . . precisely the only way in which it is possible to communicate to [a] society and to its authorities that it is Christ who is Lord and not they."[19] It appears then that, just as patience presents an alternative to speed and commitment to community presents an alternative to autonomy, Yoder's emphasis on the Christian predisposition toward suffering stands in stark contrast to the automobile's emphasis on comfort.

---

16. Yoder, *Politics of Jesus*, 129.

17. As Gaillardetz puts it, "Dangerously, many technological advances rob human existence of 'friction.' Yet the experience of friction is one of the essential qualities that gives ordinary human existence texture—it is what makes our existence 'real.' He goes on to argue that "it is only through that willingness to feel pain, to suffer, to know real loss, that we can know delight, gratitude, and the joy of life that the Spirit offers us" (*Transforming Our Days*, 42, 75).

18. Yoder, *For the Nations*, 111; italics in original. Yoder went on to say that this alternative perspective is "precisely why the change [that servanthood] brings about is real and durable" (ibid.).

19. Yoder, "People in the World," 271.

Genetically Modified Food

As with the automobile, the discussion of genetically modified food in the previous chapter demonstrates that assessments have, for the most part, overlooked the larger moral significance of this emerging technology. Genetically modified food can also be seen as a profound manifestation of the biblical concept of the principalities and powers. Like the automobile, genetically modified food is comprised of numerous particular technologies and depends on numerous elements of a complex technological system. Critics and foes alike recognize that products such as the Flavr Savr tomato, Roundup Ready soybeans, and Golden Rice could not have come into existence without new technologies such as gene transfer technology, not to mention a network of scientific research labs, seed marketers, farmers, and food processors. Each piece of this system is built on the back of modern industrial agriculture, and yet it further develops existing systems by adding layers of complexity in academic, business, and regulatory spheres. Indeed, while it is still possible for hobbyists and individual farmers to develop unique breeds of fruits and vegetables using traditional techniques, genetic engineering is something that is not likely to be within reach of the backyard gardener.

Most importantly, the system that has led to the genetic modification of food is clearly more than the sum of its particular technologies, for it embodies and encourages the distinctive characteristics of a technological way of thinking. Following Samuel Wells and Gerald McKenny, I have argued that the genetic modification of food has moral implications apart from concerns with safety, environmental impact, and economics. And, as with the automobile, key characteristics of Yoder's theological stance place these moral implications in sharp relief. In short, Yoder's emphasis on the marks of vulnerability, humility, and nonconformity provide an alternative vision to the technological traits of control, mastery, and conformity that are embodied in and encouraged by genetically modified food. It is this alternative moral vision—more than simply improving the safety, environmental impact, or economic benefits of genetically modified food—that is crucial to transforming the power manifested by genetically modified food.

Vulnerability

The word "control" is typically used in a pejorative way throughout Yoder's writing, which suggests he would have been uncomfortable with the terms of recent debates surrounding genetically modified foods. One glimpse into Yoder's perspective on control can be found in his reflections on the "racial revolution" of the 1960s, where he warns churches of the dangers of allowing their identity to become too closely wrapped up in political causes. He suggests that "instead of blessing this or that cause in a blanket way, the church might be the conscience of a movement whose dynamism the church neither completely supplies nor expects to control."[20] For Yoder, a preoccupation with control can be traced to the Constantinian shift, to the marriage of religious and political power that detracted from the mission of the church as laid out in the New Testament. Access to power created the illusion that control of history was found in human rather than divine hands: "That the church should be a state church is not the most important concern; what matters is that Christianity is the Church of a culture and assumes that it is at the steering wheel of history."[21] This created an illusion that overlooked the reality of the life, death, and resurrection of Jesus—the reality that God redeemed history not by seizing political power, but through vulnerability to political power.

A concern for control is also what Yoder found problematic about the field of social ethics:

> One way to characterize thinking about social ethics in our time is to say that Christians in our age are obsessed with the meaning and direction of history. Social ethical concern is moved by a deep desire to make things move in the right direction. Whether a given action is right or not seems to be inseparable from the question of what effects it will cause. Thus part if not all of social concern has to do with looking for the right 'handle' by which we can 'get a hold on' the course of history and move it in the right direction.[22]

Interestingly, from Yoder's perspective, some justification for this critical attitude toward grabbing hold of the "steering wheel" or the "handles" of history can be found in the growing empirical evidence of the impact of

---

20. Yoder, *For the Nations*, 120. While clearly supportive of the movement to overcome racial oppression, Yoder sought to help churches frame the movement in theological terms apart from the language of natural rights. For example, he wrote: "God's bias in favor of the victims is not based on their merit, their capacity, or their claims. If it were, we would be off the hook; those would be arguments based on control. But God is on the side of victims because he is a God of grace, and that's a very different reason" (see Yoder, "Power and the Powerless," 33).

21. Yoder, *Karl Barth and the Problem of War*, 30–31.

22. Yoder, *Politics of Jesus*, 228–29. There are numerous places where Yoder makes this point—one of the more interesting examples is when he distinguishes himself from someone who would otherwise appear to be an intellectual ally: "As to a social style [Stanley Fish] makes constantinian control of the culture a model rather than a mistake" (Yoder, "Responding to Stanley Fish lecture," 4).

technology. In his words, "somehow, as we know more, we find out that we are not after all in better control. The machines we create . . . take on a character of their own and produce results other than those we had asked for."[23] Yet there are also profound theological reasons for this attitude toward control.

Indeed, an under-appreciated dimension of Yoder's perspective on human history, as revealed in his discussion of principalities and powers, is his providential view of God. His ecclesiology, indeed, even his Christology, only makes sense when viewed against the backdrop of God's providence—the reality that God is ultimately in control of all that is. More specifically, Yoder's providential perspective is reflected in his understanding not only of the church's general posture toward society in general and the world in particular, but in his understanding of the way the church does everything from interpreting the Bible to structuring its leadership. It is because God is in control that the followers of Christ can choose to remain vulnerable.

Humility

If control for Yoder is ultimately illusionary when it is assumed to rest in human hands, then mastery is even more so. The idea that we could not only steer any dimension of human history, but that we could steer it toward a successful outcome in which contingency and chance are eliminated is nothing less than absurd. Thus, in addition to always remaining vulnerable, he insisted that Christians must assume an attitude of humility.

One illustration of Yoder's preference for a posture marked by vulnerability and humility rather than control and mastery is found in his discussion of power. Yoder is under no illusion that the church, like any institution, is immune from the exercise of power. That is, we cannot deny that the church has the ability to make things happen. Indeed, he points out that "power in the simplest sense of the word was Jesus' agenda."[24] The

---

23. Yoder, *For the Nations*, 142. On another occasion Yoder argued that

    Ever since Constantine in principle, and ever since Aquinas in spelled-out theory, the relationship of nature and grace or of technique and morality has been such that we trust the people who know about nature to tell us where to start. We trust the economists to tell us about economic development and the nutritionists to tell us what people should have to eat. Then the religionists try to stir us up to do those good things. That smooth division of labor fits well within the progress imagery of a Christendom getting more and more on top of its problems. It fits less in a world out of control, or even in a world out of sync ("Theological Perspectives on 'Growth with Equity,'" 14).

24. Yoder, "Jesus and Power," 448.

crucial contribution Yoder makes to discussions of power is to complicate the picture of power as a "unity . . . a fluid like the water in a hose which you can point in any direction, morally neutral, with its value depending on what you use it for."[25] Not only can power be used in myriad of ways, some of which are more helpful and some of which are more destructive, there are a myriad of types of power, some of which are closer and some of which are further from the kind of power exercised by Jesus.[26] In becoming vulnerable to the world rather than grabbing control of the world using the levers of political power, the church is not simply rejecting the use of power but is aligning itself with a different kind of power. In short, "control should not be the goal."[27] As Yoder put it, "Jesus did not free his disciples from violence to make them pure and weak, but because he called them to use other, stronger resources."[28] These "other, stronger resources" are alternative dimensions of power that are typically left out of the equation by political theorists, advocates of social change, and even theological ethicists.

It is in large part in order to clarify this situation that Yoder attempted to reintroduce the Pauline language of principalities and powers. Ordinary power becomes a "Power" in the biblical sense of the term when it is reified and thus comes to control us rather than enabling us to simply make things happen. How does Christ transform the powers? As we have seen, Yoder insists that Christ "does not destroy them; he makes them *sober* and *modest*. He does not deny their place; he makes them serve people instead of enslaving us, by decreasing their pretentiousness."[29] It is with a strong dose of humility that the principalities and powers can once again become ordinary powers.

Throughout Yoder's work one gets the sense that even if it *appears* as though an instrumental connection can be drawn between the actions of the church and outcomes in the world at large, we must never be too quick to attempt to set it down in ink. In one article he stresses that whenever we attempt to discern the presence of God's kingdom in the midst of the

---

25. Yoder, "Moral Theology Miscellany #19," 5. This is reminiscent of Yoder's contribution to discussions about culture.

26. Yoder suggested that "some power is good, natural, like skills: the skill of mothering, the skill of gardening. Some power is very good, redemptive: the power of love, of the spirit. Some power is imply destructive: defamation, violence. Some is potentially harmful but may be harnessed to prevent worse evils; the power of office, of community consensus, of the communication media" ("Moral Theology Miscellany #19," 6).

27. Yoder, *For the Nations*, 190.

28. Yoder, "Jesus and Power," 453. Yoder's chapter on "Revolutionary Subordination" in *The Politics of Jesus* is perhaps the best illustration of this dimension of his thought.

29. Yoder, "Moral Theology Miscellany #19," 6; italics added.

world we must remember that "what God is really doing will usually be a surprise" and that "providence remains inscrutable."[30] Thus we need to be cautious about trying to predict the outcome of our actions, much less the modest contribution that they may make toward building up God's kingdom. Yoder insists that, at most, "the course of events in the world can give us cues (signals as to when to speak) and clues (hints of larger meanings), echoes or projected images of the Gospel of the kingdom coming."[31] To put it in stronger terms: "The lunge for the large view is often the beginning of self-deception."[32]

Nonconformity

Yoder's humility in evaluating the impact of even well-intentioned human efforts in the world, and his desire to remain vulnerable even in the face of ill-intentioned political forces was shaped by his belonging to a minority church tradition. Indeed, as a church historian with particular expertise in the radical wing of the Protestant Reformation, he was convinced that minority voices had much to offer to the mainstream. After all, Mennonites and other Anabaptists were post-Constantinian long before the end of Christendom. And their rejection of warfare led to experiences of persecution and frequent migrations, further entrenching their identity as people willing to stick to an alternative way of life even at great personal cost. As Yoder was quick to point out, however, the history of the church is filled with many additional examples where faithfulness to the gospel message demanded that people question the dominant perspective or commonly held assumptions. Perhaps then it is not surprising that, rather than conformity, Yoder emphasized nonconformity in his thinking.[33]

Yoder's appreciation for nonconformists in history does not mean he valued nonconformity for the sake of nonconformity. It is unlikely, for example, that he would have been swayed by the anti-establishment,

---

30. Yoder, "Discerning the Kingdom of God," 370.

31. Ibid., 372.

32. Ibid., 370. There are several other marks of the church that counter the preoccupation with control and mastery encouraged by technologies such as genetically modified food. As Harry Huebner, a Mennonite theologian who has been strongly influenced by Yoder's theology, puts it: "Hope and amazement are embarrassing to the modern mind because they come from an imagination which acknowledges that we are not in control and that we do not know everything. When we know everything we cannot be amazed. When we are in control we do not need hope" (*Echoes of the Word*, 196).

33. Perhaps then it is all the more surprising that contemporary Mennonites have conformed so easily to the ways of modern technology.

libertarian arguments used by some critics of genetically modified food. And, as noted in chapter 2, unlike Jacques Ellul, Yoder was not attracted to political anarchism. In one essay he compiled a list of seven things that Anabaptist-Mennonites are called to proclaim liberation from, starting with the dominion of Mars (the cult of war), money, and a "me-centered" existence. In Yoder's words, "if you follow the risen Jesus, *you don't have to* do your own thing."[34] His concern is less with finding or preserving a unique identity as it is with being faithful. Indeed, perhaps it is better to say he was nonconformist because he favored a particular kind of conformity—conforming to the ways of Jesus at all costs. Yoder also went on to talk about the need to proclaim liberation from the dominion of "the mass," insisting that "if you follow the risen Jesus, *you don't have to* follow the crowd."[35] Once again, we follow an alternative path not because we have turned the individual into an absolute, but because we choose to identify with a "particular people" or a "particular strand" within the mass. When we are incorporated into the body of Christ we are liberated from the crowd, and, as Yoder wrote, "the sociological name for this liberation is 'nonconformity.'"[36] In the rest of this article Yoder continues to carve out space for a nonconformist posture that cannot be reduced to either individualism or collectivism, arguing that we also need liberation from the dominion of the milieu ("*you don't have to* be one of the gang"), the mold ("*we don't have to* stay the way we have been"), and the moment ("*you don't have to* be 'with it'"). He distinguishes between participating in and becoming defined by a movement or smaller mass that confines us to a ghetto or enclave, between acknowledging and allowing ourselves to be defined by the matrix that precedes us, and between being aware of the present and claiming that our situation demands that we behave in a certain way. For Yoder, this discussion of how the various guises of nonconformity can liberate us from these less-obvious idols provides a "more concrete picture of what it means to be *redeemed*." Like peacemaking, caring for the poor, and yielding to the authority of the church, they "sketch an alternative *Gesalt*."[37]

Yoder's perspective on the ecumenical movement provides a good illustration of the shape of his kind of nonconformity. In contrast to most of the Protestant reformers, whom Yoder describes with the slogan "break-in-order-to-be-faithful," Yoder lifted up the Anabaptists as the model for how

---

34. Yoder, "Anabaptist Shape of Liberation," 341; italics in original. Most of the examples Yoder lifts up are of peoples not people, of churches not individuals choosing to follow an alternative path. See also *Christian Attitudes to War, Peace, and Revolution*.

35. Yoder, "Anabaptist Shape of Liberation.," 343; italics in original.

36. Ibid., 344.

37. Ibid., 343.

to pursue church unity.³⁸ The radical reformers insisted that "if there must be a break within the church, between the unfaithful church and the faithful church, the initiative must come from the unfaithful side."³⁹ Perhaps this is why, even when their opponents resorted to violence, the Anabaptists repeatedly and openly appealed for reconsideration.⁴⁰ Thus Yoder's exemplars for nonconformity are the very same people he points to as the pioneers of the ecumenical movement—unity is not the same thing as conformity.⁴¹

The Internet

As discussed in chapter 3, of the three examples discussed in this book, the Internet is the clearest example of a technological system. It is a network of networks upon which individuals and institutions depend to transmit digital information—unlike genetically modified food, the Internet is not simply *part* of a larger system because of the way it is developed and delivered to end users, and unlike the automobile, the Internet does not simply rely on a larger infrastructure in order to perform as designed. As such, one would think that it might also be the clearest example of a principality or power, a structure that is both necessary and fallen. However, as we have also seen, the general tenor of reflections on the Internet suggests that this is one system that is far from needing to be transformed. Indeed, it is often held up as a pathway *toward* various kinds of transformation. Clearly, this should be a warning sign for anyone who shares Yoder's perspective on the seductive nature of the powers.

Servanthood

As with control and mastery, Yoder was not enamored with efficiency, a cultural priority that is reflected in the rapid embrace of the Internet as a

---

38. Yoder, *Ecumenical Movement and the Faithful Church*, 29.

39. Ibid., 33.

40. In fact, for over a year the Swiss Brethren refused to, in Yoder's words, "accept a break that was already there" with Zwingli's church in Zurich (Yoder, *Ecumenical Movement and the Faithful Church*, 31).

41. Yoder's perspective is fleshed out by his simultaneous affirmation of the unity of all who confess Christ as Lord, and the local congregation as the location where the work of God's Spirit is most clearly evident. He was convinced that Christian unity is not something we create or preserve, but something we obey or observe. Following the pattern of scripture, sanctification is the goal not the prerequisite of Christian fellowship, and discipline or excommunication is something that can only be applied locally to individuals within a congregation.

medium for communication. Indeed, as reflected in the above discussion of effectiveness, this is the place where he is in closest agreement with Jacques Ellul's critique of technological systems and ways of thinking. Recall that Ellul defined technique as the *"totality of methods rationally arrived at and having absolute efficiency* (for a given stage of development) in *every* field of human activity."[42] The fact that efficiency is not only the motivation for the development of new technology, but has become the primary measure for economic and political policy, for educational and social service programs, and for innumerable decisions made by individuals on a daily basis, would seem to confirm Ellul's worst fears about the dominance of technique. Furthermore, as with technology in general, the ideal of efficiency is commonly assumed to be morally neutral. Indeed, if authority is defined as the ability to impact individual and collective decision-making, efficiency data is the closest thing we have to an absolute authority in a time when absolutes have virtually disappeared.[43]

As in the above discussion of the automobile and genetically modified foods, however, the contrast between Yoder and the ideals embodied and encouraged by the Internet is made clear not so much by his critique of things like efficiency, but by his affirmation of an alternative moral vision that is marked by things like servanthood.[44] Indeed, while Yoder's seminal work *The Politics of Jesus* was intended to demonstrate the relevance of the life of Jesus for social ethics, he did not reduce discipleship to some general notion of following the way of Jesus. For Yoder, to be a disciple of Jesus means we imitate him only in one very specific way:

> There is no *general* concept of living like Jesus in the New Testament . . . There is but one realm in which the concept of imitation holds—but there it holds for every strand of the New Testament literature and all the more strikingly by virtue of the absence of parallels in other realms. This is at the point of the concrete social meaning of the cross in relation to enmity and

---

42. Ellul, *Technological Society*, xxv.

43. Skeptical voices can be found—for example, some environmentalists have noted that traditional measures of efficiency tend to be bound to existing paradigms and thus a concern for efficiency on its own is a dead end. In the words of William McDonough and Michael Braungart: "Relying on eco-efficiency to save the environment will in fact achieve the opposite; it will let industry finish off everything, quietly, persistently, and completely . . . Plainly put, eco-efficiency only works to make the old, destructive system a bit less so" (*Cradle to Cradle*, 62).

44. Clearly Yoder's nonconformist tendencies would also lead him to be suspicious of the ideal of efficiency. Once again, this discussion of the marks of the church and technological ideals is not intended to set them up as binary opposites, but simply as points of tension—in fact, Yoder tended to contrast "servanthood" with "dominion" or "idolatry."

power. Servanthood replaces dominion, forgiveness absorbs hostility. Thus—and only thus—are we bound by New Testament thought to "be like Jesus."[45]

Yoder underlines this point in a number of ways. For example, in an essay on the ministry of the church, he writes: "If there is in fact a 'center' from which on biblical grounds one should seek to illuminate and orient all of the ministries of the community, it would have to be the notion of servanthood itself."[46] He subsequently came to talk about servanthood as not only the definition of Christian ministry, but as the "counterpart" to power: "The servant stance is therefore the model for the servant community's renunciation of dominion, even of dominion in the name of well-doing."[47] Of course, power cannot be reduced to dominion, and so Yoder ends up framing servanthood as a particular kind of power rather than the counterpart to power. This means that "the church is called to discriminate . . . to know which kinds of power in a given context are faithful instruments of servanthood and which would represent in that context the kind of dominion over others which [Jesus] rejects."[48]

As should now be clear, the most significant way in which servanthood contrasts with efficiency is that it is grounded in a concern for obedience rather than a concern for outcomes, although this is not as simple as a contrast between deontological and consequentialist reasoning. As Yoder put it, "Servanthood is not a position of nonpower or weakness; it is an alternative mode of power."[49] It is through this alternative mode of power that God works in the world, even though in the short term its efficacy may not be apparent. It is in giving up our urge to run the world for God, yielding ourselves not only to God's will but to each other, that our obedience becomes something more than following rules. Obedience can thus become praise, pointing to what God is already doing, and can also thus free us from despair.

At the same time, for Yoder choosing the path of servanthood does not completely usurp any concern for efficiency as much as it relativizes it. The priority of servanthood is made clear in the example of Jesus, in the instances when he refused kingly power or stooped to wash the feet of his disciples. Surely if human actions are more important for what they point to

---

45. Yoder, *Politics of Jesus*, 130, 131.
46. Yoder, *Fullness of Christ*, 66–67.
47. Yoder, "Behold My Servant Shall Prosper," in *Karl Barth and the Problem of War*, 153. This essay was originally the third of five "Stone Lectures" that Yoder presented at Princeton Theological Seminary in February, 1980.
48. Ibid., 157.
49. Yoder, *For the Nations*, 191.

than what they cause, efficiency can never be elevated to a higher power. At the same time, doing the best we can with the available resources was only common sense to Yoder, and so taking the long view should never mean disregard for a certain kind of efficiency:

> None of these considerations sets aside the need to think practically, to weigh the likely effects and the relative costs of available strategies. But they may help diminish the arbitrariness, the self-confidence, and the short sightedness with which deeper values tend to be given up for apparent immediate effect.[50]

In light of Ellul's perspective on *technique*, Yoder may have even argued that efficiency itself was a principality or power, something that was created good and is necessary to a certain extent, but that has become reified and thus fallen. The transformation of this power comes when the church refuses its idolatry and puts it in its place by celebrating servanthood.[51] It comes when the church is a community that does things without the expectation of reward, placing the needs of others ahead of its own needs. In short, the church is a community that is most inefficient.[52]

---

50. Ibid., 196.

51. Yoder, "God's Good News and the Runaway powers," 8.

52. In Yoder's words, "Instead of choosing between the ghetto and the world as it is, we choose the world to come. In the face of apparently insoluble social problems, that means finding previously unseen solutions . . . A scientist . . . deals with the predictable, the repeatable, with what standard models of causation and analogy make one expect . . . Yet history is the record of the impossible" ("God's Good News and the Runaway powers," 8–9).

Yoder was also skeptical of attempts to institutionalize service or turn it into a science as disaster relief and international development initiatives grew rapidly in the Mennonite church following World War II. In response to a request to help develop a "theology of service" for one of these initiatives, Yoder replied that "when it has been valid," Mennonite service was "a spontaneous response to seen need." In short, Christians should serve because they are called to be servants, to "render service," not because they are called to "produce . . . results." As Yoder put it, "The need itself is imperative enough. If we serve only because our minds have affirmed a logical or causative connection between the service and these results, our service won't have holding power and [ironically] won't achieve much." He went on to say: "Since the strong points of Mennonitism are the spontaneity and the broad base of participation, one should consciously avoid a rigid organization with overhead and central management. Decentralized initiative with voluntary local leadership should be fostered; only enough organization should be set up to enable moving quickly when a need arises" (Yoder, Letter to Lester Glick). I will revisit Yoder's perspective on service and effectiveness in chapter 5.

Visibility

Another mark that Yoder sees as crucial for the church to display if it is to transform the powers is transparency or visibility. While technological systems such as the Internet are seen to be better the more they recede in the background, for Yoder the practices of the church are seen to be better the more they open up the church to scrutiny. Prominent commentators on the Internet such as Nicholas Negroponte have argued that "the medium is not the message in a digital world," and thus seek to overturn the influential work of the media theorist Marshall McLuhan.[53] In contrast, Yoder sounds downright McLuhanesque when, as noted already in chapter 2, he says: "Ethics is more than ethics . . . actions proclaim . . . the medium and the message are inseparable . . . *How* God is doing it is indistinguishable from *what* God is doing, and *how the world can know* about it is again the same thing."[54] Yoder is emphatic that what matters is not simply the outcome, but the process that leads to the outcome. Thus he is convinced that the church "is a pulpit."[55] The church does not simply proclaim God's message to the world, it *is* God's message to the world. It is the means of God's transformation of the world, more than it is an end.

In Yoder's view then, the church is the opposite of a "black box." As we have already seen in the above paragraphs, the most faithful church is certainly *not* the one that demands the least of its members. Furthermore, its work must never be hidden from sight or disappear from our consciousness. Yoder's particular vision of evangelicalism pervaded his theological reflections—once again, as we have already seen in chapter 2, he insisted not only that ethics were for Christians, but that ethics were by definition missional. Thus to do ethics is to do mission. Indeed, Yoder's ecclesial reflections did not dwell on the longstanding distinction between the visible and invisible church, but focused entirely on the former, on "the Christian community as a visible body within history."[56] He insisted that "to say the church must be visible demands an existence, a structure, a sociology of

---

53. Negroponte, *Being Digital*, 71. McLuhan's well known expression is: "The medium is the message." See *Understanding Media*, 7.

54. Yoder, *For the Nations*, 41.

55. Ibid.

56. Ibid., 185. Yoder stressed that, as with the Jewish tradition, many of the marks of the early church were visible. For example, there was a visible decision to join the community as marked by baptism; there were clearly defined borders to the community; and the church did not conform to the ways of the world in terms of political allegiance, economic practices, slavery, the role of women, etc. See Yoder, *Jewish-Christian Schism Revisited*, 125.

its own, independent of the other structures of society."[57] Finally, and even more concretely, he pointed out that the activities undertaken by the church are not "opaque rituals," they are not secret or magical, but are visible and "lend themselves to being observed, imitated, [and] extrapolated."[58] The church is, by definition for Yoder, something that is restricted in both time and place, and so meeting face to face is crucial, not optional.

Simplicity

The final mark of the church noted by Yoder that will be discussed in this chapter is simplicity, a mark that contrasts with the technological ideal of novelty. It might be argued, however, that Yoder's resistance to novelty is open to challenge. After all, given his appreciation for nonconformity and the resulting readiness for reform that this prompts in both the church and society, it is not surprising that critics have accused him of helping create an expectation and receptivity for change. Furthermore, unlike traits such as nonconformity, vulnerability, and patience, to my knowledge Yoder never wrote about simplicity in a substantive way. Nonetheless, on several occasions Yoder did point to simplicity, along with nonviolence and servanthood, as one of the defining marks of the Anabaptist-Mennonite tradition.

For example, in the late 1970s Yoder joined a small group of Mennonite academics and development experts in starting a not-for-profit company called International Development Enterprises. The purpose of this organization was to connect Western technical expertise with needs in the so-called Third World.[59] In an early memo to his partners, Yoder provided an explanation for why this kind of venture was congruent not only with the concerns of the Mennonite church, but why a theologian was interested in it. Aside from his personal relationship with Paul Polak, the driving force

---

57. Yoder, *Royal Priesthood*, 170.

58. Yoder, "Concluding Observations," 4.

59. Incorporation papers filed on Oct. 1, 1982 declared the intention to serve the following purposes:
- A. To identify, manufacture and market appropriate services and technology for the representatives of third world communities.
- B. To facilitate the rational distribution of human and natural resources.
- C. To provide opportunity for modest grass roots technological and community development.
- D. To provide access to technological, business, and professional expertise and experience.
- E. To publish information regarding international economic development.

behind the venture,⁶⁰ Yoder pointed to a shared "ideology." He begins by describing a development conundrum: many problems "can only be dealt with by grass roots modest technology and community development," and yet those with the "mobility of experience in technology" who could help in this regard tend to be part of governments, non-governmental organizations, and multi-national corporations who "necessarily prefer higher technologies." This need could be addressed, Yoder suggests, by a different kind of multi-national corporation capable of serving "local development possibilities by bringing to bear medium level expertise and technology and interfacing with the global system." It is the proposal for a more appropriate level of technology, as well as the possibility of being "'in but not of' the world market systems; using their channels without sharing their values" that Yoder sees as a parallel to "the peace/service/self-help/simplicity/stewardship strands in the ideal Mennonite identity."⁶¹

A second occasion where Yoder highlights the mark of simplicity is in his discussion of the need for liberation from the "dominion of the moment." As he puts it: "If you follow the risen Jesus *you don't have to* be 'with it.'"⁶² Yoder suggests that we tend to be preoccupied with the present rather than the past or future, with keeping up with the latest and greatest rather than the eternal. Although he was writing before the Internet era had begun, Yoder noted that "our culture has exacerbated this tendency by the growth of instantaneous communications media."⁶³ Once again, his commitment to the church, more specifically to local, face-to-face relationships within the church, demands authenticity and stability, and thus challenges virtuality and the pursuit of novel experiences.⁶⁴

60. Polak is now a leading figure in international development circles in the U.S. See, for example, his book *Out of Poverty*.

61. Yoder, "Paul Polak Project," 5.

62. Yoder, "Anabaptist Shape of Liberation," 347. Yoder also makes a connection between simplicity and liberation or freedom in an unpublished review of two books on simplicity, Vernard Eller's *The Simple Life*, and Arthur G. Gish's *Beyond the Rat Race*.

63. Yoder, "Anabaptist Shape of Liberation," 347.

64. Yoder's perspective on the Internet may also be fleshed out by his actual practice with regard to what was for him a novel way of communicating. E-mail use among academics was becoming commonplace in the final few years of his life, and, as the records in the Yoder archive demonstrate, he was not averse to using it. While some scholars have rejected the use of e-mail on principle or simply because they were not inclined to change long-established communication practices, Yoder appeared to feel some sense of responsibility to keep up with this technology, if for no other reason that those he communicated with had embraced it. For someone who maintained an enormous volume of correspondence by regular mail, one might have expected him to be more enthusiastic about the possibilities presented by e-mail. However, overall his attitude seemed to be cautious and measured, and he was a far cry from "going digital."

TECHNOLOGY IS CONSCIENTIOUSLY ENGAGED THROUGH THE PRACTICES OF THE CHURCH

By this point it should be clear that the marks of the church discussed above have broader implications than the contrasts that were drawn with the ideals embodied and encouraged by automobiles, genetically modified food, and the Internet. After all, the desire for speed, control, and efficiency may be clearly associated with particular technologies, but they also transcend particular technologies. And I should make it clear once again that although the range of the marks of the church that have been highlighted is broad, it is not comprehensive. Indeed, I have not even grappled with the one trait that is most commonly associated with Yoder's thought: nonviolence.

The key question that needs to be addressed at this point is what to do with the obvious tension that has been put on display in the previous section. The moral landscape painted by Yoder provides an alternative vision that puts the particular technologies under consideration in this project in a different light. Cars, crops, and computers look very different when viewed through the lens of Yoder's theological ethic as compared to the lens provided by scientific, economic, or sociological data. What then do we do with this alternative vision? Is it simply one more compelling critique of technology, or is it something more?

There is still much more that Yoder enables us to say about, and to do with technological artifacts, systems, and ways of thinking. Recall that the point of the church's existence in Yoder's view is to give testimony to the fact that the principalities and powers have been defeated, or have been humbled, by the work of Jesus Christ. The church provides this testimony most profoundly not through words, not by talking about an alternative vision, but by embodying a new way of life, by living out an alternative vision. Thus the next step is to ask how it is possible for a church community to share the gifts of patience, vulnerability, and servanthood. For it is by sharing these gifts in the midst of a context driven by the imperatives of speed,

---

For example, his concern about maintaining records of his communication, and fear about losing information when software became obsolete, led him to retain hard copies of numerous messages. And he seemed rather unimpressed with the immediacy of e-mail communication—with so much on the go, perhaps he was happy to wait a month or two for a response to a mailed inquiry.

If anything excited Yoder about the Internet, it was the possibility of making articles and papers widely available by serving as an online archive of his files. To serve that end he was one of the first professors in the Department of Theology at Notre Dame to have a personal web page, a page that was maintained by his family for several years after his death.

control, and efficiency that particular technologies such as the automobile, genetically modified food, and the Internet can be put in their rightful place.

Technology and Practices

Before proceeding any further, however, a few general comments about the relationship between moral vision and practices are in order. As mentioned in chapter 1, my own perspective on this relationship has been influenced by philosophers such as Alasdair MacIntyre and Charles Taylor, and theologians such as George Lindbeck and Vincent J. Miller.

MacIntyre argues that traditions alone are capable of settling moral disputes, and, since traditions are constituted by practices, these disputes ultimately come to reside in competing practices.[65] It is important to note, however, that MacIntyre has something quite precise in mind when he speaks of practices:

> By a 'practice' I am going to mean any coherent and complex form of socially established cooperative human activity through which goods internal to that form of activity are realized in the course of trying to achieve those standards of excellence which are appropriate to, and partially definitive of, that form of activity, with the result that human powers to achieve excellence, and human conceptions of the ends and goods involved, are systematically extended.[66]

Thus "practices" for MacIntyre do not refer to just any type of action—they include architecture but not bricklaying, farming but not planting, and the game of football but not throwing a ball. It would seem then that the development of technologies such as automobiles, genetically modified food, or the Internet could each be distinct practices, although the *use* of these same technologies would not be. That is, automotive engineering is a practice but driving a car is not, genetic engineering is a practice but choosing crop characteristics from a seed catalog is not, and software engineering is a practice but clicking a link on a web site is not.[67] Indeed, it would seem

---

65. Of course, MacInytre's concern is not new. As Kallenberg has noted, "Throughout church history there have been persistent witnesses (St. Francis, Philip Jacob Spener, Kierkegaard) to the view that right living (praxis) is logically prior to right thinking. Voices like these remind us of the ways in which ethics is rooted in practice." See "Positioning MacIntyre within Christian Ethics," chapter 3 in Murphy, Kallenberg, and Nation, *Virtues and Practices in the Christian Tradition*, 74.

66. MacIntyre, *After Virtue*, 187.

67. As Gaillardetz points out, each of these practices could also be viewed as *focal* practices: "Our difficulty does not lie with the technological artisans. For the software

that technologies enhance our capability to act in the world while at the same time diminishing our engagement with traditional practices. Cars may enhance mobility while undermining our ability to sustain households and neighborhoods; genetically modified foods may enhance agricultural productivity while undermining the need for excellence in farming, and the Internet may enhance access to information while undermining any sense of historical context for that information. In short, technology itself comes to undermine the possibility of nurturing the kind of tradition that presents any alternative to technological ideals.

Charles Taylor focuses on what he calls "social imaginaries" rather than traditions, although the end result is a similar elevation of the significance of practices for philosophers and intellectual historians. Taylor writes: "We can think of the social imaginary of a people at a given time as a kind of repertory . . . including the ensemble of practices they can make sense of."[68] He thinks that talking about ideas or theories on their own is nonsensical since theories are "glossed" or "given a particular shape" by the very practices they try to make sense of;[69] theories thus "need to be 'schematized,' to receive some concrete interpretation in the domain of practice, if they are to be operative in history."[70] The implication is that modern malaises such as individualism and instrumental reason cannot be addressed by re-casting

---

designer or the electrical engineer, the invention and perfection of technological devices is doubtless itself a focal practice that expresses the ingenuity of human creativity. But the vast majority of us engage technology as consumers, not designers or inventors, and it is as consumers that we most experience technology reshaping our lives" (*Transforming Our Days*, 136).

68. Taylor, *Modern Social Imaginaries*, 115.

69. Ibid., 29.

70. Ibid., 115. Taylor's perspective on practices is also more balanced than MacIntyre, or at least than the way MacIntyre is often used to not simply elevate the significance of practices relative to theory, but to elevate practices *over* theory. Several quotes from *Modern Social Imaginaries* makes this clear:

> "It is a false dichotomy to view ideas and material factors as rival causal agents . . . they are inseparable" (ibid., 30).
>
> "Because human practices are the kind of thing that makes sense, certain ideas are internal to them; one cannot distinguish the two in order to ask: Which causes which?" (ibid.).
>
> "Certain moral self-understandings are embedded in certain practices, which can mean both that they are promoted by the spread of these practices and that they shape the practices and help them get established. It is equally absurd to believe that the practices always come first, or to adopt the opposite view, that ideas somehow drive history" (ibid., 63).

Given the portrayal of Yoder in chapter 2, he seems to be closer to Taylor than MacIntyre.

our philosophy because they have become entrenched within the institutions of technological society.[71]

Theologians as well as philosophers have also urged that increased attention be paid to practices. For example, George Lindbeck, one of the pioneering voices of what became the broader movement known as postliberal theology, stresses that religions are best thought of as cultural-linguistic rather than cognitive-propositional or experiential-expressive movements. That is, religious faith should not be pictured as a decision to be guided by either known propositions or inner experience:

> Rather, to become religious—no less than to become culturally or linguistically competent—is to interiorize a set of skills by practice and training. One learns how to feel, act, and think in conformity with a religious tradition that is, in its inner structure, far richer and more subtle than can be explicitly articulated.[72]

Thus things such as rituals and examples are far more important for religious formation than rules and ideas. And thus Lindbeck encourages theologians to focus on following rather than interpreting doctrines in order to become "directly relevant to the praxis of the church."[73]

If MacIntyre, Taylor, and Lindbeck provide a philosophical and theological perspective that elevates the significance of practices in general,[74] Vincent Miller elevates the significance of a particular set of practices. In short, Miller makes a compelling argument for why the standard practices of consumer culture undermine religious belief. Indeed, he demonstrates that "consumer culture is best diagnosed not as a deformation of belief but as a particular way of engaging religious beliefs that divorces them from practice."[75] As consumers awash in a sea of commodities, we are trained to treat everything we encounter, including religion, as "things to be played

---

71. See Taylor, "An Iron Cage?," chapter 9 in *Ethics of Authenticity*. Once again, over and against technological determinists, Taylor insists that despite the strong push of technology, we do retain some measure of freedom. In fact, he argues that technology can also be seen to embody values such as benevolence.

72. Lindbeck, *Nature of Doctrine*, 35.

73. Ibid., 107.

74. My interest in practices has also been shaped by the work of philosophical pragmatists—see, for example, Hickman, *John Dewey's Pragmatic Technology*; and Fish, *Trouble with Principle*. Of course, thanks to the work of liberation theologians, there has also been a great deal of interest in *praxis* in recent years. For a comprehensive look at the theological appropriation of the notions of both practice and praxis, see Pilario, *Back to the Rough Grounds of Praxis*.

75. Miller, *Consuming Religion*, 12.

with, explored, tried on, and, in the end, discarded."[76] We have developed "a set of habits of interpretation and use . . . that renders the 'content' of beliefs and values less important."[77] Furthermore, this culture is even capable of co-opting or domesticating criticism, since "ideas are so easily abstracted from practice."[78] Miller points out that "this abstraction impedes the translation of ethical concerns into action, reducing ethics to sentiment."[79] In order to counter this reality, Miller does not propose a revised metaphysicis or anthropology,[80] but alternative practices that will counter the formative influence of consumerism.

While I agree with Miller that our obligation to consume influences the underlying form of our lives, the first half of this chapter makes it clear that prominent dimensions of our technological culture also undermine religious convictions. The point to be underlined here is that technology provides a profound illustration of the extent to which practices shape our moral vision. Certainly ideals such as autonomy, control, and efficiency transcend our technological era—they were around long before the automobile, genetically modified food, and the Internet. Yet they have also been embodied by these particular technologies is a significant way, and, moreover, they have flourished along with these technologies, growing in status and authority. In addition, other ideals such as speed, conformity, and novelty seem more like the product of, rather than the impetus for, new technologies such as those discussed in this book.

Finally, I would add that there are significant parallels between the overall structure of this effort and Miller's book, as I demonstrate the significance of an important cultural phenomenon, and then attempt to move beyond analysis to engagement. Significant parallels can also be found between Miller's discussion of commodification and the work of Albert Borgmann.[81] Indeed, at times Borgmann appears to be more concerned about commodification and consumerism than he is about technology. And yet for Borgmann, commodification is a symptom of a deeper problem, it is not the root of the problem—commodification is the consequence of our be-

---

76. Ibid., 6.
77. Ibid., 1.
78. Ibid., 32.
79. Ibid., 76.

80. Indeed, Miller is convinced that traditional theological skills such as the hermeneutics of retrieval and suspicion, conceptual clarification, and systematic elaboration are all susceptible to commodification and therefore build up rather than undermine consumerism (see ibid., 180).

81. Miller does mention Borgmann, although only in one brief reference that accuses him of being "overly romantic." See ibid., 47.

conscientiously engaging technology

ing shaped by technological devices rather than focal things and practices. Technological devices and systems mediate our experiences, insulating us from each other and from the world, and producing abstracted goods that lack any connection to traditional practices. What MacIntyre's work can be seen to suggest, Borgmann's work demonstrates: technology undermines the possibility of nurturing the kind of tradition that presents any alternative to a technological worldview.

Yoder's Perspective on the Practices of the Church

As mentioned in chapter 2, Yoder's ecclesial focus, coupled with his conviction that ethics and theology are two sides of the same coin, leads him to view the practices of the church as the starting point for Christian ethics.[82] Throughout his corpus he talks about the things that Christians do together as the body of Christ, and the following paragraphs will trace the emergence of five central practices in this discussion.[83] As with the discussion of the marks of the church in the previous chapter, several alternative paths could have been taken if this was a more general project—for example, we could explore the technological implications of the seven traditional sacraments of the church. Or we could explore the implications of practices unique to particular religious orders such as the Rule of St. Benedict, or St. Ignatius of Loyola's Spiritual Exercises. Once again, however, I will be utilizing Yoder's terms of reference in my discussion.

The obvious source to turn to in order to summarize Yoder's perspective on the practices of the church is *Body Politics*, a short volume first

---

82. This a sharp difference with Borgmann's concern to nurture focal practices through "communities of celebration" in the public sphere. See "Communities of Celebration," chapter 3 in *Power Failure*.

In this regard Yoder would have more in common with theological interpreters of Borgmann such as Gaillardetz, who argues that "the Christian community itself possesses a distinctive set of such 'focal' practices," seen most clearly in liturgy (*Transforming Our Days*, 105). Dawn agrees, insisting that "Christianity provides focal concerns worthy of our creation as human beings and efficacious for dealing with the encroachments and fetterings of our technologized, commodified milieu" (*Unfettered Hope*, 76).

83. Despite the obvious resonance with MacIntyre, on one occasion Yoder noted that he "chose the term 'practice' as the most neutral word available; yet at the same time one might note that the contemporary philosopher Alasdair MacIntyre has made of this ordinary word a very technical term, his key to the complex renewal of the understanding of how moral thinking works." Yoder's definition of "practice" was much more generic. See Yoder, "Concluding Observations," 7.

published in 1992.[84] As significant as this book is, however, it has a long history, a history that helps to provide a fuller picture of Yoder's perspective.

Yoder's most comprehensive discussion of church practices is found in a report he prepared for a Mennonite church consultation in 1967.[85] As an appendix he included a "Checklist of the Functions of the Church," where, starting with Luther's brief summary of the church as the place "where the word of God is properly preached" and "where the sacraments are properly administered," he surveyed eight additional thinkers. Calvin, for example, added correct discipline or church order to Luther's two functions; Menno Simons added holy living, brotherly love, confession of faith, and suffering. Another Anabaptist, Balthasar Hubmaier, insisted on his own list of four functions: baptism, Lord's supper, discipline (restoration or exclusion), and teaching (catechism). A more recent figure, Yoder's teacher Harold S. Bender, reduced the functions of the church to three: discipleship, brotherhood, and nonresistance. Yoder also looked to the Anglican bishop Stephen Neill, to the former World Council of Churches General Secretary Willem Visser 't Hooft, to contributors to a Believers' church conference statement, and to the Mennonite sociologist Cal Redekop, before concluding with his own list based on material from a seminary course on the nature of the church he had been teaching for several years. Yoder's list of seven functions or practices included sharing, unity, worship or prayer, testing the truth, making disciples, binding and loosing, and serving.

In his summary Yoder attempts to synthesize insights from each of these perspectives in a "combination check list," utilizing another seven-fold outline to hold them all together. He recognizes that each individual list was "established with a view to those points at which Christians differ," and thus (with the exception of his own list) each "have a gap at the point of what all Christians would have in common . . . the requirement that Christians gather for worship." Furthermore, Yoder only claims to have achieved "relative completeness and orderliness," not "a polished outline from either a literary or logical perspective."[86] Despite these qualifications, it is interesting to note that a rough correspondence can be found with his own list of seven marks or functions of the church:

---

84. This book was republished in 2001, and it from this latter edition that all quotations will be taken.

85. Yoder, "Anabaptist Understandings of the Nature and Mission of the Church." Yoder subsequently addressed many of the same themes in "A People in the World."

86. Yoder, "Checklist of the Functions of the Church," 4.

> The Faithful Church is a missionary Church: baptism
> The Faithful Church is a loving brotherhood: bread and wine (see Yoder's "sharing" and "unity")
> The Church gathers to praise God: prayer and song (see: "worship or prayer")
> The Church is renewed by the Word: preaching (see: "testing the truth")
> The Church is a band of Disciples: forsaking all (see: "making disciples")
> The Church speaks God's binding and loosing word: fraternal address (see: "binding and loosing")
> The Church is servant: towel and basin (see "serving")

Yoder's report proper focuses on another gap he identifies in his synthesis, patterns of church organization and leadership. In drawing upon insights from the sixteenth-century Anabaptist movement, he acknowledges that this is another area in which competing church traditions can be distinguished. He also points out that his retrieval is not intended to inflate the egos of the Mennonite church leaders he was addressing: "If Anabaptism is the flag we fly it would have to become as well a norm to judge us."[87] The main point Yoder goes on to stress is that reconciliation is a basic need not only in a world rife with violence, but within the church, and even when that church is earnestly seeking to follow the Prince of Peace. Thus the primary goal of any organizational structures in the church must be to serve as an instrument of reconciliation. Following the path of the Anabaptists means that:

> We will not think about our organizations from the perspective of how they may work most smoothly and efficiently where there are no problems. Nor will we ask how they can work in spite of problems by not being stopped or tripped up when there are difficulties. We will rather ask what kind of organizational relationship is most fruitful for actually solving serious problems with a truly reconciling solution.[88]

Recognizing Yoder's early emphasis on the inevitability of the need for reconciliation is crucial for understanding his subsequent emphasis on practices such as binding and loosing. He did not focus on this practice out of a concern for purity or perfection, or to make sure that the church was "without spot or wrinkle." Rather, he recognized that, at least until the eschaton, the church would always be dealing with its fallibility. Indeed, the special contribution that the church has to offer to a world in need of

---

87. Yoder, "Anabaptist Understandings of the Nature and Mission of the Church," 1.
88. Ibid., 3.

reconciliation is not a model community free of problems so much as a community process for dealing with problems.[89] As he put it in his report to the Mennonite church: "So what we ask is not 'how can we organize for maximum smoothness in the carrying out of our regular tasks?' But rather 'how can we catch issues soon enough to bring to bear on them a reconciling concern before it is too late?'"[90]

A second emphasis of Yoder's that can be seen already in this early work is the authority of the local congregation, and this too is necessary to make sense of the kinds of church practices he discusses. Put negatively, although he recognized it was necessary, Yoder harbored a deep suspicion of the institutional church as manifest in denominational structures, hierarchies, and offices. Indeed, he pointed out that "one of the definitions of an institution is that it provides for its own survival . . . This is one point at which the Christian church should be different."[91] How might the church be different? Yoder's suggestion was to adopt an organization that was not only minimal, but fragile: "the best kind of church organization would be the kind which collapses most rapidly when there is no Holy Spirit or when there is no vision or when the brethren cease to love each other."[92] Put positively, Yoder claimed to be following the insistence of the New Testament account of the early church, as well as the Anabaptist witness, that "the Holy Spirit works wherever men gather." This does not mean that "congregations have nothing to do with each other," but that unity is a fruit of the Holy Spirit more than the product of institution-building. In Yoder's words, "there can be separate centers without chaos."[93]

Yoder continued to refine his list of the functions of the church as he taught related courses both at a Mennonite seminary and a Catholic university, and presented lectures on the topic at Lutheran retreat center, two Methodist church conferences, and a Methodist divinity school. He published his first journal article on the topic in 1991,[94] which became the basis

89. This dimension of Yoder's thought is amplified by Sider in *To See History Doxologically*.

90. Yoder, "Anabaptist Understandings of the Nature and Mission of the Church," 4. See also numerous published and unpublished writings such as: "Jesus and Lifestyle"; "Historiography as a Ministry to Renewal"; "If It's Not Broke, Fix It"; and "Methodological Miscellany #2."

91. Yoder, "Anabaptist Understandings of the Nature and Mission of the Church," 6. Earlier he made this point using sharper language: "Shuffling and creating structures is for administrators what intellectual gymnastics are for the academic; a powerful temptation to hide from fraternal encounter" (ibid., 4).

92. Ibid., 6.

93. Ibid., 9. See also: Yoder, *As You Go*.

94. Yoder, "Sacrament as Social Process." This article was republished twice, and

for *Body Politics*, a monograph originally published by a United Methodist church press. All that is to say that Yoder's perspective on the practices of the church was informed by, and was intended to speak to more than a Mennonite or Anabaptist audience.[95]

By the time of his first article, Yoder's was talking about five instead of seven key practices of the church: fraternal admonition, induction into the new humanity, the Spirit's freedom in the meeting, the universality of charisma, and breaking bread. While three of his original seven practices are clearly represented (sharing, testing the truth, and binding and loosing), as well as one of the practices added in his 1967 synthesis (baptism), he dropped other worship-related items such as prayer, song, and preaching, and discipleship-related items such as forsaking all, and towel and basin. He also added a new item related to church leadership. From this point on in Yoder's work the labels would change, but the basic categories remained the same—in *Body Politics* we read about:

Yoder presented the material in a number of contexts, including a lecture at the Duke University Divinity School in February, 1986, the Presidential Address at the Western Regional Meeting of the Society of Christian Ethics in February, 1987, a lecture at Boston University in April, 1987, and lectures at two United Church of Christ Seminaries, Eden Theological Seminary in October, 1987, and Bangor Theological Seminary in February, 1988.

Yoder had published essays on individual church practices prior to this point, although those pieces focused on issues related to those particular practices rather than making an argument about the social significance of church practices. For example, an earlier essay entitled "Binding and Loosing" was published in the *Concern* pamphlet series in February, 1967, as well as in the book *Healing the Wounded*. An earlier essay on the multiplicity of gifts was published as "The Fullness of Christ" in the *Concern* pamphlet series in February, 1969, and was based on "The One and the Many," a presentation Yoder made to a gathering of the InterSeminary Movement at The Ecumenical Institute, Evanston, IL, March 4, 1961. This essay was subsequently released as a monograph entitled *The Fullness of Christ* for the Believers' Church Conference on Ministry at Bethany Theological Seminary, Oak Brook, IL, Sept. 2–5, 1987.

95. Yoder thanked individuals from each of these contexts in the preface to *Body Politics*, where he also noted that he had "treated some of the themes elsewhere." In fact, there were many other occasions where Yoder shared his perspective on the practices of the church. This includes the "Stone Lectures" he gave at Princeton Theological Seminary in January, 1980, as well as the "Morgan Lectures" he gave at Fuller Theological Seminary and an unnamed lecture series at Loyola University in New Orleans later that same year—the fifth lecture in each case was entitled "Body Politics." He also managed to squeeze in a trip to Australia in 1980 to present related material to Baptist church leaders. Finally, Yoder continued to develop his thinking after *Body Politics* was published, for example, in lectures given at the Presbyterian Theological Seminary of Taipei (Taiwan). Taking into consideration the histories of both "Sacrament as Social Process" and *Body Politics*, Yoder tested his perspective on the practices of the church in at least eight different denominational settings representing a very broad range of ecclesiologies.

Binding and loosing
Baptism, or "Baptism and the new humanity"
Open meeting or "The rule of Paul"
Multiplicity of gifts or "The fullness of Christ"
Eucharist or "Disciples break bread together"

One reason that the practices Yoder examined had shifted was that his reason for talking about church practices had shifted. Not only was he intending to speak to an ecumenical audience, but he was increasingly interested in demonstrating how the practices of the church addressed "the issue of involvement in the structural processes of wider society."[96] Yoder was convinced that the practices of New Testament believers "can be spoken of in social process terms easily translatable into nonreligious terms" and thus were empirically accessible.[97] In other words, church practices are not only sacramental, they are social and ethical as well—even though they "are formally rooted in the order of redemption . . . that by no means makes them less public."[98] To be clear, this is not to deny that the things believers do together are given meaning by God's presence, or to completely reduce sacraments to sociological practices, but to insist that they also have political implications.[99]

Yoder chose the expression "body politics" to describe his perspective on church practices because "it obligates us to deal with the life of the church in ordinary human language." He wanted to make it clear that "the difference between church and state or between a faithful and an unfaithful church is not that one is political and the other not, but that they are political in different ways."[100] Thus these practices are politically relevant not because they offer alternative ways to administer the world, but because they are "modes of vulnerable but also provocative, creative presence" in the midst of the world.[101] Finally, he noted that he was focusing on "five sample ways" that the church was called to operate as a political body, adding: "There could be others, but the five cases should suffice to make the pattern clear."[102]

96. Yoder, *Body Politics*, ix.

97. Yoder, *Royal Priesthood*, 364.

98. Ibid., 371. Yoder is trying to overcome the common way of describing the autonomy of the political realm by confining it to the doctrine of creation (we know God's will by looking at the shape of the world as it is).

99. This is a point that seems to be lost on critics—see, for example, Martens, "Problematic Development of the Sacraments," and *Heterodox Yoder*.

100. Yoder, *Body Politics*, ix. Another apt quote from the same page: "Church and world are not two compartments under separate legislation or two institutions with contradictory assignments, but two levels of the pertinence of the same Lordship. The people of God is called to be today what the world is called to be ultimately."

101. Yoder, *Royal Priesthood*, 373.

102. Yoder, *Body Politics*, ix. Indeed, in a subsequent lecture on this topic

The Technological Implications of Yoder's Discussion of Church Practices

The marks of the church discussed in the first half of this chapter are not simply theological principles or moral ideals that can be advertised in a brochure or stamped on the foreheads of Christians. They are not simply general traits or characteristics that can be distilled from their embodiment in the church, but rather are manifestations of the body of Christ in action. To put it another way, the marks of commitment, patience, suffering, vulnerability, humility, nonconformity, servanthood, visibility, and simplicity are more than traits or characteristics. Each are also helpfully thought of as a particular kind of posture or disposition, and as a particular kind of skill or habit. The simplest way of saying this is that they are virtues. At the same time, however, the church bears witness to these key marks not simply through its general stance or through actions in general, but through its participation in particular practices. Thus the concluding section of this chapter will briefly summarize Yoder's discussion of the key practices of the church, pointing to the various marks of the church that they bear witness to. Given the connections that have already been drawn between these marks and the ideals embodied and encouraged by particular technologies, it should be clear that the practices of the church have technological implications. Indeed, it is through these practices that the church is able to conscientiously engage technological artifacts, systems, and ways of thinking. It is through these practices that the church is able to proclaim the power of Christ and resist the seduction of the power of technology.

Binding and Loosing

The practice of binding and loosing is grounded in Jesus' instructions to his disciples in Matthew 18:15: "If another member of the church sins against you, go and point out the fault when the two of you are alone. If the member listens to you, you have regained that one." The sacramental nature of this practice is made clear by the fact that if the disciples followed these "simple instructions, their activity would at the same time be the activity of God."[103] For in verse 18 they are told: "Whatever you bind on earth will be bound in heaven, and whatever you loose on earth will be loosed in heaven." And yet there is also broader social significance to this practice. As Yoder

---

Yoder added a sixth practice to the discussion—enemy love. See Yoder, "Concluding Observations."

103. Yoder, *Body Politics*, 1.

writes, "The way God wants believers to live together should be a model as well for other social relationships."[104] The Christian community is equipped not with a code or with rules for discipline so much as with a process for "ongoing moral discernment in the face of questions which could not have been answered substantially ahead of time."[105] Furthermore, this process has given birth to social sciences such as conflict resolution, for, after all, "to be human is to be in conflict, to offend and to be offended. To be human in light of the gospel is to face conflict in redemptive dialogue."[106] The engagement in a disciplinary practice such as this clearly makes visible distinctive marks of the church such as commitment, patience, vulnerability, and humility.

Breaking Bread

Yoder notes that breaking bread together, the second key practice he examines, is also based on specific instructions given by Jesus to his disciples, this time as recorded in Luke 22. Whatever else may have been implied by these instructions, Yoder insists that they applied to common meals: "The meal Jesus blessed . . . and claimed as his memorial was their *ordinary* partaking of food for the body."[107] Rather than diminishing the significance of the Lord's supper, this perspective amplifies it. Yoder reminds us that "every meal in a Jewish household was an act of worship."[108] He also points out that only because the common meal was at the center of the life of the early church "could it extend into the formation of economic community."[109] The "common purse" was really a common table—sharing was the natural extension of table fellowship. This then is the social and ethical significance of the practice of the Eucharist: "Bread eaten together *is* economic sharing, not merely symbolically, but also in fact."[110] This practice has thus given birth to an economic ethic, to the application of sharing in all areas of life. As Yoder put it, the Eucharist as celebrated in the context of worship is one sign of the "real presence" of Christ, but so too is the act of feeding the hungry. Engagement in this practice shines a spotlight on marks of the church such as commitment, vulnerability, nonconformity, and servanthood.

104. Ibid., 11.
105. Ibid., 8.
106. Ibid., 13.
107. Ibid., 16.
108. Ibid., 19.
109. Ibid., 16.
110. Ibid., 20.

Baptism

The third key practice discussed by Yoder, baptism, is also a sign of the real presence of Christ—in this case in the new humanity, the new creation that is the body of Christ. Just as breaking bread together *is* an economic act, so too baptism *is* the formation of a new society, "inducting all kinds of people into the same people." It thus "serves as a model for the world's moving in the same direction."[111] Baptism provided a profound witness of the Christian message of equality, a message that Yoder saw as "rooted in the work of Christ, not in creation or providence."[112] Once again, as with binding and loosing and the Eucharist, Yoder points to the sacramental nature of baptism even as he stresses that it relies on ordinary human behavior and thus is an example of a publicly accessible practice. Baptism is clearly both a consequence and a sign of marks of the church such as commitment, vulnerability, nonconformity, and visibility.

Multiplicity of Gifts

The fourth key practice discussed by Yoder is the multiplicity of gifts or the fullness of Christ, and this is certainly a less commonly identified practice. Indeed, Yoder claims that it is the first practice under consideration "whose adequate concrete form has still to be retrieved."[113] In short:

> The Paul of Ephesians [4:11–13] uses the term *the fullness of Christ* to describe a new mode of group relationships, in which every member of a body has a distinctly identifiable, divinely validated and empowered role.[114]

This image of the body[115] is filled out in 1 Corinthians 12:7 when Paul says: "To each is given the manifestation of the Spirit for the common good;" and

---

111. Ibid., 32.
112. Ibid., 40.
113. Ibid., 59.
114. Ibid., 47.

115. Yoder notes that Paul may have coined the metaphor of "body" to describe a social group, and made an effort to contrast the individualistic nature of contemporary missions with the social nature of Paul's missionary efforts: "The reconciliation of Jew and Gentile in the 'new humanity' is first a *community* event. It *cannot* happen to a lone individual." Yoder does make clear that his intention "is not to deny a personal or subjective or inward dimension to the experience of becoming a Christian, but to challenge the normative claim made for a view which would reduce it to only that dimension, or make that dimension the essential center." See Yoder, "Apostle's Apology Revisited," 132–33.

in Romans 12:4–5 when he says: "For as in one body we have many members, and not all the members have the same function, so we, who are many, are one body in Christ, and individually we are members one of another." For Yoder these are clear instructions to see the diversity of gifts "as a specific working of God the Spirit, present in, with, and under a particular pattern of social process," instructions that clearly differed from the patterns of the day.[116] The radicalness of this practice of sharing roles, of gifted individuals working together in a kind of organic interdependence, may be lost on us today, shaped as we are by models of cooperation and teamwork rather than hierarchy. Yet Yoder wonders whether these contemporary models may in fact be indebted to this practice of the early church. Furthermore, Paul proclaims that the dignity of each individual is found in their complementarity. Thus Yoder points out: "This is not an anti-structural stance; it is the affirmation of a structure analogous to the human organism. God has done this not by making everyone the same, but by empowering each member differently although equally."[117] The multiplicity of gifts focuses attention on marks of the church such as humility, nonconformity, servanthood, and visibility.

Open Meeting

The fifth and final practice discussed in *Body Politics* is the Open Meeting or the Rule of Paul. With reference to 1 Corinthians 14 as well as Acts 15, Yoder argues that the early church followed a particular practice in the way they held meetings. This practice was grounded in the conviction that the unity of the body depended upon the leading of the Holy Spirit, and thus all members were to be given the freedom to speak. Within this freedom priority was given to those prompted to offer words of prophecy, that is, words that "speak to other people for their upbuilding and encouragement and consolation" (1 Corinthians 14:3). The only further instructions are that the meeting should be orderly and that people should only speak in unknown tongues if a translation is also provided. Most notable for its absence is any mention of a minister, elder, deacon, or apostle to provide leadership for these meetings. It appears as though the Holy Spirit was the only guide needed to lead the body to consensus. As Yoder put it, "because God the Spirit speaks in the meeting, conversation is the setting for truth-finding."[118] He points out that this practice was not only followed at the level of local congregations, but it also served to guide larger church-wide meet-

---

116. Yoder, *Body Politics*, 48.
117. Ibid., 55.
118. Ibid., 70.

ings—early synods and councils reflected this pattern of decision making through open conversations.[119] And this practice of coming to agreement through conversation has been shown to have relevance for groups outside the church as well. The practice of open meetings clearly reflects marks of the church such as patience, vulnerability, humility, and visibility.

As helpful as the above five practices may be, there is no reason to stop here. Indeed, on several occasions Yoder went on to discuss additional practices that "make the Christian life a matter of direct attention and intention," and this chapter will conclude by briefly reviewing four practices that Yoder included in his original checklist of the functions of the church.[120]

Praise

Yoder emphasized that praise is the one thing that all Christians have in common. Exactly what counts as worship is open for debate, and what is viewed as the high point of worship varies from tradition to tradition. Furthermore, the manner or style in which praise is expressed through things such as prayer and song is also open for debate.[121] Yet there is no doubt that the faithful church will gather in order to praise God. At its root, Yoder argues, praise permits the "recital of the mighty deeds of God," and the "reaffirmation of the covenant by the people."[122] As noted by J. Alexander Sider, Yoder was also certain that the church's praise "enacts God's grace by making it public and accessible, by making it available in a way that it can be responded to by the outsiders of every age."[123] The key point to emphasize here is that praise witnesses to the message of God's salvation by welcoming others into the body of Christ. The practice of praise thus reflects marks of the church such as commitment, vulnerability, nonconformity, and visibility.

---

119. Ibid., 63–64. Yoder develops this perspective in several essays advocating a community-centered approach to hermeneutics—see, for example, Yoder, "The Hermeneutics of the Anabaptists"; "Authority of the Canon"; and "Hermeneutics of Peoplehood," chapter 1 in *Priestly Kingdom*.

120. Yoder, "Concluding Observations," 3. In this particular lecture series Yoder also discussed a sixth practice, love of the enemy, and also proposed truth-telling, freeing slaves, and serving instead of ruling as additional examples.

121. If celebrating the Eucharist is the high point of Roman Catholic worship, and preaching the Word is the high point for many Protestants, singing is the most sacred and crucial component of worship for many Mennonites. For a discussion of the significance of acappella four-part congregational singing for Mennonite worship, see Kropf and Nafziger, *Singing*; and Kropf, "Singing as Sacrament."

122. Yoder, "Checklist of the Functions of the Church," 4.

123. Sider, *To See History Doxologically*, 55.

Preaching

Another crucial practice of the church that is also a component of worship for most Christians is preaching the Word of God. Not only did Yoder note that the church is "renewed by the Word," that is, that a tradition can be transmitted and tested through preaching, but in the process the church bears witness to its particular and peculiar way of being.[124] Indeed, the good news is preached not simply for the benefit of those who make up the church, but for the purpose of welcoming others into the church. The social significance of this practice is centered on the affirmation it provides for meaningful speech. Teaching is possible in all sorts of realms; communication is possible between people even if they belong to different religious, cultural, and linguistic groups. Yoder did not subsequently reflect on preaching as a practice, but the social-process meaning of preaching is underlined by his extensive writings in the area of missiology.[125] In one essay he wrote that "valid trans-community communication . . . is therefore not merely something optional or accessory that we can take or leave." Rather, "the calling to witness to the Other has been a constitutive component of the self definition of . . . Christianity since Pentecost."[126] Preaching thus bears witness to the marks of patience, vulnerability, servanthood, and visibility.

Serving

One of the practices of the church that has a unique place of significance in the worship tradition of Anabaptist-Mennonites is footwashing. Drawing upon Jesus' actions and instructions in John 13, the traditional biannual celebration of communion in many Mennonite churches is followed by a ritual "washing of the saints feet." Members divide up into pairs, remove their shoes, and then "wash" (rinse and then dry) each other's feet. The ritual is concluded with a greeting, typically an embrace or holy kiss along with words of blessing.[127] At first glance it is surprising that Yoder did not choose to expand on his discussion of the "towel and basin" in his original checklist

---

124. Yoder, "Checklist of the Functions of the Church," 4.

125. See, for example, Yoder, *To Hear the Word*; "Meaning After Babble"; "On Not Being Ashamed of the Gospel"; and *He Came Preaching Peace*.

126. Yoder, "Meaning After Babble," 137–38.

127. For a discussion of the history of the Mennonite understanding and practice of footwashing, see Miller, "Mennonite Footwashing." In recent years the frequency of communion has increased, and the frequency of footwashing has decreased in most Mennonite churches.

of the functions of the church.¹²⁸ The most likely explanation is that the particularity of footwashing would have worked against Yoder's ecumenical concerns. Another explanation is suggested by one of Yoder's few published comment on footwashing—the social significance of this ritual was better illustrated in other forms of service:

> When Jesus washed the feet of his disciples he made no abiding contribution to the hygiene of Palestine. Nevertheless, this act took a position in the world that has in itself both spiritual and ethical value. Similarly, when Christians devote themselves to the care of the seriously ill, of the mentally retarded, of the unproductive aged, the fruitfulness of this service cannot be measured by any statistical index of economic efficacy. Whether evaluated from the perspective of the individual or the society, the meaning of this deed is what it signifies, the reality for which it is *the sign*, namely, that this man is here to be the servant of his neighbor.¹²⁹

In any case, the practice of service both in its ritualized and everyday forms puts marks of the church such as commitment, humility, servanthood, and simplicity¹³⁰ on display to a watching world.

Making Disciples

Preaching, praise, and washing feet have become, along with baptism and breaking bread, important rituals in Christian worship. However, for Yoder there are also additional practices of the church which, like binding and loosing, the multiplicity of gifts, and open meetings, are not typically recognized as liturgical or sacramental even though they involve both divine and human action. This chapter will conclude with a brief discussion of one such practice—the making of disciples. According to Yoder, one crucial element for a church that "is a band of disciples" is that members are committed to "forsaking all."¹³¹ It is important to view this radical practice as more

---

128. Yoder, "Checklist of the Functions of the Church," 5.

129. Yoder, *Royal Priesthood*, 365. This explanation is discussed by Bob Brenneman in "Embodied Forgiveness." Another explanation proposed by Brennemen is the discomfort Yoder many have had with the intimate, embodied nature of this ritual. As Mark Thiessen Nation puts it, "having our feet washed by others is decidedly not common" ("Washing Feet," 448).

130. In Nation's words, the ritual of "footwashing cannot easily be made beautiful. It is simply earthy, no matter how clean the bowl or crisp the towel" ("Washing Feet," 449).

131. Yoder, "Checklist of the Functions of the Church," 4.

than simply an act of human obedience—in following "the pattern of true humanity" established by Jesus Christ, Yoder frames "the disciple's newness of life" as "a work of God."[132] This situating of discipleship firmly in the realm of the sacramental or the spiritual serves as one more reminder that Yoder did not harbor some sort of agenda to reduce theology to ethics:

> This is not about some legalistic approach to copying Jesus, but rather about participating in Christ. We are already part of his body; we do not become so through following him. Following Jesus is the result, not the means, of our fellowship with Christ.[133]

At the same time, the process of making disciples is something that can still make sense to those who are unable to comprehend the working of the Holy Spirit. Forsaking all for Christ, or, better put, forsaking all *thanks* to Christ, is a social and political act that makes visible marks of the church such as suffering, nonconformity, servanthood, and simplicity.

CONCLUSION

This chapter has attempted to articulate the way in which the marks of the church contrast with the technological ideals embodied and encouraged by automobiles, genetically modified food, and the Internet, and to point to the way that practices of the church bear witness to these marks. Indeed, these practices should thus be recognized as being crucial for resisting the seduction of principalities and powers. However, bringing Yoder's thought to bear on the topic of technology also has implications for understanding and going beyond his important work. This is the task that will be taken up in the final two chapters of this book.

---

132. Ibid.

133. Yoder, *Discipleship as Political Responsibility*, 61. See also: "The Disciple of Christ and the Way of Jesus," chapter 7 in *Politics of Jesus*.

5

Not Engineering, but Doxology?

To this point the work of John Howard Yoder has been held up as a promising resource for thinking theologically about technology, and what follows should not undercut that portrayal. Given the constructive nature of this project, however, it should come as no surprise that drawing upon Yoder to re-frame our perspective on technology will also have the potential to re-frame our understanding of Yoder. Thus the concluding two chapters of this book will explore the ways it is important to go beyond Yoder in order to further the conscientious engagement with technology that his work compels us to pursue.

Engineers are not spoken of highly in the work of John Howard Yoder, to put it mildly. Engineering is characterized as being preoccupied with effectiveness, and is thus contrasted with the kind of witness the church is called to embody. In short, for Yoder, Christians are called to proclaim, not to produce, the kingdom of God. After describing Yoder's criticism of engineering in the opening section, the second section of this chapter goes on to argue that Yoder himself appears to betray the mind of an engineer. This becomes most clear when we shift our focus from his work on how the church is called to relate to the world, to his work on the history of the church. Indeed, there appears to be a significant point of tension between Yoder's providential view of the world on the one hand, and his "radical reformation" view of church history on the other. The third section will provide an enriched depiction of the practice of engineering, setting up the concluding section which argues that having the mind of an engineer is not necessarily a bad thing for a theologian, assuming that we correctly understand engineering as a practice more akin to artistry than science. Thus the overall argument of this chapter may come as a surprise given its starting point: John Howard Yoder is appropriately characterized as an engineer of the church, and is appropriately criticized when he is not a good enough engineer. In my view, being pragmatic about the history and direction of the church is not necessarily problematic, provided we are prepared to acknowledge the ultimate mysteriousness of the way this history develops. Like Yoder, I think that both the faithfulness and the effectiveness of the church depend upon the working of God's Spirit in our midst. Going beyond Yoder, I think theologians can say much about the ways this Spirit comes to form the followers of Christ.

YODER DID NOT APPROVE OF ENGINEERING

John Howard Yoder's pejorative use of the term "engineering" is quite striking. In every case that I am aware of, when Yoder invokes the term "engineering" or the phrase "to engineer," he is contrasting engineering with his preferred stance or posture toward the world. That is, he is contrasting an engineering approach to the world with his concern to emphasize God's control of history, or, to put it more directly, the providence of God. This has led people, quite rightly, to focus on the positive end of the pairing, to try, for example, to unpack what Yoder had in mind when he lifted up doxology.[1] Given that this book is focused on the topic of technology, however, examining the negative end of this pairing can also help us get inside Yoder's mind.

This negative portrayal of engineering is most obvious in one of the final chapters of the last collection of essays Yoder published before his death in 1997.[2] Yoder's task in "Are You the One Who Is to Come?" is to reflect on the witness of the Gospel regarding God's concern for, and participation in, human history. While he wants to avoid making "a few timeless generalizations about a vision for history," Yoder is convinced that the story of Jesus "implies and affirms deep certainties about God's intention for the human

1. See, for example, Sider, *To See History Doxologically*. Paul Martens has argued that Yoder's use of language evolved significantly throughout his career, moving from a focus on eschatology to doxology to worship—see "Universal History and a Not-Particularly-Christian Particularity." Although I disagree with Martens' assessment, the focus of this chapter means that the distinction he tries to make between these terms does not affect my argument.

2. Yoder, *For the Nations*. All the essays included in this collection were previously presented and/or published elsewhere, and were arranged thematically, not chronologically.

story."³ The bottom line is that with Christ's resurrection the redemption of all of history has been secured; the final victory has been won. As followers of Jesus we are part of a community that is made possible by this victory, and thus "our life is to proclaim, not to produce, the new world."⁴

Yoder begins to flesh out this catchy phrase in a section entitled "Not Engineering, but Doxology." Just what then does Yoder mean by "engineering"? While social ethics has typically been concerned with setting broad goals that describe the kind of world we want to live in, he tells us that engineering is "bringing to bear toward that end whatever power we have available." Put another way, he writes that engineering is what we are doing when we ask the question "How do we get from here to there?"⁵ Yoder argues that Jesus was not interested in the questions of either engineering or modern social ethics, but in asking a third question. Jesus did not ask what kind of world we want, or how we can get it, he asked how we can recognize the new world that has already been born in our midst: "How can the lordship of YHWH, affirmed in principle from all eternity, be worthily confessed as grace through faith? How can the present world be rendered transparent to the reality already there, that the sick are to be healed and the prisoners freed?"⁶

Once again, this is a point that Yoder makes in many different ways in many of his writings. The key point to note here is the terminology he uses in this particular case in order to provide a sharp contrast with the approach of Jesus. Yoder tells us that salvation is *not* a "product," it is a "presupposition"; it is *not* something that we "bring . . . about," it is something we "accept . . . as a gift." Likewise, shalom is *not* something we "achieve," it is something we "accept"; it is *not* something we "engineer," it is something we "proclaim." This list suggests that another definition of engineering for Yoder is to produce, to bring about, or to achieve something.⁷

There are several additional references in *For the Nations* that provide further substance to Yoder's depiction of engineering. For example, in "The Racial Revolution in Theological Perspective," he correlates the

3. Ibid., 201.
4. Ibid., 209.
5. Ibid., 210.
6. Ibid.
7. Since producing, bringing about, or achieving things is clearly the preoccupation for contemporary capitalist societies, it appears that Yoder is making a stronger and broader critique of culture than is typical of his work. Still, rather than making a blanket statement about "modernity" or "liberalism" or "capitalism" in the fashion of Stanley Hauerwas, Alasdair MacIntyre, or John Milbank, Yoder points to an underlying symptom or root cause of the problem with modern, liberal, capitalist societies.

Constantinian model for Christian ethics with "social engineering," since "thinking about right and wrong must now be tailored to fit everyone, singly and collectively."[8] Thus, in addition to re-stating the more obvious connections between engineering and the pragmatist concern with "effectiveness,"[9] and with those who strive for actions that are "instrumental,"[10] Yoder implicates engineering in the modern impulse toward, to use one of his terms, "generalizability."[11] And yet he goes even further in this essay; engineering is also connected to those who focus on "theoretical sketches of the new order toward which we must move."[12] Thus for Yoder engineering is not just about trying to achieve an end in any way possible, it is about generalizing or standardizing—a one-size-fits-all approach to problem solving. And it is about about theorizing and systematizing—an abstract and aloof approach to problem solving. It seems as though an engineer could serve as a good stand-in for Constantine as the chief symbol in Yoder's work for all that has gone wrong in the history of the church.

Numerous additional references in Yoder's corpus point to, or at least allude to this pejorative view of engineering. For example, in *The Priestly Kingdom* Yoder lists "A New Value for Effectiveness" as one of six "Constantinian Sources of Western Ethics."[13] Here he is pointing to "the transformation of moral deliberation into utilitarianism," whereby "any ethic, any tactic, is . . . to be tested by its promised results." He refers to this as "the engineering approach to ethics," something that is "a long-range echo of the Constantinian wedding of piety with power."[14] After all, in biblical times it would have been senseless to think that a few powerless believers could ever promise, much less produce results of any kind. In Yoder's view, the early followers of Jesus could never have had an engineering mindset.

In a paper presented at a conference on "Human Values and the Environment," Yoder argues that the intractable nature of environmental problems is reason enough to be suspicious of any claims that we can "administer" or lay "claim to sovereignty" over the natural world, much less subject it to "our viceregal management." He writes that "to think that we are able (arbitrarily) to control the system will mean seeing the (relative) control

---

8. Yoder, *For the Nations*, 104.
9. Ibid., 108.
10. Ibid., 122.
11. Ibid., 81.
12. Ibid., 119.
13. Yoder, *Priestly Kingdom*, 140. Other sources include: a new ecclesiology, a new eschatology, a new "servant of the Lord," a new universality, and a new metaphysic.
14. Ibid.

not engineering, but doxology? 159

we did have slip from our grasp."¹⁵ Yoder acknowledges that "modern technology comes closer to 'mastering' *some* of the angles of the way the world works, but thereby it sets loose a larger set of surprising imponderables." He goes on to say that, despite the scale and scope of modern technology, there is really nothing fundamentally new about our situation. As suggested by the Promethean myth, humanity has long been tempted—and has long been vulnerable to—"the idea that we might master the secrets of physical causation."¹⁶ It appears then that for Yoder technological optimism is one of the most significant manifestations of our mistaken drive to grab hold of the handles of history. As one of the most pervasive disciplines (and preeminent professions) in a technological age, engineering would thus appear to run counter to the very nature of the new world that was inaugurated by Jesus.

It would seem then that Yoder had more to say about engineering than he did about technology. It would seem that he was more concerned with technological ways of thinking—exemplified by Constantinianism—than he was with the artifacts and systems that were produced by that thinking. Indeed, despite the close connection suggested by the sources discussed above, at one point he argues that the "constantinian turn" is more basic than the "technological turn."¹⁷ Like Ghandi and King, Yoder's pacifism is grounded in the theological claim that ends and means, and thus effectiveness and faithfulness, are inseparable. And he thus rejects the tendency of pragmatists—and, one would suppose, engineers—to prioritize the former over the latter: "The unity of means and ends is ultimately a religious world view, one which incorporates rather than rejects pragmatic wisdom. It thereby rejects the pragmatist's question (effectiveness or faithfulness?) rather than the pragmatist's answer (effectiveness)."¹⁸ Furthermore, Yoder resists the tendency to let the supposed newness of our situation dictate the terms of the debate, commending, for example, the biblical genre of apocalyptic witness to "relativize both the gloomy and confident determinisms to which we have been captive."¹⁹ For Yoder, it is the "experts," the

15. Yoder, "On Generating Alternative Paradigms," 58.

16. Ibid., 61.

17. Yoder, "Armaments and Eschatology," 44.

18. Yoder, "Nuclear Arms in Christian Pacifist Perspective," 29. In this discussion Yoder is also trying to sidestep classic philosophical debates between consequentialists and deontologists.

19. Yoder, "Armaments and Eschatology," 56. In "Nuclear Arms in Christian Pacifist Perspective" Yoder discusses the impact of nuclear weapons technology on the ethical analysis of war, and, although the threat of global annihilation has brought pacifists, just warriors, and realists together in opposition to nuclear weapons, he insists that this new technology has resulted in only "superficial" changes to the ethical basis for these three positions. On this occasion Yoder takes issue with the U.S. Catholic Bishops, although

"planners," the "specialists," the "technicians," and the "systematicians" who are responsible for our captivity.[20] Although he did not call them by name on this occasion, engineers are often viewed as the quintessential experts, planners, specialists, and systematicians of our age.

YODER WAS AN ENGINEER OF THE CHURCH
Qualifying Yoder's Pejorative View of Engineering

To be sure, there are times when Yoder actually demonstrated some enthusiasm for engineering-related work. For example, as noted in chapter 4, in the late 1970s Yoder joined a small group of Mennonite academics and development experts in starting a not-for-profit company called International Development Enterprises. Although Yoder's role was to provide a theological perspective for this project, his correspondence demonstrates a surprising level of interest in technical details. It includes marked up drawings of a new water pump design, and letters asking for clarification of specifications. Yoder even sent off a design to his son, then an engineering student at Purdue University, asking him to double-check some calculations and look into the possibility of testing a prototype in one of the university labs.[21]

Qualifications to Yoder's pejorative view of engineering can also be found in his published work. In another essay in *For the Nations*, "The Believer's Church and the Arms Race," he writes: "When I say we are free from the engineering model of the social process, that does not mean we stand its analysis on its head and say we don't care about planning, thinking, analyzing." Indeed, he insists that it is important to consider "mechanisms, causality, [and] probabilities" provided that this "fosters concern" rather than "despair."[22] And in "The Biblical Mandate for Evangelical Social Action," he insists that praising God does not mean we can avoid "the need to think practically, weighing likely effects and relative costs of available strategies."[23]

Further qualifications can be found in some of the words and phrases that Yoder uses to describe the way the church should relate to its

---

he could have just as easily criticized the approach taken by Gordon D. Kaufman in *Theology for a Nuclear Age*.

20. Yoder, "Armaments and Eschatology," 43, 45, 47, 50, 55.
21. Yoder, "Paul Polak Project."
22. Yoder, *For the Nations*, 150.
23. Ibid., 196.

surrounding society. In response to the charge that the vision of the church he describes is sectarian, at various times Yoder insisted that the church is:

> The beginning, the *pilot run*, the *bridgehead* of the new world on the way.[24]
>
> God's *beachhead* in the world as it is; the downpayment, the *prototype*, the herald, the midwife of the new world on the way.[25]
>
> Concerned for the *relative improvement* of society.[26]
>
> A ministry of *constant inventive vision* for the good of the larger society.[27]

Phrases like "relative improvement" and "constant inventive vision" evoke images of the church as a laboratory developing the next generation of a computer operating system. "Pilot run" and "prototype" evoke images of the church as a new vehicle design being driven off the assembly line for the first time, ready to be subjected to close scrutiny and possibly even some destructive testing. And of course "bridgehead" and "beachhead" evoke images of the church as a technological artifact of military significance.

Technological metaphors for the way the church works in the world aside, Yoder sounds rather pragmatic when he insists that the church "concentrates on the identification and removal of one abuse at a time rather than on theoretical sketches of the new order toward which we must move."[28] Furthermore, as much as Yoder relativizes the importance of instrumental thinking when it comes to societal practices, at times he seems to verge on instrumental thinking when it comes to ecclesial practices. The most obvious reference point is *Body Politics*, a book that, as discussed in chapter 4, was written to highlight the public witness of key church practices such as binding and loosing, the Eucharist, baptism, recognizing the multiplicity of gifts, and open meetings.[29] Yoder's non-sacramental, functional, or, as he put it, "moderately realistic"[30] view of church practices has already been subject to numerous challenges. Although I would take issue with some of these challenges, it is interesting that Yoder's focus on the socio-political dimension of church practices, much like his concern to identify and remove one abuse at a time, sounds like the church is "bringing to bear toward that

24. Ibid., 216; italics added.
25. Ibid., 218; italics added.
26. Ibid., 118; italics added.
27. Yoder, *Christian Witness to the State*, 19; italics added.
28. Yoder, *For the Nations*, 119.
29. Yoder, *Body Politics*.
30. Ibid., 11.

end whatever power we have available." It sounds like the answer to the question "How do we get from here to there?" It sounds like something an engineer might say.

Shifting Attention to Yoder's Focus on the Life of the Church

Even more significantly, however, throughout his work Yoder sounds like an engineer when he shifts his focus from the relationship of the church to the world, to the life of the church. For as much as he downplays the priority of mechanisms, causality, and probabilities when it comes to social history writ large, a case can be made that he is very interested in mechanisms, causality, and probabilities when it comes to church history. Indeed, it would appear there is a significant point of tension between Yoder's providential perspective on the history of the world, and his interventionist perspective on the history of the church. Yoder's life work called the church to be more faithful in following Jesus Christ, pointing out where it had come close, where it had fallen short, and the direction it needed to go in the moment under consideration.

The clearest sign of this perspective is Yoder's "posture of radical reformation."[31] Certainly, as Yoder notes in *The Priestly Kingdom*, all Protestants are united by "the conviction that in the earlier history of Christianity something had gone wrong."[32] However, according to Yoder the correct response to this analysis is not to seek to return the church to its pre-fallen state as restitutionists insist, for "there will always have to be change."[33] The correct response is to recognize that the church is "not only fallible but in fact peccable."[34] Thus the church should be subjected to continuous, never-ending critique—to put it even stronger, it should embody "a constant potential for reformation, and in the more dramatic situations, a readiness for the reformation even to be 'radical.'"[35] As Yoder says:

> Checking how we went wrong and asking how to get back on track is thus not an odd emergency, a rare glitch along the triumphal way . . . Salvation becomes history not with the rigidity of the railroad, but with the balanced momentum of the bicycle or the walker. Every step calls for balance to be restored.[36]

31. Yoder, *Priestly Kingdom*, 5.
32. Ibid., 16.
33. Yoder, "Historiography as a Ministry to Renewal," 217.
34. Yoder, *Priestly Kingdom*, 5.
35. Ibid.
36. Yoder, "Historiography as a Ministry to Renewal," 217.

In one unpublished memo entitled "If It's Not Broke, Fix It," Yoder even appears to apply insights from the relatively new field of reliability engineering to the church:

> That folk wisdom, which postpones corrective intervention on the grounds that the process will correct itself if it just goes on, becomes false when the stakes are higher and the processes in question are more complex. Aircraft engines maintenance does not await breakdown. Parts likely to wear out are replaced well before the time they would normally fail . . . The point behind reversing the old slogan is that human relations, in complex social organisms like marriage, like the village, the church, or the corporation, are more like the aircraft engine than they are like the Model A Ford. Human relations are more like preventive maintenance than like repairs.

However, he also found other ways to argue for the need to embrace rather than avoid correcting problems in the church. One of the best known is from *The Priestly Kingdom*: "Far from being an ongoing growth like a tree . . . the wholesome growth of a tradition is like a vine: a story of constant interruption of organic growth in favor of pruning and a new chance for the roots." As a result, the appeal to origins is properly seen to be "a 'looping back,' a glance over the shoulder to enable a midcourse correction."[37] Thus Yoder's use of the image of a "vinedresser" reminds us that the potential for radical reformation is not only a critical, but a renewing posture.

The point to be emphasized here is that, whether the image is mechanistic or organic, Yoder was most definitely motivated by a desire to renew the church, both for the benefit of local congregations, and for the sake of Christian unity. He constantly asked: "How did we get from there to here?" and "How do we get from here to there?" And he tried to encourage effective change in the church—to produce, achieve, or bring about a desired end—while recognizing there will always be new challenges that cannot be anticipated in advance. It thus seems appropriate to go so far as to call Yoder an "engineer of the church."

ENGINEERING, PROPERLY UNDERSTOOD

Until now the discussion of engineering in this chapter has been confined to the terms utilized by Yoder, although I have attempted to demonstrate there are times when Yoder himself appears to betray the mind of an engineer

37. Yoder, *Priestly Kingdom*, 69. The use of this image by Yoder has been highlighted by, among others, Romand Coles—see "The Wild Patience of John Howard Yoder," 310.

according to these terms. The following paragraphs will sketch an enriched understanding of the practice of engineering, an understanding based on a loose consensus among a wide range of more philosophically-minded engineers. Before going any further, however, it should be made clear that I will be talking about engineering as a "practice" in the way that the philosopher Alasdair MacIntyre uses this word. As discussed in chapter 4, engineering—like architecture, farming, and football—is properly viewed as a practice because it is a "cooperative human activity" that develops over time in the threefold sense of achieving particular ends, cultivating particular skills in its practitioners, and making measured progress in these skills from generation to generation.[38] One advantage of viewing engineering as a practice is that it becomes possible to talk about engineers and the work of engineers in a collective way even though engineers do not typically comprise a clearly defined or autonomous group. It is also a broader term than knowledge-focused alternatives such as "discipline," or organization-focused alternatives such as "profession."[39]

A Nonconstantinian Preoccupation with Effectiveness

The crucial point I want to make about the practice of engineering is that while it *is* often preoccupied with effectiveness, it is *not* Constantinian. Engineering, properly understood, is *not* a one-size-fits-all, abstract, and aloof approach to problem solving; the practice of engineering does *not* hinge upon generalizations, or even on the application of theory.

---

38. See *After Virtue*, 187. Although engineering was an established practice long before the dawning of the modern scientific method, exactly *when* what we think of today as engineering originated is debatable. Lynn White Jr. credits the interest of medieval monks in technology for the birth of engineering in the Middle Ages—see "Technology, Western"; Eugene Ferguson credits the invention of technical drawing in the Renaissance in *Engineering and the Mind's Eye*; Michael Davis credits the size and organization of the French army in the seventeenth century in *Thinking Like an Engineer*, 10; and David F. Noble stresses the continued interconnection of engineering and the military in the 20th Century—see *Forces of Production*. In any case, engineering is a fairly recent addition to the scholarly guilds. While the National Academy of Sciences was established in 1863, the National Academy of Engineering did not come in existence until 1964, more than a century later.

39. Davis, *Thinking Like an Engineer*, viii. Certainly many engineers have organized into self-regulating professional groups in North America. However, the majority of engineers apply their skills, along with both fellow engineers and non-engineering colleagues, to ends determined and evaluated by the organization they are employed by. In this way engineering differs from law or medicine, where professionals typically work directly with clients or patients who are counting on the profession to determine the worthiness of ends (and the competency of the professional in striving for these ends).

A preoccupation with effectiveness can be seen clearly in most definitions of engineering. For example, the aeronautical engineer Walter Vincenti follows his colleague Gordon F.C. Rogers in defining engineering as "the practice of organizing the design and construction [and operation] of any artifice which transforms the physical world around us to meet some recognized need."[40] Like most people—including Yoder—for Rogers and Vincenti, engineering is all about producing, bringing about, or achieving something. This focus on getting the job done is echoed by the historian of technology and civil engineer Henry Petroski, who, by way of a quote from a nineteenth-century railroad engineer, defines engineering as "the art of doing well for one dollar, what any bungler can do with two."[41] It is also echoed by Samuel C. Florman, another civil engineer, who argues that while scientists loftily seek what is "True," engineers "merely" seek what is "Good."[42]

A similarly pragmatic, yet more developed definition of engineering is provided by the nuclear engineer Billy Vaughn Koen, who defines the engineering method as "the strategy for causing the best change in a poorly understood situation within the available resources."[43] The key, of course, is fleshing out just what the strategy is for doing this. Koen argues that it is the use of heuristics, that is, "anything that provides a plausible aid or direction in the solution of a problem but is in the final analysis unjustified, incapable of justification, and potentially fallible."[44] To put it more simply, he tells us that engineering is really just an "ad hoc method of 'doing the best you can with what you've got.'"[45] The several dozen engineering heuristics discussed by Koen include rules of thumb for specific applications,[46] but most have broad relevance. Examples of the latter include: "At some point in the project,

---

40. Vincenti, *What Engineers Know*, 6.

41. Petroski, *Invention by Design*, 141.

42. Florman, "Subsumed by Science?," 59. In this quotation Florman is affirming an attempted snub of engineering by the scientist John Horgan.

43. Koen, *Discussion of the Method*, 7.

44. Ibid., 28.

45. Ibid., 93.

46. For example, "The cost of building construction scales as the price of meat;" and: "Use a factor of safety of 1.5 for commercial airplanes (in the military a factor of safety of 1.25 is more appropriate)." See Koen, *Discussion of the Method*, 67, 69. Koen's use of expressions such as "ad hoc" and "rules of thumb" is reminiscent of Yoder's use of these terms in contrasting his own approach to theology with more systematic methodologies (see chapter 2).

freeze the design;"[47] "Solve problems by successive approximations;"[48] and "Work at the margin of solvable problems."[49]

Koen's main concern is to emphasize that while engineers will use whatever works to solve a problem, they also implicitly recognize the fallibility of their strategy—they are interminable doubters when it comes to assuming that a particular strategy is true for all times and places. Thus engineers have no illusions about mastering the natural world or possessing solutions to every problem, much less about controlling human history. Indeed, for all his effort to clarify what he means by heuristics, Koen only serves to highlight the complexity and messiness of engineering. Almost every heuristic requires an engineer to make significant judgments: they still have to determine *when* to freeze a design; they still have to determine *which* approximations are appropriate; and they still have to determine *where* the margins of a solvable problem are to be found. Most importantly, engineering designs are always being evaluated according to a moving target—the best practices or, as Koen likes to call them, the "state of the art," are in constant flux.[50] For all the effort engineers expend trying to develop and propagate these best practices, as evident in libraries full of design handbooks, not to mention the myriad of regulatory policies and laws, engineers are only ever necessary to the extent that ambiguity and uncertainty are present in the design process.[51] And the ever-increasing numbers of

---

47. Ibid., 35.
48. Ibid., 38.
49. Ibid., 72.

50. Although heuristics can never assume ontological status for Koen, he does think that they themselves can also be judged according to the state of the art in a particular time and place. This means that engineers are obligated "in every instance to choose the best heuristic for use" from what appears to be the state of the art in heuristics, or the best engineering practice at the time. See *Discussion of the Method*, 57.

Furthermore, Koen is not content to stop with engineering heuristics. Indeed, in the second half of his book he sets out to generalize the engineering method, arguing that it is the prototype of a universal method—that it is the underlying method employed by all human endeavors. Koen is convinced that all of us rely on heuristics ranging from time to language to truth in order to find our way through life. And since all disciplines employ heuristics, whether they recognize it or not, all disciplines are thus nothing more than different versions of "applied engineering." In this respect there is some similarity between Koen and Jacques Ellul—both find a common underlying methodology in all human pursuits.

51. As Bucciarelli puts it: "Uncertainty is what gives designers an opportunity to develop creative, cost-effective, robust, and innovative designs. The design process is about the new and the uncertain by its very nature. If the process is sure from the start, you can be sure that it is not a design process" (*Designing Engineers*, 118).

engineers graduating from universities around the world suggests that there is no shortage of ambiguity and uncertainty on the horizon.

The Ambiguity of Engineering Design

What then can be said about what happens "on the margins" of a problem being addressed by an engineer? How are engineering judgments made? What can be said beyond the insistence of engineers such as Jack Swearengen that "design is not a purely objective and rational process"?[52] Vincenti argues that, in addition to varieties of explicit knowledge, "we must add the implicit, wordless, pictureless knowledge essential to engineering judgment . . . tacit knowledge."[53] The historian of technology Eugene Ferguson agrees, pointing out that "successful design still requires the stores of expert tacit knowledge and intuitive 'feel' of experience."[54] Thus,

> No matter how vigorously a 'science' of design may be pushed, the successful design of real things in a contingent world will always be based more on art than on science. Unquantifiable judgments and choices are the elements that determine the way a design comes together.[55]

Underlining this point, the civil engineer Samuel C. Florman argues that "engineers agree that intuition, practical experience, and artistic sensibility are at least as important to their work as is the application of scientific theory."[56] Indeed, he insists that "although engineering is serious and methodical, it contains elements of spontaneity. Engineering is an art as well as a science, and good engineering depends upon leaps of imagination as well as painstaking care."[57]

52. *Beyond Paradise*, 194. To be clear, Swearengen does not lament this state of affairs—he goes on to say that design "is not intended to be" objective, "and it cannot be."

53. *What Engineers Know*, 198.

54. *Engineering and the Mind's Eye*, 171. Ferguson stresses the nonverbal nature of this experience: "Many features and qualities of the objects that a technologist thinks about cannot be reduced to unambiguous verbal descriptions; therefore, they are dealt with in the mind by a visual, nonverbal process" (ibid., xi). He thinks it is crucial that we recognize this, because "an engineering education that ignores its rich heritage of nonverbal learning will produce graduates who are dangerously ignorant of the myriad subtle ways in which the real world differs from the mathematical world their professors teach them" (ibid., xii).

55. Ibid., 194.

56. Florman, "Subsumed by Science?," 59.

57. Florman, *Existential Pleasures of Engineering*, 182. Although the Jesuit astronomer Guy Consolmagno lumps together engineers and scientists as "technies,"

Emotion

These references to the artistic dimension of engineering design provide further clues to the kinds of things that influence engineering judgment in the midst of "leaps of imagination"—one obvious example is emotion. As Florman puts it, "The fact that engineers are inarticulate does not signify that engineering does not evoke strong emotions."[58] He goes on to say that "analysis, rationality, materialism, and practical creativity do not preclude emotional fulfillment; they are pathways to such fulfillment. They do not 'reduce' experience, they expand it."[59] Other characterizations of the impulse that makes engineering pleasurable for those who practice it include John Kenneth Galbraith's notion of "technological virtuosity,"[60] Herbert F. York's use of the expression "technological exuberance,"[61] and Robert C. Post's discussion of "technological enthusiasm."[62] Finally, Arthur P. Molella has applied insights from psychology to the process of innovation, emphasizing that invention is "not a step-by-step logical process but the complex fruit of the unconscious mind's ability to perceive and form patterns, or gestalts."[63] He thus sought to draw attention to the engineer's emotional, spiritual, and aesthetic sides.

---

his description of innovation resonates with what Vincenti, Ferguson, and Florman have written:

> When you take a hard look, you realize that most of our work is shot through with nonrational behavior. When I say 'nonrational,' I don't mean 'irrational.' Our nonrationality is in fact quite reasonable. It's necessary, because our very rationality itself relies on insight: we techies usually start our problem solving with a hunch—an insight about where we should look to find the solution, what the answer is going to look like, how this problem will parallel or differ from similar problems of our experience. Without those hunches, we have no idea where to start. And without knowing ahead of time what the solution is going to look like, we would have no way of recognizing it once we found it; we'd have no idea when to stop looking (*God's Mechanics*, 16).

58. *Existential Pleasures of Engineering*, 98.

59. Ibid., 101. Florman connects emotional dimension of engineering design to religion: "Not only cathedrals, but every great engineering work is an expression of motivation and purpose which cannot be divorced from religious implications . . . man cannot help but transcend himself as soon as he begins to design and construct" (ibid., 126).

60. See chapter 15 in *New Industrial State*.

61. *Advisors*, 81.

62. *High Performance*, x–xii. Post goes on to frame technological enthusiasm with an apt quote from Eugene Ferguson: "To plumb the depths of human motivation with measuring rods precisely calibrated in economic terms is to miss the strong romantic and emotional strains of life" (ibid., 10).

63. See "Inventing the History of Invention," 23–30.

Of course, the emotional side of engineering is also revealed by the fact that, for the most part, it is a collective, not an individual pursuit. Engineers do not face constraints imposed solely by the natural world, but constraints such as cost, time, and personality conflicts—all of which are subjective, and involve personal relationships. Aerospace engineer Louis Bucciarelli's study of three different engineering firms makes this point clearly:

> The process of designing is a process of achieving consensus among participants with different 'interests' in the design . . . [it] is necessarily social and requires the participants to negotiate their differences and construct meaning through direct, and preferably face-to-face, exchange.[64]

Bucciarelli highlights this social reality throughout the design process, including the negotiation of performance specifications, the selection of a short list of promising design concepts, the assessment of data from prototype testing, and the implementation of a chosen design. As he puts it: "The design is the shared vision, and the shared vision is the design—a (temporary) synthesis of the different participants' work."[65] For this reason the philosopher Michael Davis suggests that although "engineers often describe themselves as applying natural science to practical problems, they could just as easily, and more accurately, describe themselves as applying knowledge of how people work in a certain industry." Thus "engineering is as much management as it is natural science."[66]

Aesthetics

Another significant influence on engineering judgment is aesthetics. Cyril Stanley Smith, the renowned metallurgist and historian of science, has argued that "order per se is not art, and neither is complexity, but the finding of order in complexity is." He goes on to suggest that "it is obvious that engineers . . . have always had a rich and valid aesthetic experience

---

64. *Designing Engineers*, 159.
65. Ibid.
66. Davis, *Thinking Like an Engineer*, 24. Providing further support for this point, David F. Noble has pointed out the strong connection between engineers and managers in the U.S. in *America by Design*. Between 1884 and 1924, roughly two thirds of engineering graduates had become managers within fifteen years of graduating from college. This marked trend "reflected the unprecedented demand for technically trained managers in modern industry." At the same time, it clearly indicated that it had become "almost always necessary for an engineer to leave the engineering of materials and enter the engineering of men in order to become very successful financially and socially" (ibid., 41).

in building their structures and devising their machines."⁶⁷ For example, "The strength of steel and concrete and the beauty of a streamlined surface are proper aesthetic experiences in today's world, and they become more so as artists explore their meaning."⁶⁸ Echoing Smith, David P. Billington uses the work of the Swiss bridge designer Robert Maillart to emphasize that "engineering form is the result of human imagination, not rational choices." Thus "the essence of the artist as engineer does not lie in his or her need to deny the analytic side of structural engineering, but to see calculation as merely means."⁶⁹

Theologian and engineering ethicist Brad Kallenberg has picked up on this point, suggesting that the arts and engineering actually have much in common because both require skills in "seeing." He thinks that the tacit skills that go into, for example, reading a complex mechanism—the ability to see simply and plainly what others must work to interpret—demonstrates that engineers have the capacity for other tacit skills. Furthermore, Kallenberg agrees with Ferguson that an engineer's tacit or "embodied knowledge is both chronologically and logically prior to theoretical reasoning," and so "when a practice such as engineering is on its cutting edge, theoretical explanations of a good design frequently follow rather than precede the design."⁷⁰

67. Smith, "Art, Technology and Science," 537.
68. Ibid., 548.
69. Billington, *Robert Maillart's Bridges*, 105, 107.

70. Kallenberg, *God and Gadgets*, 149–50. Kallenberg has pursued the implications of the closeness of engineering and the arts in a provocative way, drawing upon the work of the engineer-philosopher Ludwig Wittgenstein to argue that engineering method is analogous to moral reasoning—Christian ethicists, like engineers, are more concerned with *phronesis* than *theoria*, and thus ethics is design. This also reflects the influence of Stanley Hauerwas' view that moral judgment is not "computational prowess but as a skill akin to aesthetic taste." See "Ethics as Aesthetics," chapter 2 in *Ethics as Grammar*, 51.

Deane-Drummond and Szerszynski provide support for Kallenberg's perspective on the role of practical reasoning in ethics: "Moral judgment involves the slow, steady development of craft skills and tacit knowledge, rather than the learning of rules and procedures." See *Re-ordering Nature*, 321–22. And Bucciarelli provides support for Kallenberg's perspective on the role of theory in design: "As you approach the here and now, the more diffuse, unclear, uncertain, and ambiguous do events appear. The further back in time you go, the less diffuse, the more clear, certain, and unambiguous they seem" (*Designing Engineers*, 178). See also: "What Engineers Don't Know and Why They Believe It," chapter 3 in *Engineering Philosophy*.

ENGINEERING THE CHURCH, PROPERLY UNDERSTOOD

What then do these insights into the practice of engineering mean for my portrayal of Yoder as a harsh critic of engineering who at the same time appeared to think like an engineer? What are the implications of labeling Yoder an engineer of the church? First, I would argue that the issues Yoder is confronting in his critique of engineering are valid, but misplaced, for good engineering does not exhibit the characteristics he thinks it does. Good engineering can be seen to counter, rather than elevate the problematic tendencies of Constantinianism that Yoder was so attuned to, in the sense that it is marked by heuristics and tacit skills rather than the drive for control and mastery. Engineering is more accurately thought of as a kind of artistry rather than the straightforward application of theoretical reasoning. Thus the practice of engineering is not, as Yoder suggests, diametrically opposed to his own understanding of the way the church should relate to the world. A concern for effectiveness that recognizes the subjectivity and the fallibility of the means utilized—which is what good engineering is really all about—may be able to work *with* rather than against God's purposes. In short, engineering-like practices provide a glimpse of one way the church may be able to move beyond the deep-rooted tension between calls for effectiveness and calls for faithfulness.

Second, I would argue that the characteristics of the practice of engineering can enrich Yoder's approach to the life of the church. In my view, when Yoder falls short as a theologian it is not because he is trying to engineer the church, but because he is not a good enough engineer. To the extent that Yoder's posture of radical reform fails to do more than highlight the need for effective change in the church—stopping short of trying to flesh out how it may be possible to help produce, achieve, or bring about a desired end—it remains inadequate.

Traces of this critique can be found in other readings of Yoder. For example, Conrad Brunk has argued that Yoder's insistence that "the church must avoid the temptation to 'take charge' and 'engineer' society" is inadequate, because, "if the church is to establish an alternative moral community, then it must 'take charge' of its own institutions and 'engineer' them in certain ways."[71] And yet Brunk's own perspective is problematic, given that he is willing to accept and apply Yoder's skewed understanding of engineering directly to the church—thus he equates engineering the church with "taking charge" of it. Even if the church really was an institution like any

---

71. Brunk, Review of *For the Nations*, 131.

other, we have seen that engineers would recognize the futility of this kind of grasping for control, if not mastery.

However, there is still an important insight in Brunk's critique, an insight that Michael Cartwright makes clear when he accuses Yoder of not adequately appreciating the importance of Christian formation. As Cartwright puts it, "Yoder can explain what church looks like, when it happens, but he does not bother to describe how it comes into being over time."[72] As eloquent as he is when it comes to explaining the potential impact of the practices of the church on the watching world, Yoder does not talk about the way these same practices come to impact those who make up the church.[73] As Cartwright points out, Yoder even makes his *disinclination* to address this need clear in two early unpublished presentations on education. In the first presentation, Yoder framed church-administered education as a problem for Mennonites:

> The Christian faith which we are interested in expressing, preserving, propagating and transmitting to our children, is a personal relationship of fellowship and obedience with God in Christ through the Spirit. This relationship cannot be established by proofs and defenses, nor can it be ensured by pedagogical and psychological influences. It is the work of a Spirit who blows where He will, and it calls forth a fully personal, fully free, fully individual response in the believer.[74]

Yoder goes on to argue against the notion that "Christian nurture is an alternative procedure to conversion," insisting that "if the church does not live by miracles she does not live at all."[75] A few years later in a presentation on church-administered colleges, Yoder suggested that religiously homogeneous student bodies and compulsory chapel attendance "reflects a defensive and

---

72. Cartwright, "Sharing the House of God," 610. Kotva Jr., hints at this critique when he says that "Yoder's work evidences little actual interest in the acquisition of virtue or personal growth and sanctification" (*Christian Case for Virtue Ethics*, 158).

73. In fact, Yoder explicitly situates his essay "Sacrament as Social Process" as an alternative to the connections that others were making between liturgy and ethics following Paul Ramsey's landmark article "Liturgy and Ethics." Yoder was grateful but "unsatisfied" with efforts, for example, to emphasize the way worship forms the character of persons or communities, or provides motivation for ethical practices. Thus his account of the social significance of sacraments was intended to provide a "simpler account . . . that at least complements [earlier efforts] and might partially correct them." See *Royal Priesthood*, 360–61.

74. Yoder, "Christian Education," 4.

75. Ibid., 7–8.

non-missionary vision of the church."⁷⁶ More significantly, he challenged the claims made by Christian colleges that their interest in the liberal arts goes beyond a utilitarian approach to education to include a commitment to general "religious concern" or a vague sense of "character building":

> I submit that this glorification of the gratuitousness of character formation is not only morally questionable but in fact not an accurate description of what the Christian schools have been doing. The liberal arts curriculum, in the first place, was generally established because of its usefulness in preparing persons for the Christian ministry and the other professions . . . [Thus] it is not only morally but also pedagogically preferable to build "character" around preparation for a clearly defined social task than for its own sake.⁷⁷

In short, Yoder did not deny that formation happened at Christian colleges, but he challenged the assumption that this formation was—and that it should be—primarily concerned with Christian discipleship. This was the job of the Holy Spirit, not the liberal arts.

I agree that making Christian disciples is the job of the Holy Spirit, and I agree that the Holy Spirit "blows where it will." However, I do not think this means we must deny that the Holy Spirit works through the church (or in other ways) to accomplish this goal. The making of disciples is a process—a messy, complicated, and often tenuous process—not simply the instantaneous transformation resulting from a "fully personal, fully free, fully individual" decision. Thus my depiction of Yoder as an engineer of the church shines a spotlight on the need for further exploration into the way the practices of the church contribute to the formation of faithful witnesses to Christ. It compels further exploration into what makes something like, for example, Yoder's posture of radical reformation possible.⁷⁸

To sum up, I do not think we should try to circumvent Yoder's concern to bring about effective change in the church. Nor do I think that we should be under any illusions that the moving of God's Spirit can be fully explained by an examination of the practices of the church. The key is that, just as good engineers are aware of their dependence on heuristics and tacit skills, good theologians—good engineers of the church—must acknowledge

---

76. Yoder, "Syllabus of Issues Facing the Church College," 22.

77. Ibid., 19.

78. Schlabach draws on the above unpublished sources in his recent critique of Yoder's inability to recognize the extent to which his own posture of dissent was the result of his standing point within a "tradition of dissent." See "Continuity and Sacrament, or Not," 189.

their own dependence on heuristics and tacit skills, proclaiming their trust that God is at work in ways they hardly imagine. What the church needs is doxology *and* engineering.

CONCLUSION

Arguing that theologians are appropriately conceived of as engineers of the church is not where someone influenced by the work of John Howard Yoder would expect to end up, given the pejorative view of engineering that it displays. And no doubt much more needs to be said about the kind of engineering that the church should pursue.

For example, we need to be careful when talking about the formative nature of church practices—they are not simply instruments, tools, or techniques.[79] Indeed, following Craig Dykstra, I think the point of Christian practices, unlike most practices, are not human achievement or excellence:

> Christian practice is different. And that is because its story is different. While achievement is valued in the Christian story, it has a different place and meaning. The human task is not fundamentally mastery. It is rather the right use of gifts graciously bestowed by a loving God for the sake of the good that God intends—*and ultimately assures*... So our basic task is not mastery and control. It is instead trust and grateful receptivity. Our exemplars are not heroes; they are saints. Our epitome is not excellence; our honor is in faithfulness.[80]

Indeed, in another essay Dykstra highlights the problematic way that "theology is commonly depicted as a form of technology."[81] What Dykstra is most concerned about is the vision that a "lone theologian is a technician who through technical expertise (preaching the sermon, teaching the class, writing the article) causally effects change in the generic recipients of these activities." After all, "human relations are not necessarily mechanical, nor is knowledge necessarily technical," and so this view of theology as technological is "harmfully individualistic," not to mention "ahistorical" and "abstract."[82] In contrast then, Dykstra argues that we should think

---

79. As Consolmagno puts it in *God's Mechanics*: "Indeed, the scientist's or engineer's mind-set can be susceptible to a particular and subtle kind of narrow-mindedness. Given their 'how does it work?' functional mind-set, what a religion is can become equated with what a religion does" (ibid., 73).

80. Dykstra, *Growing in the Life of Faith*, 76.

81. Dykstra, "Reconceiving Practice in Theological Inquiry," 161.

82. Ibid.

of the process of doing theology as a practical skill, and by this he means much more than the application of theory to a problem: "Far from being an abstract enterprise, theology is a very practical exercise whose goal is nothing less than a way of life."[83] Although Dykstra sees himself as thus abandoning the "technological criterion (effecting change)" for theology, I don't think he would disagree with the parallel I have drawn between a more enriched perspective on engineering and the proper task of theology. Although, as I have depicted it, theology continues to be about making something happen, it is also pursued within the context of community and ambiguity. Once again, rather than overcoming individual subjectivity with the abstract, a-historical application of theory, good theologians—like good engineers—depend upon heuristics and tacit skills to solve problems. And, just as importantly, what makes a theologian an engineer of the church is his or her principal focus on making things happen in a very particular context—the church, not in society at large.[84]

However, perhaps the most promising direction that the above portrayal of Yoder as an engineer of the church leads is not to help the church re-conceive the work of the theologian, but to carve out space for a conversation between theologians and engineers. After all, it appears that not only do theologians have something to bring to the table in discussions about technology, but engineers have something to bring to the table in discussions about moral reasoning and problem solving in the church. It is this kind of conversation that has the potential to further the conscientious engagement of technology that has been modeled in previous chapters. In particular, this conversation could broaden our scope to include a concern for the *development* of technological artifacts, systems, and ways of thinking. Indeed, Joel Shuman suggests that a close examination of technology should lead theologians to recognize that "the first and most basic question to be asked of any given technology must be whether the story of its *development* and proposed use(s) can readily be taken up into and made part of the broader narrative of the Christian God's saving work in history."[85] Pursuing further dialogue between engineers and theologians is beyond the scope of this project, but the concluding chapter will discuss additional ways in which the topic of technology can lead to the enrichment of Yoder's theological ethics.

83. Ibid., 162.

84. One alternative to my depiction of theologians as "engineers of the church" can be found in Hauerwas's recent attempt to connect theology with hard work or physical labor, although I don't think our views are irreconcilable. More specifically, Hauerwas suspects that "theologians are more like laborers than bricklayers; that is, the theologian's task is to serve those who are masters of the craft of being Christian." See *The State of the University*, 109.

85. Shuman, *To Live is to Worship*, 13–14; italics added.

6

Continuing to Test Yoder with Technology

THE PREVIOUS CHAPTER ARGUED that there is a significant shortcoming in John Howard Yoder's perspective on the practices of the church. Yoder falls short as an engineer of the church because he fails to appreciate the way in which the practices of the church form faithful followers of Christ. As demonstrated in chapter 4, Yoder elevated the potential impact of these practices on "the watching world," and thus they are properly viewed as the clearest indication of the way the church conscientiously engages technology. However, in my view these practices are more than signs; they do more than bear witness to the fact that Christ has defeated the principalities and powers. The practices of the church are also morally formative for those who participate in these practices. The practices of the church help build up the body of Christ, and as such play a crucial role in the formation of the alternative power that Yoder has taught us is crucial for resisting the seduction of the power of technology. The objective of this concluding chapter is to complicate this point in two ways, and in the process offer a further enrichment to Yoder's thought.

The opening section in what follows will note the way in which Yoder's vision of the church is complicated by the fragmented nature of identity and belonging in our contemporary context. Yoder never denied that Christians have multiple commitments and multiple involvements, but it would appear that he underestimated the difficulty of distinguishing the church from both competing and congruent dimensions of our existence. I think that the pervasiveness of technological systems and ways of thinking shine a spotlight on this difficulty—principalities and powers are more akin to overlapping spheres of influence, to forces that interpenetrate and build upon each other in complex ways, as opposed to discrete, parallel vectors that exert themselves upon us in isolation from each other. What then does it mean to talk about technology, or the church, as a power in the biblical sense of the term? In my view, this complexity suggests some important nuances to a Yoderian perspective on the principalities and powers as applied to the realm of technology.

The second section of this chapter will build upon Albert Borgmann's insistence that we go beyond talking about the importance of practices to focus on what he calls "reality." He argues that ethics should be concerned not only with practices, and certainly not only with theory, but also with ordinary experiences. On the one hand this focus dovetails nicely with Yoder's resistance to both "punctualism," where ethics is reduced to momentary decisions, and quandary ethics, where the discussion is driven by extreme cases. On the other hand, Borgmann's focus also highlights a lacuna in contemporary theological reflection, including Yoder's own theological reflection on the practices of the church. In short, after pointing to the broader relevance of what the church does together as a worshiping community, Yoder fails to discuss everyday practices that are characteristic of the social engagement of the church—the kinds of things Christians do in schools and hospitals or in soup kitchens and refugee camps, not to mention the kinds of things Christians do as households and as neighborhoods. Thus, going beyond Yoder, I think it is important to talk about additional tactics for engaging technology, tactics that are rooted in Christian worship, but are not restricted to typical liturgical practices. This importance is amplified by the fact that these tactics enable the conscientious engagement of technology not simply through their social witness, but most profoundly through the role they play in moral formation.

THE POWERS ARE PERVASIVE AND INTERRELATED

It should be clear by this point that the central role that Yoder's understanding of the principalities and powers plays in his theological ethics has been under-appreciated. It provides the context for his vision of the church, his analysis of the world, and the relationship between these two realms. In other words, it explains his providential view of history, as well as the role that the people of God play in witnessing to God's kingdom. It also provides a clear indication of the theological nature of Yoder's apparent preoccupation with ethics—the transformation of the world depends upon the church bearing witness to the work that Christ has done in defeating the powers, a witness that does not depend simply upon a human decision or obedience, but upon the working of God's spirit.

As helpful as I think Yoder's perspective on the powers is, and this should be clear by the way previous chapters have drawn upon some of his unpublished writings, there is still something left to be desired in his depiction of the church and the world. As discussed in chapter 2, Yoder has often been dismissed as a sectarian, in part because of what people like Jeffrey Stout characterize as a "rigid church-world dualism."[1] Once again, this is based on a misunderstanding of terms—for Yoder a clear distinction between the church and the world *can* be made, indeed, it *must* be made. Yet not everything that exists apart from the church necessarily opposes the church, and thus, according to Yoder, there is much that belongs in neither of the realms of church or world. This is no simple dualism because for Yoder there are more than two categories of allegiance.

One problem that persists, however, is that despite Yoder's narrow definition of the realms of church and world, he pays relatively little attention to the broad swath of people and institutions that do not belong neatly in either. As mentioned in chapter 2, this is a criticism that A. James Reimer has made in recent years, although it is not insurmountable.[2] Indeed, Yoder himself was the first to acknowledge that his work was shaped primarily by the nature of his assignments, and thus he was concerned primarily with ecclesial issues on the one hand, and the problem of war and conflict on the other. I will be returning to this point in the following section when I discuss additional tactics for engaging technology.

I think the more intractable problem with Yoder's discussion of the church and world is that the people who make up the church are the same people who compose or contribute to many of the other structures or institutions in our society. They belong to both the new and the old society. Those who form the body of Christ, those who make manifest the power of Christ, are often the same people who form fallen bodies, and who therefore make manifest powers that are in need of Christ's transformation. As mentioned above, Yoder never denied that Christians have multiple commitments and multiple involvements, and thus I think he would agree completely when

---

1. Stout, *Democracy and Tradition*, 147.

2. Once again, Reimer criticizes Yoder's lack of attention to "numerous issues raised by science and cosmology," and "music and the arts." See "Theological Orthodoxy and Jewish Christianity," 433. More recently, Reimer's focus on dimensions of culture such as the law was also intended to highlight a blind spot in contemporary Mennonite theology. See "'I came not to abolish the law but to fulfill it,'" 246–48.

Stout insists that "Christians rightly find themselves members of many communities."³ Indeed, in *The Politics of Jesus* he wrote: "The claim is not that there is immediately a new world regime which violently replaces the old; rather, the old and the new order exist concurrently on different levels."⁴ Nonetheless, it would appear that he underestimated the difficulty not of distinguishing the *church* from both competing and congruent dimensions of our existence, but of distinguishing the allegiance of the *individuals* who make up the church to both competing and congruent dimensions of their existence. Even if our primary allegiance is to the body of Christ, we continue to have numerous secondary allegiances.

To be clear, I am not trying to undercut the way Yoder has helpfully refocused attention on the social rather than the personal dimension of faithfulness—I am not advocating an atomistic conception of community where the basic unit is the individual. I agree entirely when Yoder argues that we can, like the Apostle Paul, continue to speak of the powers because "we acknowledge that there are bodies of meaning not reducible to individual thoughts and experiences. Every whole is more than its parts."⁵ Likewise, I agree when he argues that "the fallenness of the world is not just the fallenness of individual sinners."⁶

Furthermore, I appreciate the way Yoder's congregational focus for the church allowed him to prioritize the community without losing sight of the individual. For example, his discussion of practices such as binding and loosing stressed that discipline was to be applied individually rather than on the level of inter-church or denominational sanctions: "The discipline procedure prescribed by Christ applies to one person at a time."⁷ And yet he was also clear that practices such as this "do not make the individual the pivot of change." Instead he argued that "the fulcrum/leverage for change and the forum for discernment is the moral independence of the believing community as a body."⁸ Thus, for Yoder, focusing on the local community

---

3. Stout, *Democracy and Tradition*, 147. Hauerwas seems more susceptible to Stout's critique—in his response to Stout he seems to affirm Stout's categories, focusing instead on the permeable nature of the boundary between the church and world. See "Postscript: A Response to Jeff Stout's *Democracy and Tradition*," in *Performing the Faith*, 231.

4. Yoder, *Politics of Jesus*, 186. In this case Yoder is explaining how the New Testament writers could make sense of the radical new social reality in the Body of Christ in the midst of a culture that oppressed slaves and women.

5. Yoder, "God's Good News and the Runaway Powers," 5.

6. Yoder, *Jewish-Christian Schism Revisited*, 175.

7. Yoder, *Ecumenical Movement and the Faithful Church*, 24.

8. Yoder, "Concluding Observations," 5.

is neither a "distancing mental move" or a move that "heightens individual autonomy."[9] It is simply the result of recognizing the continued reality of the incarnation: "There is a particular point where the redeemed individual and social structure are both present, namely in the Christian community as a visible body within history."[10]

It should also be clear that I am not trying to resurrect the charge of perfectionism under a new guise—I do not think that the fallenness or fallibility of the church means we must give up an understanding of the church as a visible social reality. As discussed in chapter 2, those who critique Yoder in this fashion are ignoring his frequent acknowledgment of the peccability of the church. The church is not distinguished from the world by the absence of sin, but by the presence of a new way to address sin. Thus those who have argued that Yoder's vision of the church can be disregarded because it is nothing more than a vision are missing the crucial point of this vision.

The more apt critique is that Yoder fails to recognize the complex nature of identity, and, as a result, his analysis of and response to the principalities and powers lacks some necessary nuance. In my view, this nuance can be provided by incorporating insights from prominent communitarian philosophers such as Charles Taylor and Michael Walzer.

Taylor would seem to agree with Yoder's critique of those who assume that what we call "culture" or "society" or "public" is a monolithic entity. Try as we might, it is not possible to describe "culture-in-general" without excluding or distorting crucial fragments with unique histories. Thus instead of talking about a unitary public sphere, Taylor suggests that we envision a "multiplicity of public spheres nested within each other."[11] This multiplicity has implications for the identity of the modern citizen—Taylor points out that a key "thrust of modern democracy" has sought to "shift the balance within the identity of the modern citizen, so that being a citizen will take precedence over a host of other poles of identity, such as family, class, gender, and even (perhaps especially) religion."[12] The key point here is that multiple commitments create multiple points of tension not just between social structures and institutions, but within individuals.[13]

9. Yoder, "Creation and Gospel," 9.
10. Yoder, *For the Nations*, 185.
11. Taylor, "Liberal Politics and the Public Sphere," 208–9.
12. Taylor, "Nationalism and Morality," 40.

13. A related discussion can be found among legal scholars and political theorists who apply the idea of "intersectionality" to the relationship between race, gender, class, and sexuality. All of these dimensions of identity interact in complex ways to shape the experiences of, for example, African America women in their workplaces. See Crenshaw, "Mapping the Margins."

Michael Walzer makes this reality even more explicit in his discussion of identity in a postmodern age, a time when "people have begun to experience life without clear boundaries and without secure or singular identities," and where "difference is dispersed, and encountered everywhere, everyday." One significant factor is that we are increasingly living in what Walzer characterizes as "immigrant societies." It is due to the resulting "highly intensive multiculturalism" that we experience "a constant co-mingling of ambiguously identified individuals in society and in families."[14] After all, as a result of common practices such as inter-cultural marriage "a literal multiculturalism [is] instantiated not only in the society as a whole but in each family and even each individual."[15] In Walzer's view, the postmodern project thus "undercuts every sort of common identity and standard behavior."[16] Put another way: "There are still boundaries, but they are blurred by all the crossings."[17]

Clearly, this reshaping of identity can be seen to be a result not simply of a larger cultural or political shift, but, as hinted at in chapter 3, the result of the impact of developments in transportation and communications technologies. Sherry Turkle echoes Taylor and Walzer when she notes that "in postmodern times, multiple identities are no longer so much at the margins of things. Many more people experience identity as a set of roles that can be mixed and matched, whose diverse demands need to be negotiated."[18] Turkle's research demonstrates that "the Internet has become a significant social laboratory for experimenting with the constructions and reconstructions of self that characterize postmodern life." Furthermore, it is in this "virtual reality" that we learn best how to "self-fashion and self-create."[19]

Nonetheless, this brief discussion of Taylor and Walzer also prompts a couple of suggestions for nuancing a Yoderian approach to technology. First, if principalities and powers are also more akin to overlapping spheres of influence, or better, to spheres of influence "nested within each other," to

14. Walzer, *On Toleration*, 87.
15. Walzer, "The Politics of Difference," 256.
16. Walzer, *On Toleration* , 87.
17. Ibid., 90. Randels Jr. echoes Walzer when he argues that "fragmentation is an unavoidable aspect of the postmodern condition," and he points toward my critique of Yoder when he argues that "internal fragmentation means that both church and world exist in individual Christians." See "Cyberspace and Christian Ethics," 172, 174. Ward also provides support for my critique of Yoder when he argues that Christian anthropologies and ecclesiologies have "assumed modern notions of subjectivity . . . stable, core identities." He goes on to say that "international persons of the network . . . are more synchretistic, malleable, and performative." See "Between Virtue and Virtuality," 62.
18. Turkle, *Life on the Screen*, 180.
19. Ibid.

use Taylor's expression, then I think discerning the fallenness and redeemability of these powers becomes much trickier. If the power of technology cannot be clearly distinguished from the powers of economic, political, academic, and other social structures, then it becomes more difficult to imagine where to best focus our energy in attempting to resist the seduction of these powers. To put it more concretely, automobiles, genetically engineered food, and the Internet cannot be put in their proper place without recognizing the contributions made by the institutions that undergird global capitalism, agencies that develop regulatory frameworks, and research programs that continue to drive further developments in these areas. If I have been arguing all along that technology needs to be recognized as significant power, I do not want to lapse into the pattern of those philosophers and commentators who give the impression that everything starts and stops with technology. Thus it is also important to emphasize that technology cannot be neatly distinguished from other powers.

The second nuance I want to make is to stress that the cause of the divisions within our identities—the reason why dimensions of our identity as persons remains ambiguous—goes beyond structural factors. As much as the social reality of sin may be under-appreciated, focusing on that reality should not make it possible to subsume the reality of personal sin. Indeed, I think that the fallenness of all the powers of our society, including that of technology, can be traced at least in part to failings that do not necessarily have anything to do with the powers themselves. The fallenness of technologies can be attributed not only to the particular ideals they embody and encourage, but to the ways they are corrupted by evils such as materialism, consumerism, militarism, sexism, and racism. Indeed, in contrast to the way in which many scholars, for example, Walter Wink, make use of principalities and powers language to suggest that militarism and other "isms" can be thought of themselves as principalities and powers, in my view they are better thought of as *signs* of the fallen nature of the principalities and powers. In other words, a phenomenon such as racism is a systemic or structural problem not because it is itself a system or structure (or a principality or power), but because it lives within and corrupts all of the systems and structures that rule our existence. The crucial contribution that this distinction makes is that the transformation of all principalities and powers, including that of technology, thus depends in a crucial way upon healing the wounds caused by things such as militarism and racism.[20] While addressing these

20. Not only is it important for reflections on technology to take into consideration things like militarism, sexism, and racism, but it is also important for those considering these evils to take into consideration the impact of technology. See, for example, Hawkin, *Twenty-First Century Confronts Its Gods*; Rothschild, *Machino Ex Dea*; and

needs is clearly beyond the scope of this project, I think it provides helpful perspective on the technological impact of the preceding discussion of the practices of the church, and the following discussion of additional tactics. Beyond their intrinsic power, there are reasons why we cannot resist the seductions of cars, crops, and computers that have nothing to do with the nature of automobiles, genetically modified food, and the Internet.

ADDITIONAL TACTICS FOR CONSCIENTIOUSLY ENGAGING TECHNOLOGY

Another shortcoming of the discussion in the previous chapters is that although the technological implications of the practices of the church are clear, nothing has been said about how these implications might play themselves out in the everyday lives of Christians. In the absence of more concrete illustrations, there is something unsatisfying about claiming that the authentic transformation of a technology is possible when it is subordinated to the power of Christ through practices such as baptism, communion, or footwashing. In addition to bearing witness to the marks of a Christian community that is able to counter the technological ideals that have come to define society, as discussed in the previous chapter, the church also needs to recognize the important role that these practices play in forming an alternative moral vision. However, I think the church also needs to nurture the ability to conscientiously engage technology by reshaping the way we encounter technological artifacts, systems, and ways of thinking. Thus in this section I will be moving on to discuss several examples of how others have conscientiously engaged technology, examples that I think can inspire further creative, subversive, and even transformative efforts.

The work of Albert Borgmann is a key inspiration for this discussion, thanks to the attention he pays to the realm of ordinary experiences.[21] The underlying argument of virtually all of Borgmann's writing is that, as he says in his most recent book, moral conduct not only governs, but is governed by our "tangible environment."[22] To underline this point, Borgmann repeatedly quotes Winston Churchill: "We shape our buildings, and afterwards our buildings shape us."[23] "Churchill's principle" echoes and encapsulates much of Borgmann's earlier work on technology, and buildings come to

---

Sinclair, *Technology and the African-American Experience.*

21. See, for example, Borgmann's "Theory, Practice, Reality," and "Moral Significance of the Material Culture."

22. Borgmann, *Real American Ethics*, 30.

23. Ibid., 5.

serve as a metaphor for common structures that are social and political as well as physical. The complex relationship between ideas, actions, and the tangible environment means that we need to reconsider our understanding of ethics—in addition to theoretical ethics and practical ethics, Borgmann talks about what he calls "real" ethics:

> Ethics has to become real as well as theoretical and practical. It has to become a making as well as a doing. Real means tangible; real ethics is taking responsibility for the tangible setting of life. Real also means relevant, and real ethics is grounding theoretical and practical ethics in contemporary culture and making them thrive again.[24]

Put another way, "the factor that most decisively channels the daily course of life is not moral theory but material culture."[25] This is not to say that Borgmann does not appreciate the contributions philosophers such as Kant and Rawls have made to theoretical ethics, or the important role that virtues play in shaping our practices. He insists that real ethics should be thought of not as a rival but as a complement to these alternative approaches to ethics,[26] and in this regard sounds a lot like John Howard Yoder's urging that we embrace a multiplicity of approaches to moral reasoning.[27]

Yet Borgmann's discussion of the tangible environment, and his plea that we recognize the effect this environment has on moral reasoning also highlights a gap in Yoder's work. Despite the fact that, like many Mennonites, Yoder's non-sacramental outlook led him to insist that God is worshiped in the everyday lives of believers, in his writing he actually paid little attention to the everyday, to the mundane experiences that preoccupy most of us.[28] This is striking given the way Yoder seeks to draw attention to alternatives to the dominant history of the church, as well as to alternatives to the dominant, often polarizing perspectives on issues such as war. It is also striking given the way he sought to resist the preoccupation with "punctualism" in contemporary ethics—Yoder frequently reframed the dis-

---

24. Ibid., 11.

25. Borgmann, "Invisibility of Contemporary Culture," 249. Republished in *Power Failure*, 24. Building on Borgmann's work, Gaillardetz suggests that "it is when 'nothing is happening' that we will work out our salvation. It is only when we allow our 'dailiness' to be transformed by the grace of God, that we will be able to enter into the graceful living to which people of every age have been called" (*Transforming Our Days*, 145).

26. Borgmann, *Real American Ethics*, 30.

27. Recall Yoder's discomfort with approaches to ethics that claim to be able to do it all—see, for example, "Walk and Word."

28. A few exceptions from early in Yoder's career prove the rule—see "I Choose a Vocation"; "Time and the Christian"; and "Farming Among Mennonites in France."

cussion when the tendency was to reduce ethical reflection to figuring out the correct response to the most urgent issue of the day (or split-second). Furthermore, he was frustrated when ethical reflection was driven by extreme cases, as in quandary ethics.[29]

In fact, I think Yoder would have agreed with Albert Borgmann's assessment of "what circumstances are most hostile to a Christian life":

> Our circumstances are the opposite of those that made for martyrs. Where the martyrs' challenges were overt, ours are concealed; where theirs were mortal to their bodies, ours are lethal to our souls; and where theirs tore them out of their normal life, ours channel our lives between the unquestioned banks of the technological culture.[30]

Borgmann's attention to the everyday is motivated by this suspicion that the most significant source of hostility toward moral excellence in our context comes from the ordinary not the extraordinary dimensions of our existence. As Christians we should be concerned about technology not simply because we are faced with momentous decisions concerning reproductive technology or new avenues of research in medicine, not simply because of the application of advanced technologies in warfare, and not simply because of the potentially cataclysmic ecological consequences of the reliance of so many technologies on fossil fuels as a source of energy. We should be concerned about technology because of the ways in which it reshapes us in a thousand little ways. We should be concerned about the mundane just as much as, if not more than, the exotic. As Borgmann puts it, "for more than three hundred years now, modern technology has been dissolving traditional structures and indulging our weaknesses."[31]

Perhaps this is what leaves some unsatisfied with Yoder's focus on the church—that it seems to imply that so much of everyday life is not of theological concern. Church of the Brethren theologian Scott Holland uses the words of one of his parishioners to question much of contemporary Anabaptist-Mennonite theology, including that of Yoder: "Hey preacher, why can't the strange feeling of the barn and field ever enter the meeting house?"[32] Clearly the ordinary and everyday is not a realm that can be distinguished from, or somehow eludes the church, but is a realm that needs to be included in the church. The political philosopher Romand Coles makes a similar point in his critique of the "liturgical turn" that is evident in, and

29. See "What Would You Do If . . . ?"; and *What Would You Do?*
30. Borgmann, "Everyday Fortitude," 20.
31. Ibid., 18.
32. Quoted by Wiebe in "The Body Knows as Much as the Soul," 197.

had been encouraged by, the work of Stanley Hauerwas.[33] Coles argues that by emphasizing the formation that happens when the church gathers for worship, theologians have tended to ignore the formation that happens through encounters at the border of the church and world. His point is that the church has much to learn from communities and experiences beyond the church, and so it also needs to pay attention to practices that inculcate receptivity and engagement.

As pointed out in earlier chapters, Yoder goes to great pains to point out that the practices of the church have meaning beyond the context of worship. Indeed, they can even be meaningful to those with no interest in their liturgical function. Furthermore, he helpfully broadens our conception of what counts as a liturgical practice.[34] Yoder argued that, just as liturgy is ethics, so too are everyday experiences liturgical. All of life should be properly viewed as praise.[35] Thus any discussion of the implications of Yoder's theological ethics remains incomplete if we stop short of discussing the business of the church that has a more tenuous connection to the traditional elements of worship. Indeed, moving on to discuss relevant practices of everyday life is a necessary if not crucial step for fleshing out the implications of what it means to be an engineer of the church.

A second source of inspiration for this section comes from Vincent Miller's discussion of tactics in his book *Consuming Religion*. As mentioned in chapter 4, Miller argues that, much as Borgmann does with technology, consumer culture undermines religious beliefs by divorcing them from practices. In order to counter this reality, in the concluding chapter of his book Miller proposes alternative practices that will counter the formative influence of consumerism. What is most helpful is the way Miller situates these alternative practices—he is under no illusion that they will be able to overcome the overwhelming power of dominant cultural practices:

> In advanced capitalist societies, no religion or traditional culture maintains anything approaching a strategic control of the cultural field or, for that matter, control of the cultural formation of its own faithful. For that reason, theological engagement with consumer culture must take place on the tactical level.[36]

---

33. Coles, "Gentled Into Being."

34. Yoder, *Royal Priesthood*, 364.

35. The unity of worship and life, or, more specifically, the unity of worship and *work*, in the Mennonite tradition is noted by Dueck in "Critical Examination of Mennonite Worship and Ethics," 2–4. See also "Performance of Worship and the Ordering of Our Lives," 51–52.

36. Miller, *Consuming Religion*, 181.

Instead of viewing counter-cultural practices as *strategic*, which reduces them to "insignificant symbolic gestures," Miller argues that they should be viewed as *tactics*:

> Their success is measured not as miniscule enclaves amid regnant global capitalism but as mediative counterpractices that provide means for forming believer's imaginations against the logic of the commodity fetish, thus helping them swim against the broader tide of the commodification of culture that deprives religions of the power to inform a way of life.[37]

In short, tactics are less about changing the world than they are about changing us.[38] And it is in this spirit that Miller goes on to discuss fifteen "counterpractices," ranging from making connections between products and their producers and learning a handicraft, to liturgy and making connections between contemporary Christian doctrines and their historical origins.

It is in a similar spirit that the following practices are suggested in order to help the church conscientiously engage the technologies of the automobile, genetically modified food, and the Internet.[39] It should go without saying that this is by no means a comprehensive list. It should also be clear that, although some of these tactics were not *necessarily* motivated by Christian convictions, they are being discussed because of the way in which they can contribute to the marks of the church discussed in chapter 4. Finally,

---

37. Ibid., 183. There are obvious connections here to Borgmann's discussion of focal practices, even though Borgmann himself does not use the language of tactics.

38. In this regard Miller is dependent upon the work of Michel de Certeau, who defines a strategy as something that is based upon "the calculus of force-relationships which becomes possible when a subject of will and power (a proprietor, an enterprise, a city, a scientific institution) can be isolated from an 'environment.'" In contrast, a tactic involves "a calculus which cannot count on a 'proper' (a spatial or institutional localization), nor thus on a border distinguishing the other as a visible totality." In other words, a tactic: "has at its disposal no base where it can capitalize on its advantages, prepare its expansions, and secure independence with respect to circumstances. The 'proper' is a victory of space over time. On the contrary, because it does not have a place, a tactic depends on time—it is always on the watch for opportunities that must be seized 'on the wing.' Whatever it wins, it does not keep. It must constantly manipulate events in order to turn them into 'opportunities.' The weak must continually turn to their own ends forces alien to them" (*Practice of Everyday Life*, xix). See also Miller, "Certeau."

I was first introduced to Certeau's work in David Toole's *Waiting for Godot in Sarajevo* (230–31). Toole argues that, as evident in his discussion of "revolutionary subordination," Yoder portrayed Jesus as a "tactical master." Yoder also encouraged Christians to look to "non-imperial strategies and tactics" rather than political might in order to find God's movement in history. See "Armaments and Eschatology," 56.

39. It must be emphasized, however, that where Miller focuses on the formation of individuals, I am more interested in the formation of the church, i.e., a particular kind of *social* reality.

I am not inventing anything new, but simply discussing ideas that others have already tried. It is my hope that Christian communities could—as they become better versed in these sorts of experiments and as a result become more discerning in their own engagement of technology—become fertile incubators for additional tactics.

Tactics for Conscientiously Engaging Automobiles

First and foremost, commitment to the church should have implications for the ownership of automobiles. In my view, one reason why the technological ideal of autonomy is magnified by automobiles is because they are most often at the disposal of a single individual. This reality is demonstrated by our language—if someone asked me how I traveled to school or work today, they might expect me to tell them either that I caught *the* bus or that I drove *my* car. Recognizing that automobiles will often be necessary for many people in North America for the foreseeable future, the value of autonomy could be diminished if the church was a place that made it possible for its members to get by with less than one car per adult in every household.[40] People within households could be encouraged to find ways of sharing a car, but this could also extend beyond households to include other church members, or participation in local car sharing co-operatives or businesses. There are certainly good economic and environmental reasons for pursing this path, but there is also the recognition that diminishing the importance of autonomy in deciding how we travel from place to place will increase our commitment to a particular community.[41]

Furthermore, our membership in the body of Christ also has implications for how we value particular geographic places. One way that churches can build commitment to a local community is by putting down roots in a local community. Churches should encourage their members to make living in close proximity to each other a priority, and should strive to build relationships with non-members living in the neighborhood of the church. The idea that our church would dictate where we choose to live seems even more counter-cultural than the idea that it would encourage us to make do with fewer cars, but once again, it needs to be recognized that our decisions in

---

40. The radical nature of this proposal becomes clearer when we recognize that not only are there far more registered automobiles than there are households in the U.S. and Canada, in recent years there have been significantly more registered automobiles than registered *drivers*—in other words, tens of millions of drivers in North America have exclusive use of not just one, but two vehicles.

41. It is interesting to note that Amish and Old Order Mennonite communities ban the *ownership*, not the use of cars. See Kraybill, *Riddle of Amish Culture*, 219.

these areas are never about either asserting or giving up our individuality. We are simply choosing to commit ourselves to different types of community.[42]

Patience has obvious implications for the practice of driving. After all, failing to wear seat belts and speeding are, aside from alcohol impairment, the leading causes of traffic fatalities in North America.[43] Yet patience implies much more than taking the time to buckle up, follow speed limits, and contain our road rage. Patience is what allows us to focus on the task at hand rather than racing ahead to what awaits is next. Put negatively, the absence of patience opens us up to a host of sins. In a rare article in a theological journal that focuses on the automobile, John Waterson notes that "to suggest that anyone was a *sinful* driver would in general merely provoke amusement. Yet that is precisely what we all are from time to time."[44] Indeed, we are all guilty, at the very least, of a host of minor sins while behind the wheel, ranging from allowing ourselves to be distracted by children bickering in the backseat, to driving on too little sleep. We are all guilty of failing to take full responsibility for the "lethal weapon"[45] at our disposal,

---

42. In this regard, Yoder's theology, and the contemporary practice of his church tradition, are more problematic than helpful. In fact, in one essay Yoder insisted:

> The believers' church has been since its origins a group of people who have not been drawn together by geographical contiguity, but rather who were drawn together, often from considerable distances, even before the Industrial Revolution, by a common commitment. For this heritage, where the church is thought of as the people gathering from many quarters rather than as the agency ministering to an area, the greater flexibility of modern urban societies facilitates rather than undermines the expression of its unity.

He went on to say that "it is becoming increasingly more difficult for any particular segment of the population to feel itself a parish." Rather than lamenting what may have been lost, Yoder insists that "the parish pattern was questionable in the first place," and so "it can hardly be the most constructive way of meeting the modern world to accept and then update the parish assumptions." See Yoder, "A People in the World," 281.

There are a number of problems with Yoder's argument, not the least of which is that he conflates the coming together of believers over great distances through migration with the coming together of believers over great distances on a weekly basis. As demonstrated by their Amish and Old Order cousins, the kinds of church commutes that many urban Mennonites consider reasonable would have been impossible for a long time after the Industrial Revolution. In pointing appreciatively to the "greater flexibility of modern urban societies," this is the one occasion where Yoder provides a clear endorsement of the automobile.

43. Although seat belt use has increased and alcohol-related fatalities have decreased in the United States in recent decades, the percentage of fatal accidents in which speeding or inattentive drivers were a factor has actually increased over the same period. See the National Highway Traffic Safety Administration's website for accident data: http://www-nrd.nhtsa.dot.gov/.

44. Waterson, "Religion and Road Safety," 228.

45. Stoops, "Driving as Christians," 20.

and only thanks to luck, or perhaps the grace of God, have we avoided facing frightening consequences for these minor sins. The church should be a place where we take the time to identify and confess bad habits, and develop and nurture good habits, and this should certainly apply to driving. Indeed, a key characteristic of good drivers, as Waterson points out, is self-critique: "first-class drivers [are] given to continual searching examination of their own performance, with devoted striving to do better."[46]

Patience also has implications for how we relate to the automobiles we drive. As discussed in chapter 3, most of us have been taught to use or consume technology with a "black box" mentality—for the test case at hand, we turn the ignition key in our car and expect it to go. Everything that occurs in between the initial input and the desired result remains a mystery. Albert Borgmann has suggested that this mentality is the reason why technology leads to the separation of means and ends (or practices and beliefs) that is so characteristic of modern life.[47] In my view, patience makes the possibility of turning means into ends, for example, of transforming an automobile from a device into a thing (to use Borgmann's terms), much more likely. One final suggestion then is that churches encourage their members to take the time to learn the basics of automobile technology in order to become more aware of how their inputs while driving are translated into desired—as well as undesired—ends. For example, the impact of modifying one's driving style on fuel economy can be dramatic. Once again, there are good economic and environmental reasons for pursuing this path, but the larger aim is to nurture the re-connection of practice and belief that the seductive power of the automobile has divided.[48]

The elevation of meaningful suffering, especially when contrasted with maximizing comfort, is something that requires even more radical tactics. It is a concern that points us toward alternatives to driving cars altogether, rather than simply driving less, as shared vehicles and living close to our church make possible, or driving more mindfully, as the confession of our driving sins and technical knowledge make possible. If we are to conscientiously engage the automobile, we need to be able to see it as just one of

---

46. Waterson, "Religion and Road Safety," 229. One commendable example can be found in a Catholic statement on the "Moral aspects of driving" and "The Christian virtue of drivers and their 'Ten Commandments.'" Although the virtue of patience was not discussed, charity, prudence, justice, and hope were all recognized as relevant for driving. See the Pontifical Council for the Pastoral Care of Migrants and Itinerant People's "Guidelines for the Pastoral Care of the Road."

47. See "Invisibility of Contemporary Culture."

48. Matthew Crawford makes clear in *Shop Class as Soulcraft* that hands-on technical knowledge brings with it many benefits that are significant but difficult to articulate.

several transportation options. And, given the current state of urban, suburban, and rural landscapes in North America, this requires both creativity and the willingness to experience some level of discomfort as we travel. Indeed, while efforts to elevate the attention paid to fuel economy among Christian drivers may be commendable, if Jesus was around today he would probably opt for a bicycle or bus rather than a car.[49]

Alternative transportation tactics have been documented in recent years by loosely connected, grassroots movements such as the "De-motorize Your Soul" campaign.[50] Aiming to be "a spirited foray into the post-oil era," this effort framed "the move away from oil as a practical experiment and an irresistible spiritual adventure." Thus it proposed "a set of spiritual exercises that offer alternatives to the internal combustion engine while also nurturing the soul." As accounts of these exercises indicate, doing things like biking to work can be physically tiring at the best of times, and painful and dangerous on snowy winter days. Yet these moments of suffering have also led to meaningful, transformative experiences as commuters become connected to their communities in new ways. They help us "re-adjust normal" away from "motor mania," and make it possible to perceive the ways that speed may be "slowly messing us up inside." In any case, by putting into practice a tactic such as cycling, Christians are making visible an alternative to cars, and the presence of real, not just theoretical transportation options is the most profound way to diminish the power of the automobile.

A final tactic that the church should encourage is the ancient practice of pilgrimage. Defined as "religiously motivated travel for the purpose of meeting and experiencing God with hopes of being shaped and changed by that encounter,"[51] pilgrimages are traditionally related to significant destinations such as holy sites in Jerusalem, Rome, or Spain. However, pilgrimages can also be thought of as a spiritual discipline that leads practitioners toward greater engagement with their physical bodies, with fellow travelers, and with their surrounding environment. Furthermore, walking on a pilgrimage to a church either near or far has the potential to reframe the

---

49. Chris Huebner makes this point in an interview with Aaron Epp—see "Would Jesus drive . . . or ride?"

One example of a laudable but ultimately limited effort was the "What Would Jesus Drive?" campaign initiated in 2002 by Evangelicals for Social Action and the Evangelical Environmental Network that tried to convince Christians to view their transportation choices as moral choices. This led to a "What Should the Governor Drive?" campaign initiated by the Interfaith Climate and Energy Campaign that sought to improve the economy of vehicles owned by state governments.

50. http://www.demotorize.org. This was an outgrowth of the "Experiments with truth" section of *Geez* magazine.

51. Boers, *Way Is Made By Walking*, 41.

way we view transportation more generally. As one practitioner put it, "only recently [have] people come to expect travel to be restful and leisurely. Prior journeying was risky, hard, uncertain, expensive, and taxing. In fact, *travel* is closely related to *travail*, which means suffering."[52] Of course, traveling with the help of an automobile is also risky, hard, uncertain, expensive, and taxing—the problem is that as drivers and passengers we do not bear all of these burdens ourselves, but foist them on the rest of creation.

Tactics for Conscientiously Engaging Genetically Modified Food

Although this chapter groups together various tactics that are especially relevant for the three particular technologies discussed throughout this book, no doubt some of these tactics may also be helpful for conscientiously engaging a variety of technologies. For example, the "De-motorize Your Soul" movement talks about the dangers of speed in more general terms than simply in regards to transportation, pointing out that we are "stuck on fast forward" in lives with an "ever-escalating pace."[53] The "Slow Food" movement is another tactic that seeks to counter the technological ideal of speed, although I think it also speaks directly to the imperatives for control, mastery, and conformity that are embodied and encouraged by genetically engineered food.

Originating in Italy in the late 1980s as a movement that not only resisted but counteracted fast food, Slow Food is a non-profit organization that by 2013 was made up of over 100,000 members in 1,500 *convivia* or local chapters in 150 countries.[54] As the name and origins of the movement imply, Slow Food is interested in promoting the benefits of taking time to appreciate the food we eat, and to seek out company to enjoy it with. As an "eco-gastronomic" movement it is also interested in making connections "between plate, planet, people and culture" by promoting local food artisans, local flavors, and local farmers through a variety of initiatives such as "Presidia" projects to help find markets for traditional foods, the "Terra Madre" network to highlight the contributions of small-scale farmers, and the "Ark of Taste" to catalogue foods that are at risk of disappearing. In short, it is based on the philosophy that Slow Food is "good, clean and fair."

---

52. Ibid., 33.

53. Connections between the technological ideal of speed and dimensions of life beyond transportation can be found in Carl Honoré's *In Praise of Slowness*.

54. Quotations and statistics that follow come from the movement's main web site: http://www.slowfood.com/. Numerous books have been published on Slow Food, but the movement's manifesto is Carlo Petrini's *Slow Food*.

Joining a local Slow Food chapter, or participating in a workshop, holds the potential to cultivate knowledge and practices that resist not only the pace of contemporary life, but the demand that our tastes conform to the standards of a global marketplace. Rather than leading to greater diversity, the technologies that make globalization possible—and this includes the genetic modification of food—demand ever increasing uniformity and sameness. The celebration of local cuisine is a celebration of nonconformity. It is also a celebration of contingency that prompts respectful appreciation, if not outright humility. For the depth and particularity of the knowledge and skills exemplified by local food artisans counters any illusions that creation is something capable of being mastered, much less controlled.

There are several other ways that churches can help resist the tendency to confine food to the realm of consumption. Most obviously, Christians have a long tradition of feasting and fasting that can amplify a more significant role for food in our lives. Furthermore, the priority placed upon breaking bread together throughout the history of the church makes it possible to nurture a deep-seated "culture of the table," to use Albert Borgmann's expression. Indeed, for Borgmann, celebrating a "great meal" every day with family is the focal practice par excellence, for it gathers people together to prepare, to bless, to serve, and to converse over food, rather than simply to consume it.[55] The family meal is marked by communal engagement, by its disclosive power, and by having a clear center. However, while eating together as families is a good place to start, it is not place to stop. For the culture of the table is properly grounded in the traditional Christian practice of hospitality. When we open our homes and our tables up to brothers and sisters in Christ, and especially to strangers, we go beyond demonstrating our commitment to something greater than our individual needs to demonstrate a posture of vulnerability.[56]

Another tactic that can help form Christians in a way that embraces vulnerability toward creation is the practice of gardening. There is nothing like trying to grow our own food to make us appreciate, even slightly, the challenges that farmers are faced with as they struggle to control pests, weeds, and climatic conditions in order to harvest the food we depend on for nourishment every day. It seems to me that any comments—either critical or supportive—about the potential of genetically modified crops should be informed by first-hand experience in this struggle for control.

One particularly helpful reflection on the practice of gardening is Barbara Kingsolver's book, *Animal, Vegetable, Miracle*. In it she documents her family's efforts to eat, as much as possible, only what they are able to grow or

---

55. Borgmann, *Technology and the Character of Contemporary Life*, 204–5.
56. See Pineda, "Hospitality."

raise on their small Virginia farm. Even for experienced gardeners this is a monumental task, and, despite the many humorous anecdotes, Kingsolver's account clearly communicates the exhaustion caused by their endeavor. She also communicates the way this experiment strengthened connections with their local community, as they bartered, traded, and purchased items they could not raise or produce on their own such as honey and milk.[57] One of the most profound impacts of this experiment was on their diet—eating what you grow means you eat what is ripe and ready, or what you have been able to preserve, not whatever you happen to feel like that day. In the northern United States, this means eating asparagus and lettuce in the spring, green beans and tomatoes in the summer, watermelon and squash in the fall, and potatoes and beets in the winter.[58] Clearly then, in addition to forming people who must accept their own vulnerability, gardening can help form people with patience. As Kingsolver puts it:

> The main barrier standing between ourselves and a local-food culture is not price, but attitude. The most difficult requirements are patience and a pinch of restraint—virtues that are hardly the property of the wealthy ... We're raising children on the definition of promiscuity if we feed them a casual, indiscriminate mingling of foods from every season plucked from the supermarket.[59]

Kingsolver goes on to note: "If many of us would view this style of eating as deprivation, that's only because we've grown accustomed to the botanically outrageous condition of having everything, always."[60] The irony, or, in Kingsolver's words, the "sublime paradox," is that when we eat food in season we are also learning to wait "for the quality experience." Because our food both tastes better and is better for us, "restraint equals indulgence."[61]

A second irony of our present reliance upon heavily processed food that utilizes ingredients from all over the world is that instead of more

---

57. Of course, there were some basic necessities that the Kingsolver family continued to purchase that came from far away, including olive oil, grains (even though they were ground locally), and coffee.

58. Kingsolver's discussion of the "vegetannual" sums up this natural sequence nicely: "Each plant part we eat must come in its turn—leaves, buds, flowers, green fruits, ripe fruits, hard fruits [and tubors, bulbs, or roots]—because that's the necessary order of things for an annual plant. Some minor deviations and a bit of overlap are allowed, but in general, picturing an imaginary vegetannual plant is a pretty reliable guide to what will be in season, wherever you live" (*Animal, Vegetable, Miracle*, 65).

59. Ibid., 31.
60. Ibid., 32.
61. Ibid.

diversity, we actually have less variety in our diet. Kingsolver points out that "Modern U.S. consumers now get to taste less than 1 percent of the vegetable varieties that were grown here a century ago."[62] Indeed, as noted in chapter 3, most of our food now comes from a stunningly small fraction of the tens of thousands of plant species that humans have eaten throughout our history, and critics of genetically modified food such as Vandana Shiva have highlighted its complicity in accelerating the already worrisome extent of conformity in agriculture. If genetic engineering accelerates this trend toward monoculture, gardening resists it. Backyard gardeners are almost single-handedly responsible for preserving an incredible range of "heirloom species" of fruits and vegetables—species that were popular at one time but are no longer commercially grown because qualities such as shelf life have become more important than taste. In fact, through traditional breeding techniques, many gardeners are even adding to the genetic diversity of our food options.[63] Thus it seems as though encouraging the practice of gardening can help churches counter the technological ideals of control, mastery, and conformity. Gardening teaches us that we really are vulnerable to natural forces beyond our control, that we should be humble in light of the incredible diversity evident in creation, and that it is possible to resist conforming to the practices of mainstream agriculture even though they are increasingly entrenched in our society.[64]

Of course, few are in a position to be able to grow the majority of the food they consume. Nonetheless, even a small garden can be a significant tactic.[65] Indeed, Kingsolver concludes her book with this note:

> It's the worst of bad manners—and self-protection, I think, in a nervously cynical society, to ridicule the small gesture... Small, stepwise changes in personal habits aren't trivial. Ultimately they will, or won't, add up to having been the thing that mattered.[66]

Aside from joining a Slow Food chapter and planting a garden, there are numerous additional tactics that churches can encourage to connect

---

62. Ibid., 49.

63. The recent initiative to preserve seeds in a secure vault in Norway in order to preserve biological diversity is an example of a purely technological approach to the dangers of monoculture and climate change.

64. Cavanaugh points out that when we "turn our homes into sites of production, not just consumption," we are doing something profoundly counter-cultural on a wide variety of levels. See *Being Consumed*, 57.

65. Small efforts in urban settings can also lead in unexpected directions—see, for example, Carpenter, *Farm City*.

66. Kingsolver, *Animal, Vegetable, Miracle*, 346.

their members to their food sources. This includes joining a Community Supported Agriculture project, which could mean buying a share in either an urban or rural garden. The level of involvement required by CSA projects varies widely, ranging from controlling one's own garden plot to picking up a bag of fresh vegetables every week.[67] Additional tactics include shopping at farmer's markets, where we can purchase food directly from the hands that grew it. It includes joining in on bulk buys of eggs, cheese, and meat from local farmers. And it includes planning menus that conform to the ingredients readily available in our context in any given season, rather than to the expectation that food is a timeless and placeless commodity.[68] Each of these options plays a crucial role in efforts such as the "100 mile diet" and other campaigns to encourage people to eat locally. As with the tactics for conscientiously engaging cars that were discussed in the previous section, there are clearly many possible motivations for contributing to what Kingsolver calls a "local food culture," including environmental and health concerns, economic justice issues, and an interest in taste. However, as with the complex technological system that has made genetically engineered foods possible, the culture that makes local food possible cannot be reduced to what we can measure. As Kingsolver puts it:

> 'Locally grown' is a denomination whose meaning is incorruptible. Sparing the transportation fuel, packaging, and unhealthy additives is a compelling part of the story, but the plot goes well beyond that. Local food is a handshake deal in a community gathering place. It involves farmers with first names, who show up week after week. It means an open door policy on the fields, where neighborhood buyers are welcome to come have a look, and pick their food from the vine. *Local is farmers growing trust.*[69]

It seems to me that eating locally, even if it is not food that we ourselves have grown, requires us to be conscientiously engaged in a crucial dimension of our technological existence. It is hard work—we can no longer make our food choices simply on the basis of the grocery store advertisements in the local paper.[70] Not only does it require us to consider more than price, we will likely need to be willing to spend a greater portion of our income on food. Depending on the local practices of farmers, we may even eat genetically modified corn or soybeans—given the dominance of these crops

---

67. For a good introduction to CSAs, see Winne, *Closing the Food Gap*.
68. See, for example, Lind and Hockman-Wert, *Simply in Season*.
69. Kingsolver, *Animal, Vegetable, Miracle*, 123.
70. This is the key point made by Michael Pollan in *Omnivore's Dilemma*.

in North America, any hope of maintaining any kind of genetic purity is likely futile. However, in doing so we will have seen through any illusions of control and mastery harbored by the developers of these crops.

Tactics for Conscientiously Engaging the Internet

The final set of tactics I will briefly review make contributions especially relevant for conscientiously engaging the Internet, although, once again, they speak to the other technologies discussed above. For example, the practice of voluntary service is something that churches have long encouraged, and church-related institutions have long depended upon. Millions of Christians around the world dedicate a portion of their time—whether it be a few hours every week or month, a few weeks every year or two, or even several years at a time—to the work of the church in a wide variety of ways. And while these individuals no doubt gain much personally from this service, on the whole the decision to volunteer is a decidedly inefficient economic choice. Even as non-profit agencies of all types are subjected to increasing pressure to demonstrate that they are wise stewards of their resources—that they are operated as efficiently as possible—the fact that people volunteer for causes they believe in serves as a reminder that there is more to life than efficiency. Voluntary service is a profound counter-technique, and is an antidote to the apparent triumph of technological systems and ways of thinking.

What are the particular implications of living lives of service for the Internet? If the church is to form people who are marked by servanthood instead of the compulsion to pursue efficiency, there are particular ways of using the Internet that should be encouraged. For example, Christians who currently have computers with Internet connections can embrace the distributed or volunteer computing phenomena. By segmenting the tasks involved in analyzing huge quantities of data, distributed computing allows researchers to use of a large number of networked computers rather than a single large computer. In the same way, volunteer computing allows these same researchers to make use of the spare processing capacity on the ordinary personal computers of volunteers around the world via the Internet. After all, the collective processing capability of thousands or even millions of networked computers that are only partially being utilized (or are not otherwise being used at all) can dwarf even the fastest supercomputer. Paralleling the growth of the Internet, since the late 1990s the number of distributed computing projects has continued to grow, thanks in part to software that makes it easy for both volunteers and researchers to work together.[71]

71. See Rheingold, "Computation Nations and Swarm Supercomputers," chapter 3

A whole host of research projects have depended upon volunteer computers, including the design of AIDS or Dengue drugs, investigations into the cause of cancer or Alzheimer's disease, searching for patterns in climate data or for signs of extraterrestrial intelligence from radio-telescope data. The number of volunteers has been impressive—many projects rely on tens of thousands of computers, and there have been times when several million computers have supported a single project. Most of these projects actually ask very little of the volunteers—they unobtrusively work away in the background whenever their computer is connected to the Internet. Indeed, distributed computing software is like an anti-virus—vast amounts of processing power and bandwidth can be used without our awareness, only in this case for constructive rather than destructive purposes. Yet some projects also rely on volunteer brainpower as well as computer power. For example, in a few months the Galaxy Zoo project was able to recruit over one hundred thousand volunteers to classify galaxies from telescope images, a task that with minimal training people can complete with greater accuracy than a computer.[72]

Another, perhaps more obvious way in which volunteers compete with rather than elevate the drive toward efficiency is found in the open-source software movement. Technically savvy computer programmers have been able to work together to develop products to rival the offerings of Microsoft—examples include computer operating systems such as Linux, web browsers such Mozilla Firefox, and office productivity suites such as Open Office. The only difference is that so-called "free-ware" does not cost users any money.[73] Perhaps the most compelling benefit of these products is that they resist, at least to a certain degree, the opacity that is so highly valued by technological systems such as the Internet. Most users (including myself) have minimal or no involvement in the ongoing development and refine-

---

in *Smart Mobs*, and "You Got the Power."

72. See http://www.galaxyzoo.org/.

73. Thomas Goetz reminds software engineers that "for all its novelty, open source isn't new. Dust off your Isaac Newton and you'll recognize the same ideals of sharing scientific results in the late 1600s . . . Or role up your sleeves and see the same ethic in Amish barn raising, a tradition that dates to the early 18th century." Goetz goes on to quote Yochai Benkler, a law professor at Yale studying the economic impact of open source: "There's a reason we love barn raising scenes in movies. They make us feel great. We think, 'Wow! That would be amazing!' But it doesn't have to be just a romanticized notion of how to live. New technology allows it. Technology can unleash tremendous human creativity and tremendous productivity. This is basically a barn raising through a decentralized communication network." See "Open Source Everywhere," 158, 166. For a more recent and comprehensive discussion of open source technologies, see Kelty, *Two Bits*.

ment of open-source software, but the premise of this type of technology is that the source code is available to anyone who wants to access it. Indeed, as stipulated in the Free Software Federation's "Gnu Manifesto," contributors to this type of software even give up their rights to restrict the copying of their work, and the same rule applies to anyone who reproduces or adapts their work for another product. In essence these "copyleft" (as opposed to "copyright") licenses are designed to preserve access even as the reach of open-source software continues to expand and become more mainstream.[74]

Wikipedia is one of the clearest examples of how, because of the Internet, volunteers can contribute not only to complex research programs and to the development of free software, but to the content of collaborative web sites. Derived from the Hawaiian word that means "fast," "wiki" refers to a type of software that allows multiple users to easily create, edit, and link web pages together. Wikipedia has grown at a phenomenal rate since its inception in January of 2001, to the point that by 2013 there were over 22 million articles in 285 languages, and it was the sixth most popular website worldwide. The English edition alone has over four million articles, which far exceeds the half a million articles in the thirty volumes of the Encyclopedia Britannica, the oldest English-language encyclopedia still in print.[75] Although Wikipedia has been found to be remarkably reliable, given that anyone with access to the Internet can edit or create articles, favoring consensus over credentials in the editorial process continues to be controversial. It also remains unclear whether Wikipedia will continue to command the attention and energy of enough contributors to maintain an acceptable level of accuracy, much less continue to expand, once the novelty of the project has worn off.[76] Nonetheless, it continues to be an inspiration for other collaborative endeavors, both web-based and more traditional.

Wikis, Open Source software projects, and distributed computing are tactics that are accessible to many users of the Internet, including those who do not consider themselves technically savvy. And yet, as discussed above with regards to the automobile, technical literacy is precisely what is required to properly understand the implications of our use of technological artifacts and systems. This literacy is also what makes it possible to resist

---

74. See http://www.gnu.org/gnu/manifesto.html. Many of the most popular examples of this type of software are covered by the GNU Free Documentation License (GFDL) or Creative Commons public copyright licenses.

75. See http://en.wikipedia.org/wiki/Wikipedia:About.

76. In fact, the popularity of Wikipedia makes it the least collaborative of any wiki application. For example, in early 2013 Wikipedia had approximately 77,000 "active contributors"—those who made at least five monthly contributions—a tiny percentage of the 470 million monthly "unique visitors" worldwide.

letting the drive for invisibility or opacity run roughshod over our lives. Sherry Turkle talks of three categories of computer users—hackers, hobbyists, and users:

> A user is involved with the machine in a hands-on way, but is not interested in the technology except as it enables an application. Hackers are the antithesis of users. They are passionately involved in mastery of the machine itself. The hobbyists in their own way were equally enthralled.[77]

I would argue that anything that helps shift people out of the category of "user" is an appropriate tactic for helping the church conscientiously engaging the Internet. This includes tactics already discussed, but it could also include small groups to tackle projects such as designing and maintaining a congregation's web site (rather than hiring an outside contractor), or helping troubleshoot or upgrade old computers for members of the congregation[78]

If a technological system such as the Internet, like the automobile and genetically modified food, can be put in its place with greater technical knowledge and access, I think an even more profound tactic is to opt out. I don't mean to suggest that congregations should stage computer smashing sessions or get rid of their web sites, but that they should encourage people to have regular periods of Internet inaccessibility. The obvious Judeo-Christian tradition to draw upon here is keeping the Sabbath. As several theologians have recently pointed out, the tradition of the Sabbath teaches that it is through resting that we find genuine freedom, and it is through rest that we are able to affirm the goodness of creation and the goodness of our work. In the words of the prominent Anglican theologian Oliver O'Donovan: "We lay aside our making and acting and doing in order to celebrate the completeness and integrity of God's making and acting and doing, in the light of which we can dare to undertake another week of work."[79]

---

77. Turkle, *Life on the Screen*, 32. It should be noted that for Turkle and many other authors, "hacker" is not a pejorative or sinister label. For example, the Finnish philosopher Pekka Himanen defines hackers as "enthusiastic computer programmers who share their work with others," and argues that the values of these programmers have the potential to remake the work ethic of the industrial age. The individualism and drudgery nurtured by a Protestant Capitalist ethic is being replaced by free-flowing rhythms and more collaborative approaches. See *Hacker Ethic and the Spirit of the Information Age*. And Schultze asks "Why do we talk about Internet geeks, hackers, and spammers, but never about Internet mensches or saints?" (*Habits of the High-Tech Heart*, 87).

78. Indeed, Pullinger argues that Christians need to develop "situated knowledge" about technology themselves through "technical networks of concern" at the level of local congregations (*Information Technology and Cyberspace*, 133).

79. O'Donovan, *Begotten or Made?*, 12. Two more recent discussions of the Sabbath that consider the impact of technology on contemporary life include: Bass, *Receiving*

As the Internet grows increasingly accessible through the widespread use of smartphones in addition to computers, it is becoming increasingly difficult for many people to draw boundaries between their online and offline lives. In other words, as the threshold to Internet access becomes lower and lower, it becomes more and more difficult to overcome the urge to check e-mail or surf the web to check the latest news or sports scores. The result is increased distraction and less engagement both at work and home.[80] I would suggest that if large corporations can experiment with the idea of e-mail-free days in order to provide employees the freedom for greater creativity, then it is hardly radical for churches to encourage their members to avoid connecting to the Internet as one way to honor the Sabbath. The point is that keeping any kind of Sabbath is difficult to do on our own. As Dorothy C. Bass notes:

> Much as we might think our own incompetence is to blame, the vast majority of people have been swept into this uncomfortable situation by large social forces. The remedy needs to be social, too: we must pursue it in the company of other people, not just as individuals.[81]

Clearly, observing a day of rest has ramifications for a whole host of technological ideals, including speed and conformity, as well as efficiency. Perhaps observing an e-mail Sabbath is just the first place to start to conscientiously engage a whole host of technologies.

One final tactic that is especially helpful for resisting the seduction of a technological system such as the Internet, given the rapidly evolving nature of computer hardware and software, is to intentionally choose to remain at least one generation behind the latest and greatest technology. Deciding ahead of time that one will always be at least slightly out of step with the march of technology—becoming a "late adopter" or "technology laggard" in the parlance of the computer industry—is to opt for at least relative simplicity over novelty. Certainly there are also pragmatic reasons to go this route, for example, sticking with the tried-and-true while others struggle to work out the inevitable bugs of the new. However, once again, it is one small step toward putting technological systems in their proper place.

---

the Day; and Dawn, *Sense of the Call.*

80. See, for example, Freeman, *Tyranny of E-mail*; Powers, *Hamlet's Blackberry*; and Turkle, *Alone Together.*

81. Bass, *Receiving the Day*, 58.

CONCLUSION

This book began by arguing that technology is of theological significance, and that the work of John Howard Yoder is a helpful resource for theological reflection on this topic. It went on to use Yoder's work to demonstrate that the conscientious engagement of technology is really all about the church, as the body of Christ, resisting the seduction of the power of technological artifacts, systems, and ways of thinking in order to re-describe technology within the narrative of God's salvation of the world. More specifically, the church is able to testify to the reality that Christ has defeated and disarmed the powers, including the power of technology. This testimony is most clearly evident in the practices of the church, practices that make visible the distinctive marks of the church—viewed in the light of these marks, technological ideals are put in their proper place and are no longer granted the status of moral imperatives. What Yoder failed to appreciate was the extent to which these practices not only bear witness to the marks of the church, but contribute to the formation of these marks. Furthermore, there are numerous tactics related to our everyday encounters with particular technologies that can also contribute to this crucial work of moral formation.

In seeking to help followers of Christ move beyond the widespread preoccupation with being on the cutting edge of technology, this book also opens up a number of avenues for further research, and I will conclude by briefly highlighting five of them. Most obviously, it compels the church to pursue the conscientious engagement of a whole host of technologies. Automobiles, genetically modified food, and the Internet are just the tip of the iceberg when it comes to examples of technology that merit theological consideration. Second, by going beyond the typical issues that John Howard Yoder addressed, this book was also able to go beyond typical scholarly debates surrounding his work, a move that should encourage constructive developments of his thought. Yoder is properly viewed neither as a hero to idolize, nor as a giant to bring down. Third, in relating the practices of the church to technology, this effort is of particular relevance to those in both the academy and the church interested in the relationship between liturgy and ethics. Further attention to the technological implications of worship, as well as the impact of technological developments on liturgy is clearly required. A fourth avenue for further research pertains to the usefulness and the shortcomings of applying the biblical concept of the principalities and powers to the topic of technology. As mentioned earlier in this concluding chapter, more effort is needed to discern the relationship between technological, economic, political and academic powers, as well as the contribution that evils such as militarism, sexism, and racism make to the fall of these powers. Finally, it should be clear that the conscientious engagement of technology requires technical knowledge, and thus the church would benefit enormously from conversations with those who are involved in the development of new technologies. These conversations are especially important if the church is to become an incubator for the development of further tactics that can inspire transformative encounters with technology.

Bibliography

Abbate, Janet. *Inventing the Internet*. Cambridge, MA: MIT Press, 1999.
Ableman, Michael. *Fields of Plenty*. San Francisco: Chronicle, 2005.
Angus, Ian, editor. *Athens and Jerusalem: George Grant's Theology, Philosophy, and Politics*. Toronto: University of Toronto Press, 2006.
Archbishop Renato Raffaele Martino. Address to the Ministerial Conference on Science and Technology in Agriculture, Sacramento, California, June 23–25, 2003. Online: http://www.vatican.va/roman_curia/secretariat_state/2003/documents/rc_seg-st_20030625_gmo-martino_en.html.
Arendt, Hannah. *The Human Condition*. Chicago: University of Chicago Press, 1958.
Athanasiadis, Harris. *George Grant and the Theology of the Cross: The Christian Foundations of His Thought*. Toronto: University of Toronto Press, 2001.
Auletta, Ken. *Googled: The End of the World as We Know It*. New York: Penguin, 2009.
Barbour, Ian. *Ethics in an Age of Technology: The Gifford Lectures 1989–1991*. Vol. 2. San Francisco: HarperCollins, 1993.
Bass, Dorothy C. *Receiving the Day: Christian Practices for Opening the Gift of Time*. San Francisco: Jossey-Bass, 2001.
Bass, Dorothy C., editor. *On Our Way: Christian Practices for Living a Whole Life*. Nashville: Upper Room, 2010.
———. *Practicing Our Faith: A Way of Life for a Searching People*. San Francisco: Jossey-Bass, 1997.
Baum, Gregory. "Structures of Sin." In *The Logic of Solidarity: Commentaries on Pope John Paul II's Encyclical on Social Concern*, edited by Gregory Baum and Robert Ellsberg, 110–26. Maryknoll, NY: Orbis, 1989.
Bender, Harold S. "The Anabaptist Vision." *Mennonite Quarterly Review* 18/2 (1944) 67–88.
Benz, Ernst. *Evolution and Christian Hope: Man's Concept of the Future from the Early Fathers to Teilhard de Chardin*. Translated by Heinz G. Frank. Garden City, NY: Doubleday, 1966.
Berkhof, Hendrikus. *Christ and the Powers*. Translated by John Howard Yoder. Scottdale, PA: Herald, 1977.
Berners-Lee, Tim. *Weaving the Web: The Original Design and Ultimate Destiny of the World Wide Web by Its Inventor*. San Francisco: HarperSanFrancisco, 1999.
Berry, Wendell. *The Unsettling of America: Culture and Agriculture*. San Francisco: Sierra Club, 1977.

Billington, David P. *Robert Maillart's Bridges: The Art of Engineering.* Princeton: Princeton University Press, 1979.

Boers, Arthur Paul. *Living Into Focus: Changing What Matters In an Age of Distractions.* Grand Rapids: Brazos, 2012.

———. *The Way Is Made By Walking: A Pilgrimage Along the Camino de Santiago.* Downers Grove, IL: IVP, 2007.

Borgmann, Albert. "Christianity and the Cultural Center of Gravity." *Listening: Journal of Religion and Culture* 18 (1983) 93–102.

———. "Contingency and Grace in an Age of Science and Technology." *Theology Today* 59/1 (2002) 6–20.

———. "Everyday Fortitude: Beyond Heroism." *Christian Century* 118/31 (2001) 16–21.

———. *Holding On to Reality: The Nature of Information at the Turn of the Millennium.* Chicago: University of Chicago Press, 1999.

———. "Information and Education at the Turn of the Century." *Bridges* 5 (1998) 133–53.

———. "The Invisibility of Contemporary Culture." *Revue Internationale de Philosophie* 41 (1987) 234–49.

———. "Is the Internet the Solution to the Problem of Community?" In *Community in the Digital Age: Philosophy and Practice*, edited by Andrew Feenberg and Darin Barney, 53–68. Lanham, MD: Rowman & Littlefield, 2004.

———. "Liberty, Festivity, and Poverty: Harvey Cox on Christianity and Technology." *Philosophy Today* 30/3 (1986) 179–90.

———. "The Moral Significance of the Material Culture." *Inquiry: An Interdisciplinary Journal of Philosophy* 35/3–4 (1992) 291–300.]

———. *Power Failure: Christianity in the Culture of Technology.* Grand Rapids: Brazos, 2003.

———. "Prospects for the Theology of Technology." In *Theology and Technology: Essays in Christian Analysis and Exegesis*, edited by Carl Mitcham and Jim Grote, 305–22. Lanham, MD: University Press of America, 1984.

———. *Real American Ethics: Taking Responsibility for Our Country.* Chicago: University of Chicago Press, 2006.

———. *Technology and the Character of Contemporary Life: A Philosophical Inquiry.* Chicago: University of Chicago Press, 1984.

———. "Technology and Trust." *The Bible in TransMission* 8/2 (2004) 16–19.

———. "Theory, Practice, Reality." *Inquiry: An Interdisciplinary Journal of Philosophy* 38/1–2 (1995) 143–56.

Bowman, Carl D. "Emerging Biotechnologies: A Historical Perspective." In Miller et al., *Viewing New Creations with Anabaptist Eyes*, 171–74.

Brasher, Brenda E. *Give Me That Online Religion.* San Francisco: Jossey-Bass, 2001.

Brende, Eric. *Better Off: Flipping the Switch on Technology.* New York: HarperCollins, 2004.

———. "Technology Amish Style." *Technology Review* 99/2 (1996) 26–33.

Brenneman, Bob. "Embodied Forgiveness: Yoder and the (Body) Politics of Footwashing." *Mennonite Quarterly Review* 83/1 (2009) 7–28.

Brock, Brian. *Christian Ethics in a Technological Age.* Grand Rapids: Eerdmans, 2010.

Brooke, John Hedley. "Detracting from Divine Power? Religious Belief and the Appraisal of New Technologies." In *Re-ordering Nature: Theology, Society and the*

New Genetics, edited by Celia Deane-Drummond and Branislaw Szerszynski, 43–64. New York: T. & T. Clark, 2003.

Brottman, Mikita, editor. *Car Crash Culture*. New York: Palgrave, 2002.

Brunk, Conrad G. "The Biotechnology Vision: Insights from Anabaptist Values." In *Viewing New Creations with Anabaptist Eyes: Ethics of Biotechnology*, edited by Roman J. Miller et al., 106–21. Telford, PA: Cascadia, 2005.

———. "Ethical Values, the Technological Mind, and the Problem of International Peace and Security." *Conrad Grebel Review* 9/3 (1991) 293–307.

———. "Professionalism and Responsibility in the Technological Society." *Conrad Grebel Review* 3/2 (1985) 133–53.

———. "Religion, Risk, and the Technological Society." In *The Twenty-First Century Confronts Its Gods: Globalization, Technology, and War*, edited by David J. Hawkin, 45–58. Albany: State University of New York Press, 2004.

———. Review of *For the Nations* by John Howard Yoder, *Conrad Grebel Review* 16/2 (1998) 128–31.

Bucciarelli, Louis. *Designing Engineers*. Cambridge, MA: MIT Press, 1994.

———. *Engineering Philosophy*. Amsterdam: Delft University Press, 2003.

Bury, J. B. *The Idea of Progress: An Inquiry Into Its Origin and Growth*. 1920. Reprint, with an introduction by Charles A. Beard, London: Macmillan, 1932.

Cahalan, Kathleen. "Technology and Temperance." *Chicago Studies* 42/1 (2002) 26–35.

Cahill, Lisa Sowle. *Bioethics and the Common Good*. Milwaukee: Marquette University Press, 2004.

———. "Genetic Patents and Just Access." Paper presented at the Society of Christian Ethics Annual Meeting, Dallas, TX, January 5, 2007.

———. *Theological Bioethics: Participation, Justice, and Change*. Washington, DC: Georgetown University Press, 2005.

Caird, G. B. *Principalities and Powers: A Study in Pauline Theology*. 1956. Reprint, Eugene, OR: Wipf & Stock, 2003.

Caldecott, Stratford. "New Sins: Technology and Catholic Social Teaching." *Communio: International Catholic Review* 28/3 (2001) 488–504.

Campbell, Heidi. *Exploring Religious Community Online: We are One in the Network*. New York: Lang, 2005.

Carpenter, Novella. *Farm City: The Education of an Urban Gardener*. New York: Penguin, 2009.

Carr, Nicholas. *The Shallows: What the Internet is Doing to Our Brains*. New York: Norton, 2010.

Carter, Craig A. *The Politics of the Cross: The Theology and Social Ethics of John Howard Yoder*. Grand Rapids: Brazos, 2001.

Cartwright, Michael G. *Practices, Politics, and Performance: Toward a Communal Hermeneutic for Christian Ethics*. Eugene, OR: Wipf & Stock, 2006.

———. "Sharing the House of God: Learning to Read Scripture with Anabaptists," *Mennonite Quarterly Review* 74/4 (2000) 593–621.

Cassirer, Ernst. *The Philosophy of the Enlightenment*. Translated by Fritz C. A. Koelln and James P. Pettegrove. Princeton: Princeton University Press, 1951.

Catholic Bishops of South Africa. "Genetically Modified Food: The Impending Disaster." November 14, 2001. Online: http://www.mindfully.org/GE/GE3/Catholic-Bishops-Statement14nov01.htm.

Cavalier-Smith, T., editor. *The Evolution of Genome Size*. New York: John Wiley, 1985.

Cavanaugh, William T. *Being Consumed: Economics and Christian Desire*. Grand Rapids: Eerdmans, 2008.

Certeau, Michel, de. *The Practice of Everyday Life*. Translated by Steven Rendall. Berkeley: University of California Press, 1984.

Christian, William. *George Grant: A Biography*. Toronto: University of Toronto Press, 1993.

Clendenin, Daniel B. *Theological Method in Jacques Ellul*. Landham, MD: University Press of America, 1987.

Cobb, Jennifer. *Cybergrace: The Search for God in the Digital World*. New York: Crown, 1998.

Coles, Romand. "Gentled Into Being." In *Christianity, Democracy, and the Radical Ordinary: Conversations Between a Radical Democrat and a Christian*, by Stanley Hauerwas and Romand Coles, 208–27. Eugene, OR: Cascade, 2008.

———. "The Wild Patience of John Howard Yoder: 'Outsiders' and the 'Otherness of the Church.'" *Modern Theology* 18/3 (2002) 305–31.

Cole-Turner, Ronald. "Toward a Theology for the Age of Biotechnology." Chapter 11 in *Beyond Cloning: Religion and the Remaking of Humanity*, edited by Ronald Cole-Turner, 137–50. Harrisburg, PA: Trinity Press International, 2001.

Collier-Freed, Anne Marie. "Building a Case for the Communicability of Christian Experience in 'Ordinary' Workplaces: George Lindbeck, Nicholas Lash, and John Howard Yoder as they Engage Religion and Experience from Cultural-Linguistic Perspectives." PhD diss., Fuller Theological Seminary, 2000.

Comstock, Gary L. *Vexing Nature? On the Ethical Case Against Agricultural Biotechnology*. Boston: Kluwer Academic, 2000.

Conover, Ted. *The Routes of Man: How Roads Are Changing the World and the Way We Live Today*. New York: Knopf, 2010.

Consolmagno, Guy. *God's Mechanics: How Scientists and Engineers Make Sense of Religion*. Jossey-Bass, 2007.

Crawford, Matthew B. *Shop Class as Soulcraft: An Inquiry into the Value of Work*. New York: Penguin, 2009.

Crenshaw, Kimberle. "Mapping the Margins: Intersectionality, Identity Politics, and Violence Against Women of Color." *Stanford Law Review* 43 (1991) 1241–99.

Curran, Charles E. "The Catholic Moral Tradition in Bioethics." In *The Story of Bioethics: From Seminal Works to Contemporary Explorations*, edited by Jennifer K. Walter and Eran P. Klein, 113–30. Washington, DC: Georgetown University Press, 2003.

Davis, Arthur, editor. *George Grant and the Subversion of Modernity: Art, Philosophy, Politics, Religion and Education*. Toronto: University of Toronto Press, 1996.

Davis, Michael. *Thinking Like an Engineer: Studies in the Ethics of a Profession*. New York: Oxford University Press, 1998.

Dawn, Marva J. "The Biblical Concept of 'the Principalities and Powers': John Yoder Points to Jacques Ellul." In *The Wisdom of the Cross: Essays in Honor of John Howard Yoder*, edited by Stanley Hauerwas et al., 168–86. Grand Rapids: Eerdmans, 1999.

———. "The Concept of the 'The Principalities and Powers' in the Works of Jacques Ellul." PhD diss., University of Notre Dame, 1992.

———. "Introduction." In *Sources and Trajectories: Eight Early Articles by Jacques Ellul That Set the Stage*, by Jacques Ellul, translated and edited by Marva J. Dawn, 1–9. Grand Rapids: Eerdmans, 1997.

———. *Powers, Weakness, and the Tabernacling of God*. Grand Rapids: Eerdmans, 2001.

———. *The Sense of the Call: A Sabbath Way of Life for Those Who Serve God, the Church, and the World*. Grand Rapids: Eerdmans, 2006.

———. *Unfettered Hope: A Call to Faithful Living in an Affluent Society*. Louisville: Westminster John Knox, 2003.

Deane-Drummond, Celia. *Genetics and Christian Ethics*. Cambridge: Cambridge University Press, 2006.

———. *Theology and Biotechnology: Implications for a New Science*. Washington, DC: Chapman, 1997.

Deane-Drummond, Celia, and Bronislaw Szerszynski, editors. *Re-ordering Nature: Theology, Society and the New Genetics*. New York: T. & T. Clark, 2003.

Degregori, Thomas R. "Genetically Modified Foods." In *Encyclopedia of Science, Technology, and Ethics*, edited by Carl Mitcham, 2:836–38. Detroit: MacMillan Reference USA, 2005

De Vries, George. "Lessons From an Alternative Culture: The Old Order Amish." *Christian Scholar's Review* 10/3 (1981) 218–28.

Dintamen, Stephen. "The Spiritual Poverty of the Anabaptist Vision." *Conrad Grebel Review* 10/2 (1992) 205–8.

Drees, Willem. "'Playing God? Yes!' Religion in the Light of Technology." *Zygon* 37/3 (2002) 643–54.

———. "Religion in an Age of Technology." *Zygon* 37/3 (2002) 597–604.

Dueck, Irma Fast. "The Performance of Worship and the Ordering of Our Lives: Liturgy and Ethics in the Mennonite Tradition." *Mennonite Quarterly Review* 79/1 (2005) 51–68.

———. "A Critical Examination of Mennonite Worship and Ethics: A Praxis Approach." ThD diss., Emmanuel College of Victoria University, 2006.

Dunn, James A., Jr. *Driving Forces: The Automobile, Its Enemies, and the Politics of Mobility*. Washington, DC: Brookings Institution Press, 1998.

Durbin, Paul T. "Aquinas, Art as an Intellectual Virtue, and Technology." *The New Scholasticism* 55/4 (1981) 265–80.

———. "Thomism and Technology: Natural Law Theory and the Problems of a Technological Society." *Theology and Technology: Essays in Christian Analysis and Exegesis*, edited by Carl Mitcham and Jim Grote, 209–25. Lanham, MD: University Press of America, 1984.

Dykstra, Craig. *Growing in the Life of Faith: Education and Christian Practices*. Louisville: Geneva, 1999.

———. "Reconceiving Practice in Theological Inquiry and Education." In *Virtues and Practices in the Christian Tradition: Christian Ethics after MacIntyre*, edited by Nancy Murphy et al., 161–82. Harrisburg, PA: Trinity, 1997.

Dyson, Freeman. *The Sun, the Genome, and the Internet: Tools of Scientific Revolutions*. New York: Oxford University Press, 1999.

Eller, Vernard. *The Simple Life*. Grand Rapids: Eerdmans, 1973.

Ellul, Jacques. *Anarchy and Christianity*. Translated by Geoffrey W. Bromily. Grand Rapids: Eerdmans, 1988.

———. *The Ethics of Freedom*. Translated by Geoffrey W. Bromiley. Grand Rapids: Eerdmans, 1976.

———. *In Season, Out of Season: An Introduction to the Thought of Jacques Ellul*. Based on interviews by Madeleine Garrigou-Lagrange, translated by Lani K. Niles. San Francisco: Harper & Row, 1982.
———. Letter to John Howard Yoder, May 5, 1979.
———. *Money and Power*. Translated by LaVonne Neff. Downers Grove, IL: InterVarsity, 1984.
———. *Perspectives on Our Age: Jacques Ellul Speaks on His Life and Work*. Edited by William H. Vanderburg. Translated by Joachim Neugroschel. New York: Seabury, 1981.
———. *The Presence of the Kingdom*. Translated by Olive Wyon, introduction by Daniel B. Clendenin. 2nd ed. Colorado Springs: Helmers & Howard, 1989.
———. *Sources and Trajectories: Eight Early Articles by Jacques Ellul That Set the Stage*. Translated and edited by Marva J. Dawn. Grand Rapids: Eerdmans, 1997.
———. *The Technological Bluff*. Translated by Geoffrey W. Bromiley. Grand Rapids: Eerdmans, 1990.
———. *The Technological Society*. Translated by John Wilkinson, introduction by Robert K. Merton. New York: Vintage, 1964.
———. *The Technological System*. Translated by Joachim Neugroschel. New York: Continuum, 1980.
———. "Technology and the Gospel." *International Review of Mission* 66/262 (1977) 109–17.
Epp, Aaron. "Would Jesus drive . . . or ride?" *Canadian Mennonite* 11/2 (2007) 18.
Fasching, Darrell J. "The Dialectic of Apocalypse and Utopia in the Theological Ethics of Jacques Ellul." In *Technology and Religion: Research in Philosophy and Technology*, edited by Frederick Ferré, 10:149–65. Greenwich, CT: JAI, 1990.
Feenberg, Andrew. *Critical Theory of Technology*. New York: Oxford University Press, 1991.
Feenberg, Andrew, and Maria Bakardjieva. "Consumers or Citizens? The Online Community Debate." In *Community in the Digital Age: Philosophy and Practice*, edited by Andrew Feenberg and Darin Barney, 1–30. Lanham, MD: Rowman & Littlefield, 2004
Feenberg, Andrew and Darin Barney, editors. *Community in the Digital Age: Philosophy and Practice*. Lanham, MD: Rowman & Littlefield, 2004.
Ferguson, Eugene S. *Engineering and the Mind's Eye*. Cambridge, MA: MIT Press, 1992.
Ferré, Frederick. *Philosophy of Technology*. 2nd ed. Athens: University of Georgia Press, 1995.
Ferré, Frederick, editor. *Technology and Religion: Research in Philosophy and Technology*. Volume 10. Greenwich, CT: JAI, 1990.
Finch, Christopher. *Highways to Heaven: The AUTO Biography of America*. New York: HarperCollins, 1992.
Finger, Thomas N. "Did Yoder Reduce Theology to Ethics?" In *A Mind Patient and Untamed: Assessing John Howard Yoder's Contributions to Theology, Ethics, and Peacemaking*, edited by Ben C. Ollenburger and Gayle Gerber Koontz, 318–39. Telford, PA: Cascadia, 2004.
Fish, Stanley. *Is There a Text in This Class? The Authority of Interpretive Communities*. Cambridge: Harvard University Press, 1980.
———. *The Trouble with Principle*. Cambridge, MA: Harvard University Press, 1999.
Flink, James J. *The Automobile Age*. Cambridge, MA: MIT Press, 1990.

Florman, Samuel. *The Existential Pleasures of Engineering*. 2nd ed. New York: St. Martin's Griffin, 1996.
———. "Subsumed by Science?" *Technology Review* 100/3 (1997) 59.
Franklin, Ursula. *The Real World of Technology*. Toronto: CBC, 1990.
Fraser, Norman. *The Net Commandments: How to be a Righteous Nerd*. Leicester, UK: InterVarsity, 2002.
Freeman, John. *The Tyranny of E-mail: The Four-thousand Journey to your Inbox*. New York: Scribner, 2009.
Friesen, Duane K. *Artists, Citizens, Philosophers: Seeking the Peace of the City*. Scottdale, PA: Herald, 2000.
Friesen, Duane K., and Gerald W. Schlabach, editors. *At Peace And Unafraid: Public Order, Security, And the Wisdom of the Cross*. Scottdale, PA: Herald, 2005.
Gaillardetz, Richard R. *Transforming Our Days: Spirituality, Community and Liturgy in a Technological Culture*. New York: Crossroad, 2000.
Galbraith, John Kenneth. *The New Industrial State*. London: Deutsch, 1972.
Gardner, Christine J. "Tangled in the Worst of the Web." *Christianity Today* 45/4 (2001) 42–49.
Gaud, William S. "The Green Revolution: Accomplishments and Apprehensions." Address to the address to the Society for International Development, March 8, 1968. Online: http://www.agbioworld.org/biotech-info/topics/borlaug/borlaug-green.html.
Gay, Peter. *The Enlightenment, an Interpretation*. New York: Knopf, 1966.
George, Susan. *Religion and Technology in the 21st Century: Faith in the E-world*. Hershey, PA: Information Science, 2006.
Gies, Frances and Joseph. *Cathedral, Forge, and Waterwheel: Technology and Invention in the Middle Ages*. New York: HarperCollins, 1994.
Gill, David W. *Doing Right: Practicing Ethical Principles*. Downers Grove, IL: InterVarsity, 2004.
———. "Interview with Jacques Ellul." *Radix* 15/4 (1984) 4–7, 28.
———. "Jacques Ellul: Answers from a Man who asks Hard Questions." *Christianity Today* 28/7 (1984) 16–21.
———. *The Word of God in the Ethics of Jacques Ellul*. ATLA Monograph 20. Metuchen, NJ: ATLA and Scarecrow, 1984.
Gimpel, Jean. *The Medieval Machine: The Industrial Revolution of the Middle Ages*. 2nd ed. Aldershot, UK: Wildwood House, 1988.
Gingerich, Ray, and Ted Grimsrud, editors. *Transforming the Powers: Peace, Justice, and the Domination System*. Minneapolis: Fortress, 2006.
Gish, Arthur G. *Beyond the Rat Race*. Scottdale, PA: Herald, 1973.
Goetz, Thomas. "Open Source Everywhere." *Wired* 11/11 (2003) 158, 166.
Goodenough, Ursula. "Reflections on Science and Technology." *Zygon* 35/1 (2000) 5–12.
Gore, Al. *The Assault on Reason*. New York: Penguin, 2007.
Graham, Mark. "Catholic Moral Theology, Technology, and the Ethic of Use: Starting a New Conversation." Paper presented at the Society of Christian Ethics Annual Meeting, Dallas, TX, January 5, 2007.
Grant, George. "The Computer Does Not Impose on Us the Ways It Should Be Used." In *Beyond Industrial Growth*, edited by Abraham Rotstein, 117–31. Toronto: University of Toronto Press, 1976.

———. "Conversation: Intellectual Background." In *George Grant in Process: Essays and Conversations*, edited by Larry Schmidt, 61–67. Toronto: House of Anansi, 1978.

———. *The George Grant Reader*. Edited by William Christian and Sheila Grant. Toronto: University of Toronto Press, 1998.

———. *Technology and Empire: Perspectives on North America*. Toronto: House of Anansi, 1969.

———. *Time as History*. Toronto: CBC, 1969.

Groothuis, Douglas. *The Soul in Cyberspace*. Grand Rapids: Baker, 1997.

Gustafson, James M. *Intersections: Science, Theology, and Ethics*. Cleveland: Pilgrim, 1996.

Hall, Douglas John. *Thinking the Faith: Christian Theology in a North American Context*. Minneapolis: Fortress, 1989.

Halweil, Brian. "Still No Free Lunch: Nutrient Levels in U.S. Food Supply Eroded by Pursuit of High Yields." Critical Issue Report prepared for the Organic Center, September, 2007. Online: http://www.organic-center.org/reportfiles/Yield_Nutrient_Density_Final.pdf.

Harris, Nancy, editor. *Genetically Engineered Foods*. San Diego: Greenhaven, 2004.

Hauerwas, Stanley. *Performing the Faith: Bonhoeffer and the Practice of Nonviolence*. Grand Rapids: Brazos, 2004.

———. Review of *After Virtue*, by Alasdair MacIntyre. *The Thomist* 46/2 (1982) 313–21.

———. *The State of the University: Academic Knowledges and the Knowledge of God*. New York: Routledge, 2007.

———. *Suffering Presence: Theological Reflections on Medicine, the Mentally Handicapped, and the Church*. Notre Dame, IN: University of Notre Dame Press, 1986.

———. *Unleashing the Scripture: Freeing the Bible from Captivity to America*. Nashville: Abingdon, 1993.

———. "When the Politics of Jesus Makes a Difference." *Christian Century* 110/28 (1993) 982–87.

Hauerwas, Stanley, and Chris K. Huebner. "History, Theory, and Anabaptism: A Conversation on Theology after John Howard Yoder." In *The Wisdom of the Cross: Essays in Honor of John Howard Yoder*, edited by Stanley Hauerwas et al., 391–408. Grand Rapids: Eerdmans, 1999.

Hauerwas, Stanley, et al., editors. *The Wisdom of the Cross: Essays in Honor of John Howard Yoder*. Grand Rapids: Eerdmans, 1999.

Hauerwas, Stanley, and Samuel Wells, editors. *The Blackwell Companion to Christian Ethics*. Malden, MA: Blackwell, 2004.

Hawkin, David J., editor. *The Twenty-First Century Confronts Its Gods: Globalization, Technology, and War*. Albany: State University of New York Press, 2004.

Hazard, Paul. *The European Mind, 1680–1715*. Translated by J. Lewis May. New York: World, 1963.

Hefner, Philip. *The Human Factor: Evolution, Culture, and Religion*. Minneapolis: Fortress, 1993.

———. *Technology and Human Becoming*. Minneapolis: Fortress, 2003.

Heidegger, Martin. *The Question Concerning Technology and Other Essays*. Translated and introduced by William Lovitt. New York: Harper & Row, 1977.

Heilke, Thomas. "Yoder's Idea of Constantinianism: An Analytical Framework Toward Conversation." In *A Mind Patient and Untamed: Assessing John Howard Yoder's Contributions to Theology, Ethics, and Peacemaking*, edited by Ben C. Ollenburger and Gayle Gerber Koontz, 89–125. Telford, PA: Cascadia, 2004.

Henig, Robin Marantz. *The Monk in the Garden*. New York: Houghton Mifflin, 2000.

Herzfeld, Noreen. *Technology and Religion: Remaining Human in a Co-created World*. West Conshohocken, PA: Templeton, 2009.

Hickman, Larry A. *John Dewey's Pragmatic Technology*. Bloomington: Indiana University Press, 1990.

Higgs, Eric, et al., editors. *Technology and the Good Life?* Chicago: University of Chicago Press, 2000.

Himanen, Pekka. *The Hacker Ethic and the Spirit of the Information Age*. New York: Random House, 2001.

Hipps, Shane A. *The Hidden Power of Electronic Culture: How Media Shapes Faith, the Gospel, and Church*. Grand Rapids: Zondervan, 2005.

Højsgaard, Morten T. and Margit Warburg, editors. *Religion and Cyberspace*. New York: Routledge, 2005.

Holznagel, Fritz. "Of Horses, Buggies, and the Web." *Wired* online edition, April 10, 2000. Online: http://www.wired.com/techbiz/media/news/2000/04/35560.

Homer-Dixon, Thomas. *The Ingenuity Gap*. Toronto: Knopf, 2000.

Honoré, Carl. *In Praise of Slowness: How a Worldwide Movement is Challenging the Cult of Speed*. San Francisco: HarperSanFrancisco, 2004.

Hopper, David H. *Technology, Theology, and the Idea of Progress*. Louisville: Westminster John Knox, 1991.

Houston, Graham. *Virtual Morality: Christian Ethics in the Computer Age*. Leicester, UK: Apollos, 1998.

Huebner, Chris K. "Bioethics and the Church: Technology, Martyrdom, and the Moral Significance of the Ordinary." *Vision* 4/1 (2003) 74–81.

———. "Patience, Witness, and the Scattered Body of Christ: Yoder and Virilio on Knowledge, Politics, and Speed." In *A Mind Patient and Untamed: Assessing John Howard Yoder's Contributions to Theology, Ethics, and Peacemaking*, edited by Ben C. Ollenburger and Gayle Gerber Koontz, 56–74. Telford, PA: Cascadia, 2004.

———. *A Precarious Peace: Yoderian Explorations on Theology, Knowledge, and Identity*. Scottdale, PA: Herald, 2006.

———. "Unhandling History: Anti-Theory, Ethics, and the Practice of Witness." PhD diss., Duke University, 2002.

Huebner, Harry J. "The Christian Life as Gift and Patience: Why Yoder Has Trouble with Method." In *A Mind Patient and Untamed: Assessing John Howard Yoder's Contributions to Theology, Ethics, and Peacemaking*, edited by Ben C. Ollenburger and Gayle Gerber Koontz, 23–38. Telford, PA: Cascadia, 2004.

———. *Echoes of the Word: Theological Ethics and Rhetorical Practice*. Kitchener, ON: Pandora, 2005.

Hughes, Mark. *Speed Addicts: Grand Prix Racing*. London: CollinsWillow, 2005.

Hughes, Thomas P. *Human-Built World: How to Think About Technology and Culture*. Chicago: University of Chicago Press, 2004.

Hütter, Reinhard. *Suffering Divine Things: Theology as Church Practice*. Translated by Doug Stott. Grand Rapids: Eerdmans, 2000.

IAASTD. "Executive Summary of the Synthesis Report of the International Assessment of Agricultural Knowledge, Science and Technology for Development (IAASTD)." Johannesburg, South Africa, April 7–11, 2008. Online: http://www.unep.org/dewa/agassessment/reports/IAASTD/EN/Agriculture%20at%20a%20Crossroads_Synthesis%20Report%20%28English%29.pdf.

Ihde, Don. *Instrumental Realism: The Interface Between Philosophy of Science and Philosophy of Technology*. Bloomington: Indiana University Press, 1991.

———. *Philosophy of Technology: An Introduction*. New York: Paragon House, 1993.

———. *Technology and the Lifeworld: From Garden to Earth*. Bloomington: Indiana University Press, 1990.

Illich, Ivan. *Tools for Conviviality*. New York: Harper & Row, 1973.

Jacobsen, Eric O. *Sidewalks in the Kingdom: New Urbanism and the Christian Faith*. Grand Rapids: Brazos, 2003.

Jardine, Murray. *The Making and Unmaking of Technological Society: How Christianity Can Save Modernity from Itself*. Grand Rapids: Brazos, 2004.

Jewel, John P. *Wired for Ministry: How the Internet, Visual Media, and Other New Technologies Can Serve Your Church*. Grand Rapids: Brazos, 2003.

Johnson, Deborah G., and Thomas M. Powers. "Ethics and Technology: A Program for Future Research." In *Encyclopedia of Science, Technology, and Ethics*, edited by Carl Mitcham, 1:xxvii-xxxv. Detroit: MacMillan Reference USA, 2005

Jonas, Hans. *The Imperative of Responsibility: In Search of an Ethics for the Technological Age*. Chicago: University of Chicago Press, 1984.

Kallenberg, Brad J. *Ethics as Grammar: Changing the Postmodern Subject*. Notre Dame: University of Notre Dame Press, 2001.

———. *God and Gadgets: Following Jesus in a Technological World*. Eugene, OR: Cascade, 2011.

———. "Positioning MacIntyre within Christian Ethics." In *Virtues and Practices in the Christian Tradition: Christian Ethics after MacIntyre*, edited by Nancey Murphy et al., 45–81. Harrisburg, PA: Trinity, 1997.

Kaufman, Gordon D. *In Face of Mystery: A Constructive Theology*. Cambridge, MA: Harvard University Press, 1993.

———. *Theology for a Nuclear Age*. Philadelphia: Westminster, 1985.

Kay, Jane Holtz. *Asphalt Nation: How the Automobile Took Over America and How We Can Take It Back*. New York: Crown, 1997.

Kelty, Christopher M. *Two Bits: The Cultural Significance of Free Software*. Durham, NC: Duke University Press, 2008.

Kimbrell, Andrew, editor. *Fatal Harvest: The Tragedy of Industrial Agriculture*. Washington, DC: Island, 2002.

Kingsolver, Barbara, with Camille Kingsolver and Steve L. Hopp. *Animal, Vegetable, Miracle: A Year of Food Life*. New York: HarperCollins, 2007.

Klein, Naomi. *No Logo: Taking Aim at the Brand Bullies*. New York: Picador, 1999.

Kline, Stephen. "What is Technology?" *Bulletin of Science, Technology, and Society* 5/3 (1985) 215–18.

Koen, Billy Vaughn. *Discussion of the Method: Conducting the Engineer's Approach to Problem Solving*. Oxford: Oxford University Press, 2003.

Koontz, Ted. "Goshen College not China: Challenges to Mennonite Ethics." In *The Limits of Perfection: A Conversation with J. Lawrence Burkholder*, edited by Rodney

J. Sawatsky and Scott Holland, 110–14. Waterloo, ON: Institute of Anabaptist-Mennonite Studies, 1993.

Korten, David C. *When Corporations Rule the World*. West Hartford, CT: Kumarian, 1995.

Koselleck, Reinhard. *Futures Past: On the Semantics of Historical Time*. Translated by Keith Tribe. Cambridge, MA: MIT Press, 1985.

Kotva, Joseph J., Jr. *The Christian Case for Virtue Ethics*. Washington, DC: Georgetown University Press, 1996.

Kraybill, Donald B. "Plain Reservations: Amish and Mennonite Views of Media and Computers." *Journal of Mass Media Ethics* 13/2 (1998) 99–110.

———. *The Riddle of Amish Culture*. 2nd ed. Baltimore, MD: Johns Hopkins University Press, 2001.

Kraybill, Donald B., and Marc C. Olshan, editors. *The Amish Struggle With Modernity*. Hanover, NH: University Press of New England, 1994.

Kroes, Peter, and Anthonie Meijers, editors. *The Empirical Turn in the Philosophy of Technology: Research in Philosophy and Technology*. Vol. 20. New York: JAI, 2000.

Kropf, Marlene. "Singing as Sacrament: An Exploration of the Role of Hymn Singing in Mennonite Spiritual Formation." DMin thesis, The Graduate Theological Foundation, 1997.

Kropf, Marlene, and Kenneth Nafziger. *Singing: A Mennonite Voice*. Scottdale, PA: Herald, 2001.

Kundera, Milan. *The Book of Laughter and Forgetting*. Translated by Michael Henry Heim. New York: Knopf, 1980.

———. *Slowness*. Translated by Linda Asher. New York: HarperCollins, 1996.

Lambrecht, Bill. *Dinner at the New Gene Café: How Genetic Engineering is Changing What We Eat, How We Live, and the Global Politics of Food*. New York: Dunne, 2001.

Lammers, Stephen E., and Allen Verhey, editors. *On Moral Medicine*. 2nd ed. Grand Rapids: Eerdmans, 1998.

Lasch, Christopher. *The True and Only Heaven: Progress and Its Critics*. New York: Norton, 1991.

Le Goff, Jacques. *Time, Work, and Culture in the Middle Ages*. Translated by Arthur Goldhammer. Chicago: University of Chicago Press, 1980.

Levinson, Paul. "The Amish Get Wired. The Amish?" *Wired* 1/6 (1993) 124.

Liang, G.H., and D.Z. Skinner, editors. *Genetically Modified Crops: Their Development, Uses, and Risks*. New York: Food Products, 2004.

Lind, Mary Beth, and Cathleen Hockman-Wert. *Simply in Season*. Scottdale, PA: Herald, 2005.

Lindbeck, George A. *The Nature of Doctrine: Religion and Theology in a Postliberal Age*. Philadelphia: Westminster, 1984.

Lomasky, Loren E. "Autonomy and Automobility." *Independent Review* 2/1 (1997) 5–29.

Lonergan, Bernard. *Method in Theology*. Minneapolis: Seabury, 1979.

Long, D. Stephen. *Divine Economy: Theology and the Market*. Radical Orthodoxy. New York: Routledge, 2000.

———. *John Wesley's Moral Theology: The Quest for God and Goodness*. Nashville: Kingswood, 2005.

Long, D. Stephen, and Nancy Ruth Fox. *Calculated Futures: Theology, Ethics, and Economics*. Waco: Baylor University Press, 2007.

Long, Tony. "Dark Underbelly of Technology." *Wired* online edition, October 13, 2005. Online:http://www.wired.com/culture/lifestyle/commentary/theluddite/2005/10/68606.

Lurquin, Paul F. *High Tech Harvest: Understanding Genetically Modified Food Plants*. Boulder, CO: Westview, 2002.

Lysaught, M. Therese. "From Clinic to Congregation: Religious Communities and Genetic Medicine." In *On Moral Medicine*, 2nd ed., edited by Stephen E. Lammers and Allen Verhey, 547–61. Grand Rapids: Eerdmans, 1998

———. "Patient Suffering and the Anointing of the Sick." In *On Moral Medicine*, 2nd ed., edited by Stephen E. Lammers and Allen Verhey, 356–64. Grand Rapids: Eerdmans, 1998.

MacIntyre, Alasdair C. *After Virtue: A Study in Moral Theory*. 2nd ed. Notre Dame, IN: University of Notre Dame Press, 1984.

Manjoo, Farhad. *True Enough: Learning to Live in a Post-Fact Society*. New York: Wiley, 2008.

Martens, Paul. *The Heterodox Yoder*. Eugene, OR: Cascade, 2012.

———. "The Problematic Development of the Sacraments in the Thought of John Howard Yoder." *The Conrad Grebel Review* 24/3 (2006) 65–77.

———. "Universal History and a Not-Particularly-Christian Particularity: Jeremiah and John Howard Yoder's Social Gospel." In *Power and Politics: Engaging the Work of John Howard Yoder*, edited by Anthony Siegrist and Jeremy Bergen, 131–46. Scottdale, PA: Herald, 2009.

Martineau, Belinda. *First Fruit: The Creation of the Flavr Savr Tomato and the Birth of Genetically Engineered Food*. New York: McGraw-Hill, 2001.

Marx, Leo and Bruce Mazlish, eds. *Progress: Fact or Illusion?* Ann Arbor: University of Michigan Press, 1996.

May, Henry. *The Enlightenment in America*. New York: Oxford University Press, 1976.

McDonough, William, and Michael Braungart. *Cradle to Cradle: Remaking the Way We Make Things*. New York: North Point, 2002.

McGinn, Robert. "What is Technology?" In *Research in Philosophy and Technology*, edited by Carl Mitcham, Frederick Ferré, Walter C. Zimmerli, and Leonard J. Waks, 1:179–97. Greenwich, CT: JAI, 1978.

McKenny, Gerald P. *To Relieve the Human Condition: Bioethics, Technology, and the Body*. Albany: State University of New York Press, 1997.

McKibben, Bill. *Deep Economy: The Wealth of Communities and the Durable Future*. New York: Times, 2007.

McKim, Robert, and Jeff McMahan. *The Morality of Nationalism*. New York: Oxford University Press, 1997.

McLuhan, Marshall. *Understanding Media: The Extensions of Man*. New York: New American Library, 1964.

Meaton, Julia and David Morrice. "The Ethics and Politics of Private Automobile Use." *Environmental Ethics* 18/1 (1996) 39–54.

Milbank, John. *The Word Made Strange: Theology, Language, Culture*. Challenges in Contemporary Theology. Cambridge, MA: Blackwell, 1997.

Miller, Henry I., and Gregory Conko. *The Frankenfood Myth: How Protest and Politics Threaten the Biotech Revolution*. Westport, CT: Praeger, 2004.

Miller, Keith Graber. "Mennonite Footwashing: Identity Reflections and Altered Meanings." *Worship* 66/2 (1992) 148–70.

Miller, Roman J., et al., editors. *Viewing New Creations with Anabaptist Eyes: Ethics of Biotechnology*. Telford, PA: Cascadia, 2005.

Miller, Samuel. *A Brief Retrospect of the Eighteenth Century*. 2 vols. New York: T. and J. Swords, 1803. Reprint, with an introduction by Roger Fechner, Bristol, England: Thoemmes, 2001.

Miller, Vincent J. *Consuming Religion: Christian Faith and Practice in a Consumer Culture*. New York: Continuum, 2004.

———. "Certeau." In *Handbook of Postmodern Biblical Interpretation*, edited by A. K. M. Adam, 42–48. St. Louis: Chalice, 2000.

Mitcham, Carl. "Questions of Christianity and Technology: A Bibliographic Introduction." *Science, Technology and Society* 14/11 (1979) 1–7.

———. *Thinking Through Technology: The Path Between Engineering and Philosophy*. Chicago: University of Chicago Press, 1994.

Mitcham, Carl, editor. *Encyclopedia of Science, Technology, and Ethics*, 4 volumes. Detroit: MacMillan Reference USA/Thompson Gale, 2005.

Mitcham, Carl, and Jim Grote, editors. *Theology and Technology: Essays in Christian Analysis and Exegesis*. Lanham, MD: University Press of America, 1984.

Mitcham, Carl, and Robert Mackey. "Jacques Ellul and the Technological Society," in *Philosophy Today* 15/2 (1971) 102–21.

Mitcham, Carl, and Robert Mackey, editors. *Philosophy and Technology: Readings in the Philosophical Problems of Technology*. New York: Free, 1983.

Mohan, Robert Paul, ed. *Technology and Christian Culture*. Washington, DC: Catholic University of America Press, 1960.

Molella, Arthur P. "Inventing the History of Invention." *Invention & Technology* 4/1 (1988) 23–30.

Monsma, Stephen V., editor. *Responsible Technology: A Christian Perspective*. Grand Rapids: Eerdmanns, 1986.

Mullaney, Jamie L. *Everyone is NOT Doing It: Abstinence and Personal Identity*. Chicago: University of Chicago Press, 2006.

Mumford, Lewis. *Technics and Civilization*. New York: Harcourt, Brace, 1934.

Murphy, Nancey. "John Howard Yoder's Systematic Defense of Christian Pacifism." In *The Wisdom of the Cross: Essays in Honor of John Howard Yoder*, edited by Stanley Hauerwas et al., 45–68. Grand Rapids: Eerdmans, 1999.

———. *Theology in the Age of Scientific Reasoning*. Ithaca, NY: Cornell University Press, 1990.

Murphy, Nancey, et al., editors. *Virtues and Practices in the Christian Tradition: Christian Ethics after MacIntyre*. Harrisburg, PA: Trinity, 1997.

Nakaya, Andrea C., editor. *Cars in America*. Farmington Hills, MI: Greenhaven, 2006.

Nation, Mark Thiessen. "A Comprehensive Bibliography of the Writings of John Howard Yoder." *Mennonite Quarterly Review* 71/1 (1997) 93–145.

———. "John H. Yoder, Ecumenical Neo-Anabaptist: A Biographical Sketch." In *The Wisdom of the Cross: Essays in Honor of John Howard Yoder*, edited by Stanley Hauerwas et al., 1–23. Grand Rapids: Eerdmans, 1999.

———. *John Howard Yoder: Mennonite Patience, Evangelical Witness, Catholic Convictions*. Grand Rapids: Eerdmans, 2006.

———. "Supplement to 'A Comprehensive Bibliography of the Writings of John Howard Yoder.'" In *The Wisdom of the Cross: Essays in Honor of John Howard Yoder*, edited by Stanley Hauerwas et al., 472–91. Grand Rapids: Eerdmans, 1999.

———. "Theology as Witness: Reflections on Yoder, Fish, and Interpretive Communities." *Faith and Freedom* 5/1–2 (1996) 42–47.

———. "Washing Feet: Preparation for Service." In *The Blackwell Companion to Christian Ethics*, edited by Hauerwas and Wells, 441–54. Malden, MA: Blackwell, 2004.

Negroponte, Nicholas. *Being Digital*. New York: Knopf, 1995.

Newman, Jay. *Religion and Technology: A Study in the Philosophy of Culture*. Westport, CT: Praeger, 1997.

Niebuhr, H. Richard. *Christ and Culture*. New York: Harper & Row, 1951.

Nisbet, Robert. *History of the Idea of Progress*. New York: Basic, 1980.

Noble, David F. *America by Design: Science, Technology, and the Rise of Corporate Capitalism*. New York: Knopf, 1977.

———. *Forces of Production: A Social History of Industrial Automation*. New York: Knopf, 1984.

———. *Progress Without People: In Defense of Luddism*. Chicago: Kerr, 1993.

———. *The Religion of Technology: The Divinity of Man and the Spirit of Invention*. New York: Knopf, 1997.

Nordquist, Joan. *Biotechnology and Our Food: A Bibliography*. Contemporary Social Issues 59. Santa Cruz: Reference & Research Services, 2000.

Nottingham, Stephen. *Eat Your Genes: How Genetically Modified Food is Entering Our Diet*. New York: Zed, 2003.

Ollenburger, Ben C., and Gayle Gerber Koontz, editors. *A Mind Patient and Untamed: Assessing John Howard Yoder's Contributions to Theology, Ethics, and Peacemaking*. Telford, PA: Cascadia, 2004.

O'Donovan, Joan E. *George Grant and the Twilight of Justice*. Toronto: University of Toronto Press, 1984.

O'Donovan, Oliver. *Begotten or Made?* New York: Oxford University Press, 1984.

O'Rourke, P.J. *Driving Like Crazy*. New York: Atlantic Monthly, 2009.

Ovitt, George, Jr. "The Cultural Context of Western Technology: Early Christian Attitudes toward Manual Labor." *Technology and Culture* 27/2 (1986) 477–500.

———. *The Restoration of Perfection: Labor and Technology in Medieval Culture*. New Brunswick, NJ: Rutgers University Press, 1987.

Pacey, Arnold. *The Culture of Technology*. Cambridge, MA: MIT Press, 1983.

———. *The Maze of Ingenuity: Ideas and Idealism in the Development of Technology*. Cambridge, MA: MIT Press, 1976.

———. *Technology in World Civilization: a thousand year history*. Cambridge, MA: MIT Press, 1990.

Palfrey, John, and Urs Gasser. *Born Digital: Understanding the First Generation of Digital Natives*. New York: Basic, 2008.

Parham, Robert Mereman. "An Ethical Analysis of the Christian Social Strategies in the Writings of John C. Bennett, Jacques Ellul, and John Howard Yoder." PhD diss., Baylor University, 1984.

Pattison, George. *Thinking About God in an Age of Technology*. New York: Oxford University Press, 2005.

Pence, Gregory E. *Designer Food: Mutant Harvest or Breadbasket of the World?* Lanham, MD: Rowman & Littlefield, 2002.

Penner, Myron Bradley, and Hunter Barnes, editors. *A New Kind of Conversation: Blogging Toward a Postmodern Faith*. Cumbria, UK: Paternoster Publishing, 2007.

Perry, John. *Food for Thought: Catholic Insights into the Modified Food Debate*. Ottawa, ON: Novalis, 2002.

Petrini. Carlo. *Slow Food: The Case for Taste*. Translated by William McCuaig. New York: Columbia University Press, 2004.

Petroski, Henry. *Invention by Design: How Engineers Get From Thought to Thing*. Cambridge, MA: Harvard University Press, 1996.

Piatt, Christian, and Amy Piatt. *MySpace to Sacred Space: God for a New Generation*. St. Louis: Chalice, 2007.

Pilario, D. F. *Back to the Rough Grounds of Praxis: Exploring Theological Method with Pierre Bourdieu*. Leuven: Leuven University Press, 2005.

Pinches, Charles R. *Theology and Action: After Theory in Christian Ethics*. Grand Rapids: Eerdmans, 2002.

Pineda, Ana Maria. "Hospitality." In *Practicing Our Faith: A Way of Life for a Searching People*, edited by Dorothy Bass, 29–42. San Francisco: Jossey-Bass, 1997.

Pitt, Joseph C. "In Search of a New Prometheus." In *Broad and Narrow Interpretations of Philosophy of Technology*, edited by Paul T. Durbin, 3–15. Philosophy and Technology 7. Boston: Kluwer Academic, 1990.

———. *Thinking About Technology: Foundations of the Philosophy of Technology*. New York: Seven Bridges, 2000.

Pitt, Joseph C., editor. *New Directions in the Philosophy of Technology*. Philosophy and Technology 11. Boston: Kluwer Academic, 1995.

Polak, Paul. *Out of Poverty: What Works When Traditional Approaches Fail*. San Francisco: Berrett-Koehler, 2008.

Pollan, Michael. *In Defense of Food: An Eater's Manifesto*. New York: Penguin, 2008.

———. *The Omnivore's Dilemma: A Natural History of Four Meals*. New York: Penguin, 2006.

Pontifical Council for Justice and Peace. *Compendium of the Social Doctrine of the Church*. Vatican City: Libreria Editrice Vaticana, 2004.

———. Study Seminar: "GMOs: Threat or Hope?" November 10–11, 2003. Online: http://www.vatican.va/roman_curia/pontifical_councils/justpeace/documents/rc_pc_justpeace_doc_20031110_card-martino-ogm_en.html.

Pontifical Council for the Pastoral Care of Migrants and Itinerant People. "Guidelines for the Pastoral Care of the Road." August, 2007. Online: http://www.vatican.va/roman_curia/pontifical_councils/migrants/pom2007_104-suppl/rc_pc_migrants_pom104-suppl_orientamenti-en.html.

Pontifical Council for Social Communications. *Aetatis Novae: Pastoral Instruction on Social Communications on the Twentieth Anniversary of Communion et progressio*. Washington, DC: Unites States Catholic Conference, 1992.

———. "The Church and the Internet: Challenge and Opportunity." *The Pope Speaks* 47/5 (2002) 272–73.

———. "Ethics in Internet." *L'Osservatore Romano* 10 (2002) 4–6.

———. "Ethics in the Media of Social Communications." *The Pope Speaks* 45/6 (2000) 340–55.

———. "Working for Solidarity in a Cyberspace World." *The Pope Speaks* 47/5 (2002) 282–83.

Pope John Paul II. Address to "The Environment and Health" convention, March 24, 1997. *L'Osservatore Romano*, English edition, April 9, 1997, 2.

———. Address at Mercy Maternity Hospital, Melbourne, November 28, 1986. *L'Osservatore Romano*, English edition, December 9, 1986, 13.

———. Address to the National Academy of Sciences, September 21, 1982. *Insegnamenti di Giovanni Paolo II*, 5/3 (1982) 511–15.

———. Address to the Pontifical Academy of the Sciences, October 23, 1982. *Insegnamenti di Giovanni Paolo II*, 5/3 (1982) 889–93.

———. "Encyclical on the Hundredth Anniversary of Rerum Novarum, *Centesimus Annus* (May 1, 1991)." *Acta Apostolicae Sedis* 83 (1991) 793–867.

———. "The Church Must Learn to Cope With the Computer Culture." Statement on World Communications Day, May 27, 1989.

———. "Do Not Be Afraid; Use New Technology to Seek Truth." Apostolic Letter to Those Responsible for Communications. *The Pope Speaks* 50/3 (2005) 184–91.

———. Meeting with scientists and representatives of the United Nations University, Hiroshima, February 25, 1981. *Acta Apostolicae Sedis* 73 (1981) 422.

———. *Redemptoris Missio: On the Permanent Validity of the Church's Missionary Mandate*. Washington, DC: United States Catholic Conference, 1990.

Porter, Richard C. *Economics at the Wheel: The Costs of Cars and Drivers*. San Diego: Academic, 1999.

Post, Robert C. *High Performance: The Culture and Technology of Drag Racing, 1950–1990*. Baltimore: Johns Hopkins University Press, 1994.

Postman, Neil. *Technopoly: The Surrender of Culture to Technology*. New York: Vintage, 1993.

Powers, William. *Hamlet's Blackberry: A Practical Philosophy for Building a Good Life in a Digital Age*. Toronto: Harper, 2011.

Pringle, Peter. *Food, Inc.: Mendel to Monsanto—the Promises and Perils of the Biotech Harvest*. New York: Simon & Schuster, 2003.

Prokes, Mary Timothy. *At the Interface: Theology and Virtual Reality*. Tucson: Fenestra, 2004.

Pullinger, David. *Information Technology and Cyberspace: Extra-connected Living?* Cleveland: Pilgrim, 2001.

Purves, Alan C. *The Web of Text and the Web of God: An Essay on the Third Information Transformation*. New York: Guilford, 1998.

Ramsey, Paul. "Liturgy and Ethics." *Journal of Religious Ethics* 7/2 (1979) 139–72.

Randels, George D, Jr. "Cyberspace and Christian Ethics: The Virtuous and/in/of the Virtual." *Annual of the Society of Christian Ethics* 20 (2000) 165–79.

Rasmussen, Larry L. *Moral Fragments and Moral Community: A Proposal for Church in Society*. Philadelphia: Fortress, 1993.

Reames, Kent. "Histories of Reason and Revelation: With Alasdair MacIntyre and John Howard Yoder into Historicist Theology and Ethics." PhD diss., University of Chicago, 1997.

Reimer, A. James. "'I came not to abolish the law but to fulfill it': A Positive Theology of Law and Civil Institutions." In *A Mind Patient and Untamed: Assessing John Howard Yoder's Contributions to Theology, Ethics, and Peacemaking*, edited by Ben C. Ollenburger and Gayle Gerber Koontz, 245–73. Telford, PA: Cascadia, 2004.

———. "Mennonites, Christ, and Culture: The Yoder Legacy." *Conrad Grebel Review* 16/2 (1998) 5–14.

———. *Mennonites and Classical Theology: Dogmatic Foundations for Christian Ethics*. Kitchener, ON: Pandora, 2001.

———. "The Nature and Possibility of a Mennonite Theology." *Conrad Grebel Review* 1/1 (1983) 33–55.

———. "Theological Orthodoxy and Jewish Christianity: A Personal Tribute to John Howard Yoder." In *The Wisdom of the Cross: Essays in Honor of John Howard Yoder*, edited by Stanley Hauerwas et al., 430–48. Grand Rapids: Eerdmans, 1999.

Reimer, A. James, editor. *The Influence of the Frankfurt School on Contemporary Theology: Critical Theory and the Future of Religion*. Toronto Studies in Theology 64. Lewiston: Mellen, 1992.

Rheingold, Howard. "Look Who's Talking." *Wired* 7/1 (1999) 128–31, 160–63.

———. *Smart Mobs: The Next Social Revolution*. Cambridge, MA: Perseus, 2002.

———. *The Virtual Community: Homesteading on the Electronic Frontier*. Reading, MA: Addison-Wesley, 1993.

———. "You Got the Power." *Wired* 8/8 (2000) 176–84.

Rothschild, Joan, editor. *Machino Ex Dea: Feminist Perspectives on Technology*. New York: Pergamon, 1983.

Roy, Rustum. "Religion/Technology, Not Theology/Science, as the Defining Dichotomy." *Zygon* 37/3 (2002) 667–76.

———. "Scientism and Technology as Religions." *Zygon* 40/4 (2005) 835–44.

Rubin, Jeff. "The Efficiency Paradox." *CIBC World Markets StrategEcon*, November 27, 2007. Online: http://research.cibcwm.com/economic_public/download/snov07.pdf.

Russell, Robert John. "Five Attitudes Toward Nature and Technology from a Christian Perspective." *Theology and Science* 1/2 (2003) 149–59.

Sachs, Wolfgang. *For Love of the Automobile: Looking Back into the History of Our Desires*. Translated by Don Reneau. Berkeley: University of California Press, 1992.

Safranski, Rudiger. *Martin Heidegger: Between Good and Evil*. Translated by Ewald Osers. Cambridge, MA: Harvard University Press, 1998.

Sample, Tex. *The Spectacle of Worship in a Wired World: Electronic Culture and the Gathered People of God*. Nashville: Abingdon, 1998.

Scarce, Rik. *Eco-Warriors: Understanding the Radical Environmental Movement*. Updated ed. Walnut Creek, CA: Left Coast, 2006.

Schlabach, Gerald. "Anthology in Lieu of System: John H. Yoder's Ecumenical Conversations as Systematic Theology." *Mennonite Quarterly Review* 71/2 (1997) 305–9.

———. "Continuity and Sacrament, or Not: Hauerwas, Yoder, and their Deep Difference." *Journal of the Society of Christan Ethics* 27/2 (2007) 171–207.

———. "Deuteronomic or Constantinian: What Is the Most Basic Problem for Christian Social Ethics?" In *The Wisdom of the Cross: Essays in Honor of John Howard Yoder*, edited by Stanley Hauerwas et al., 449–71. Grand Rapids: Eerdmans, 1999.

Schultze, Quentin J. *Habits of the High-Tech Heart: Living Virtuously in the Information Age*. Grand Rapids: Baker Academic, 2002.

Sciadas, George. "Our Lives in Digital Times." Statistics Canada Report, November, 2006. Online: http://www5.statcan.gc.ca/bsolc/olc-cel/olc-cel?catno=56F0004MIE2006014&lang=eng.

Sclove, Richard. *Democracy and Technology*. New York: Guilford, 1995.

Scott, Peter. "Nature, Technology and the Rule of God: (En)countering the Disgracing of Nature." In *Re-ordering Nature: Theology, Society and the New Genetics*, edited by Celia Deane-Drummond and Bronislaw Szerszynski, 275–92. New York: T. & T. Clark, 2003.

———. "Response to Chapter 4—Nature to Order: But Which Nature and Whose Order?" In *Re-ordering Nature: Theology, Society and the New Genetics*, edited by Celia Deane-Drummond and Bronislaw Szerszynski, 107–14. New York: T. & T. Clark, 2003.

Segal, Howard P. *Technological Utopianism in American Culture*. Chicago: University of Chicago Press, 1985.

Shiva, Vandana. *Stolen Harvest: The Hijacking of the Global Food Supply*. Cambridge, MA: South End, 2000.

Shuman, Joel James. *The Body of Compassion: Ethics, Medicine, and the Church*. Boulder, CO: Westview, 1999.

———. *To Live is to Worship: Bioethics and the Body of Christ*. Winnipeg, MB: Canadian Mennonite University, 2007.

Sider, J. Alexander. "Constantinianism Before and After Nicea: Issues in Restitutionist Historiography." In *A Mind Patient and Untamed: Assessing John Howard Yoder's Contributions to Theology, Ethics, and Peacemaking*, edited by Ben C. Ollenburger and Gayle Gerber Koontz, 126–44. Telford, PA: Cascadia, 2004.

———. *To See History Doxologically: History and Holiness in John Howard Yoder's Ecclesiology*. Grand Rapids: Eerdmans, 2011.

Siegrist, Anthony, and Jeremy Bergen, editors. *Power and Politics: Engaging the Work of John Howard Yoder*. Scottdale, PA: Herald, 2009.

Siemens, Mark, editor. *Harvest in the Balance: Food, Justice and Biotechnology*. Akron, PA and Winnipeg, MB: Mennonite Central Committee, Food, Disaster, and Material Resources Department and International Peace Office, 2002.

Sinclair, Bruce, editor. *Technology and the African-American Experience: Needs and Opportunities for Study*. Cambridge, MA: MIT Press, 2004.

Small, Gary, and Gigi Vorgan. *iBrain: Surviving the Technological Alteration of the Modern Mind*. Collins Living, 2008.

Smith, Cyril Stanley. "Art, Technology and Science: Notes on their Historical Interaction." *Technology and Culture* 11 (1970) 493–549.

Smith, Elizabeth Bradford, and Michael Wolfe, eds. *Technology and Resource Use in Medieval Europe: Cathedrals, Mills, and Mines*. Aldershot, UK: Ashgate, 1997.

Smith, James K. A. *Desiring the Kingdom: Worship, Worldview, and Cultural Formation*. Cultural Liturgies 1. Grand Rapids: Baker Academic, 2009.

Smith, Jeffrey M. *Seeds of Deception: Exposing Industry and Government Lies About the Safety of the Genetically Engineered Foods You're Eating*. Fairfield, IA: Yes!, 2003.

Smith, Merritt Roe, and Leo Marx, editors. *Does Technology Drive History?* Cambridge, MA: MIT Press, 1994.

Song, Robert. "Sharing Communion: Hunger, Food, and Genetically Modified Foods." In *The Blackwell Companion to Christian Ethics*, edited by Hauerwas and Wells, 388–400. Malden, MA: Blackwell, 2004.

Sperling, Daniel, and Deborah Gordon. *Two Billion Cars: Driving Toward Sustainability*. New York: Oxford University Press, 2009.

Spivak, Alvin L. *Automobile Dependence and Denial: The Elephant in the Bedroom: Impacts on the Economy and Environment*. Pasadena, CA: New Paradigm, 1993.

Stahl, William. *God and the Chip: Religion and the Culture of Technology*. Waterloo, ON: Canadian Corporation for Studies in Religion, 1998.

Staudenmaier, John M. *Technology's Storytellers: Reweaving the Human Fabric.* Cambridge, MA: MIT Press, 1985.
Staudenmaier, John M., and Thomas J. Schlereth. Review of the exhibition "Made in America" at the Henry Ford Museum and Greenfield Village. *Journal of American History* 80/3 (1993) 1014–19.
Stein, Janice Gross. *The Cult of Efficiency.* Toronto: House of Anansi, 2001.
Stewart, James S. "On a Neglected Emphasis in New Testament Theology." *Scottish Journal of Theology* 4/3 (1951) 292–301.
Stoll, Clifford. *Silicon Snake Oil: Second Thoughts on the Information Highway.* New York: Doubleday, 1995.
Stone, Pat. "The Amish Answer." *Mother Earth News* 118 (1989) 56–60.
Stoops, Barbara Halton. "Driving as Christians." *Engage/Social Action* 15 (1987) 20–21.
Stout, Jeffrey. *Democracy and Tradition.* Princeton: Princeton University Press, 2004.
Swanson, Wesley. "The Cult of the Automobile." *Epoche* 18 (1983) 96–112.
Swearengen, Jack Clayton. *Beyond Paradise: Technology and the Kingdom of God.* Eugene, OR: Wipf & Stock Publishers, 2007.
Szerszynski, Bronislaw and Celia Deane-Drummond. "Re-Ordering Nature: A Postscript." In *Re-ordering Nature: Theology, Society and the New Genetics,* edited by Celia Deane-Drummond and Bronislaw Szerszynski, 312–24. New York: T. & T. Clark, 2003.
Tanner, Kathryn. "Theological Reflection and Christian Practices." In *Practicing Theology: Beliefs and Practices in Christian Life,* edited by Miroslav Volf and Dorothy C. Bass, 228–42. Grand Rapids: Eerdmans, 2002.
Taylor, Charles. *The Ethics of Authenticity.* Cambridge: Harvard University Press, 1991.
———. "Liberal Politics and the Public Sphere." In *New Communitarian Thinking: Persons, Virtues, Institutions, and Communities,* edited by Amitai Etzioni, 183–217. Charlottesville: University Press of Virginia, 1995.
———. *Modern Social Imaginaries.* Durham, NC: Duke University Press, 2004.
———. "Nationalism and Morality." In *The Morality of Nationalism,* edited by Robert McKim and Jeff McMahan, 31–55. New York: Oxford University Press, 1997.
Terlizzese, Lawrence Joseph. *Hope in the Thought of Jacques Ellul.* Eugene, OR: Cascade, 2004.
Thirsk, Joan. *Alternative Agriculture: A History from the Black Death to the Present Day.* New York: Oxford University Press, 1997.
Thompson, Clive. "Motorhead." *Fast Company* 120 (2007) 74–83.
Tierney, John. "The Way We Drive Now: The Autonomist Manifesto (Or, How I Learned to Stop Worrying and love the Road): A Social, Moral and Environmental Case for Driving More." *New York Times Magazine,* September 26, 2004, 57–65.
Tillich, Paul. *The Spiritual Situation in Our Technical Society.* Edited by J. Mark Thomas. Macon, GA: Mercer University Press, 1988.
Toole, David. *Waiting for Godot in Sarajevo: Theological Reflections on Nihilism, Tragedy, and Apocalypse.* Boulder, CO: Westview, 1998.
Tough, Paul. "What Are We Doing On-Line?" [Forum with John Perry Barlow, Sven Birkerts, Kevin Kelly, and Mark Slouka]. *Harper's Magazine* 291 (1995) 35–46.
Turkle, Sherry. *Alone Together.* New York: Basic, 2011.
———. *Life on the Screen: Identity in the Age of the Internet.* New York: Simon & Schuster, 1995.

Ullman, Ellen. *Close to the Machine: Technophilia and Its Discontents.* San Francisco: City Lights, 1997.
United States Patent and Trademark Office. "General Information Concerning Patents." November, 2011. Online: http://www.uspto.gov/patents/resources/general_info_concerning_patents.jsp.
Vaitheeswaran, Vijay, and Iain Carson. *Zoom: The Global Race to Fuel the Car of the Future.* New York: Twelve, 2007.
Van Bragt, Thieleman. *Martyrs Mirror: The Story of Fifteen Centuries of Christian Martyrdom From the Time of Christ to A.D. 1660.* Translated by Joseph F. Sohm. Scottdale, PA: Herald, 2001.
Vanderbilt, Tom. *Traffic: Why We Drive the Way We Do (and What It Says About Us).* New York: Knopf, 2008.
Second Vatican Ecumenical Council. "Pastoral Consultation on the Church in the Modern World: *Gaudium et Spes.*" *Acta Apostolicae Sedis* 58 (1966) 1025–1115.
Veith, Gene Edward, Jr., and Christopher L. Stamper. *Christians in a .com World: Getting Connected Without Being Consumed.* Wheaton, IL: Crossway, 2000.
Vincenti, Walter. *What Engineers Know and How They Know It.* Baltimore: Johns Hopkins University Press, 1990.
Virilio, Paul. *The Art of the Motor.* Translated by Julie Rose. Minneapolis: University of Minnesota Press, 1995.
———. *The Information Bomb.* Translated by Chris Turner. London: Verso, 2000.
———. *Speed and Politics: An Essay on Dromology.* Translated by Mark Polizzotti. New York: Semiotext(e), 1986.
Visser, Margaret. *Beyond Fate.* Toronto: House of Anansi, 2002.
Vogt, Virgil. *The Roots of Concern: Writings on Anabaptist Renewal, 1952–1957.* Eugene, OR: Cascade, 2009.
Volf, Miroslav. "Theology for a Way of Life." In *Practicing Theology: Beliefs and Practices in Christian Life*, edited by Miroslav Volf and Dorothy C. Bass, 245–63. Grand Rapids: Eerdmans, 2002.
Volf, Miroslav, and Dorothy C. Bass, editors. *Practicing Theology: Beliefs and Practices in Christian Life.* Grand Rapids: Eerdmans, 2002.
Walter, Jennifer K., and Eran P. Klein, editors. *The Story of Bioethics: From Seminal Works to Contemporary Explorations.* Washington, DC: Georgetown University Press, 2003.
Walzer, Michael. *On Toleration.* New Haven: Yale University Press, 1997.
———. "The Politics of Difference: Statehood and Toleration in a Multicultural World." In *The Morality of Nationalism*, edited by Robert McKim and Jeff McMahan, 245–57. New York: Oxford University Press, 1997.
Ward, Graham. "Between Virtue and Virtuality." *Theology Today* 59/1 (2002) 55–70.
———. *Cities of God.* Radical Orthodoxy. New York: Routledge, 2000.
Waters, Brent. *From Human to Posthuman: Christian Theology and Technology in a Postmodern World.* Burlington, VT: Ashgate, 2006.
———. *Reproductive Technology: Towards a Theology of Procreative Stewardship.* Cleveland: Pilgrim, 2001.
Waterson, John H.L. "Religion and Road Safety." *Theology* 64 (1961) 228–32.
Watson, J. D., and F. H. C. Crick. "Molecular Structure of Nucleic Acids: A Structure for Deoxyribose Nucleic Acid." *Nature* 171 (1953) 737–38.

Weaver-Zercher, David. *The Amish in the American Imagination.* Baltimore: Johns Hopkins University Press, 2001.
Wells, Samuel. *Improvisation: The Drama of Christian Ethics.* Grand Rapids: Brazos, 2004.
White, Hugh C., Jr., editor. *Christians in a Technological Era.* New York: Seabury, 1964.
White, Lynn, Jr. "The Historical Roots of Our Ecological Crisis." In *Philosophy and Technology: Readings in the Philosophical Problems of Technology*, edited by Carl Mitcham and Robert Mackey, 259–65. New York: Free, 1983.
———. *Medieval Religion and Technology: Collected Essays.* Berkeley: University of California Press, 1978.
———. "Technology, Western." In *Dictionary of the Middle Ages*, edited by Joseph R. Strayer, 11:660. New York: Scribner, 1982.
White, Susan J. *Christian Worship and Technological Change.* Nashville: Abingdon, 1994.
Whitney, Elspeth. *Paradise Restored: The Mechanical Arts from Antiquity through the Thirteenth Century.* Philadelphia: American Philosophical Society, 1990.
Wiebe, Rudy. "The Body Knows as Much as the Soul: On the Human Reality of Being a Writer." *Mennonite Quarterly Review* 71/2 (1997) 189–200.
Willimon, William H. "Community & Computers: Babel, Bytes & Bits." *Christian Century* 104/25 (1987) 740–41.
Wind, James P. "Crossing the Digital Divide: New Forms of Community on the Virtual Frontier." *Congregations* 27/3 (2001) 8–9, 28.
Wink, Walter. *Engaging the Powers: Discernment and Resistance in a World of Domination.* Philadelphia: Fortress, 1992.
———. *Naming the Powers: The Language of Power in the New Testament.* Philadelphia: Fortress, 1984.
———. *Unmasking the Powers: The Invisible Forces that Determine Human Existence.* Philadelphia: Fortress, 1986.
Winne, Mark. *Closing the Food Gap: Resetting the Table in the Land of Plenty.* Boston: Beacon, 2008.
Winner, Langdon. *Autonomous Technology: Technics-out-of-Control as a Theme in Political Thought.* Cambridge, MA: MIT Press, 1977.
———. "Upon Opening the Black Box and Finding It Empty: Social Constructivism and the Philosophy of Technology." *Science, Technology, & Human Values* 18/3 (1993) 362–78.
———. *The Whale and the Reactor.* Chicago: University of Chicago Press, 1986.
Wood, David. "Interview with Albert Borgmann." *Christian Century* 120/17 (2003) 22–25.
Wright, Ronald. *A Short History of Progress.* New York: Carroll & Graf, 2004.
Yoder, John Howard. *Anabaptism and Reformation in Switzerland: An Historical and Theological Analysis of the Dialogues between Anabaptists and Reformers.* Edited by C. Arnold Snyder. Translated by David Carl Stassen and C. Arnold Snyder. Kitchener, ON: Pandora, 2004.
———. "The Anabaptist Shape of Liberation." In *Why I am a Mennonite: Essays on Mennonite Identity*, edited by Harry Loewen, 338–48. Scottdale, PA: Herald, 1988.
———. "Anabaptist Understandings of the Nature and Mission of the Church, with Implications for Contemporary Mennonite Church Organization." Paper prepared

for the Consultation of Nature and Mission of Mennonite Church, Pittsburgh, PA, April 10–11, 1967.

———. "Apologia pro imagine sua." Memo "to whom it may interest," February 8, 1974.

———. "The Apostle's Apology Revisited." In *The New Way of Jesus: Essays Presented to Howard Charles*, edited by William Klassen, 115–34. Newton, KS: Faith and Life, 1980.

———. "Armaments and Eschatology." *Studies in Christian Ethics* 1 (1988) 43–61.

———. *As You Go: The Old Mission in a New Day*. Focal Pamphlet Series 5. Scottdale, PA: Herald, 1961.

———. "The Authority of the Canon." In *Essays on Biblical Interpretation: Anabaptist-Mennonite Perspectives*, edited by Willard Swartley, 265–90. Elkhart, IN: Institute of Mennonite Studies, 1984.

———. "Binding and Loosing." In *Healing the Wounded: The Costly Love of Church Discipline*, edited by John White and Ken Blue, 211–38. Downers Grove, IL: InterVarsity, 1985.

———. *Body Politics: Five Practices of the Christian Community Before the Watching World*. Scottdale, PA: Herald, 2001.

———. "Can one be methodical without methodologism?" A memo "to graduate students in ethics," June 18, 1996.

———. "The Casuistry of Violence." *The Ellul Forum* 16 (1996) 6–7.

———. *Christian Attitudes to War, Peace, and Revolution*. Edited by Theodore J. Koontz and Andy Alexis-Baker. Grand Rapids: Brazos, 2009.

———. "Christian Education; Doctrinal Orientation." Paper prepared for a conversation about Mennonite Church-administered High Schools, 1958.

———. *The Christian Witness to the State*. 1964. Reprint, Eugene, OR: Wipf & Stock, 1998.

———. "Concluding Observations: The Shape of God's People as Word to the World." Lecture presented in Taipei, Taiwan, 1994.

———. "Creation and Gospel." *Perspectives* 3/8 (1988) 8–10.

———. "Discerning the Kingdom of God in the Struggles of the World." *International Review of Mission* 68/4 (1979) 366–72.

———. *Discipleship as Political Responsibility*. Translated by Timothy J. Geddert. Scottdale, PA: Herald, 2003.

———. *The Ecumenical Movement and the Faithful Church*. Focal Pamphlet 3. Scottdale, PA: Mennonite, 1958.

———. *The End of Sacrifice: The Capital Punishment Writings of John Howard Yoder*. Edited by John Nugent. Waterloo, ON: Herald, 2011.

———. "Farming Among Mennonites in France." *Mennonite Encyclopedia*, volume 2, 306–7. Hillsboro, KS: Mennonite Brethren, 1955.

———. "A Footnote on The 'Powers' Debate." Memo "To Whom it May Interest," December 27, 1978.

———. *For the Nations: Essays Public and Evangelical*. Grand Rapids: Eerdmans, 1997.

———. "From Basic Orientation to Concrete Discernment." Paper presented at the "Valuing Life" conference, University of Winnipeg, November, 1989.

———. *The Fullness of Christ: Paul's Revolutionary Vision of Universal Ministry*. Elgen, IL: Brethren, 1987.

———. "God's Good News and the Runaway powers." Paper presented at the "Valuing Life" conference, University of Winnipeg, November, 1989.

———. *He Came Preaching Peace: Bible Lectures on Peacemaking*. 1985. Reprint, Scottdale, PA: Herald Press, 2004.

———. "The Hermeneutics of the Anabaptists." *Mennonite Quarterly Review* 41/4 (1967) 291–308.

———. "Historiography as a Ministry to Renewal." In "From Faith to Age: Historians and the Modern Church: A Festschrift for Donald F. Durnbaugh," edited by David B. Eller, special issue, *Brethren Life and Thought* 43/3–4 (1997) 216–28.

———. "How H. Richard Niebuhr Reasoned: A Critique of Christ and Culture." In *Authentic Transformation: A New Vision of Christ and Culture*, edited by Glen H. Stassen, D. M. Yeager, and John Howard Yoder, 31–89. Nashville: Abingdon, 1996.

———. "I Choose a Vocation." *The Mennonite Community* 2 (1948) 6–7.

———. "If It's Not Broke, Fix It." Unpublished paper, August 9, 1985.

———. "Jesus and Lifestyle: An Interview with John Howard Yoder." *Radix* 9 (1977) 3–4.

———. "Jesus and Power." *Ecumenical Review* 25/4 (1973) 447–54.

———. *The Jewish-Christian Schism Revisited*. Edited by Michael G. Cartwright and Peter Ochs. Grand Rapids: Eerdmans, 2003.

———. *Karl Barth and the Problem of War and Other Essays on Barth*. Edited by Mark Thiessen Nation. Eugene, OR: Cascade, 2003.

———. Letter to Jacques Ellul. March 21, 1979.

———. Letters to John R. Stott. October 27, 1976, June 28, 1978, and December 7, 1978.

———. Letter to Lester Glick, Mennonite Disaster Service Study Committee. January 25, 1958.

———. Letter to Walter Wink, April 26, 1985.

———. "Meaning After Babble: With Jeffrey Stout Beyond Relativism." *Journal of Religious Ethics* 24 (1996) 125–39.

———. "Methodological Miscellany #2: Have you ever seen a true Church?" Unpublished paper, April, 1988.

———. "Moral Theology Miscellany #19: The power of 'power' is a Power." Unpublished paper, June, 1989.

———. *Nonviolence—A Brief History: The Warsaw Lectures*. Waco: Baylor University Press, 2010.

———. "Nuclear Arms in Christian Pacifist Perspective." In *War No More? Options in Nuclear Ethics*, edited by James W. Walters, 17–32. Minneapolis: Fortress, 1989.

———. "On Generating Alternative Paradigms." In *Human Values and the Environment: Conference Proceedings*, Report 140, 56–62. Madison, WI: Wisconsin Academy of Sciences, Arts and Letters, 1992.

———. "On Not Being Ashamed of the Gospel: Particularity, Pluralism, and Validation." *Faith and Philosophy* 9/3 (1992) 285–300.

———. "The Paul Polak Project: a brainstorm about development ethics." Memo "To Whom it May Concern," October 24, 1978.

———. "'Patience' as Method in Moral Reasoning: Is an Ethic of Discipleship 'Absolute'?" In *The Wisdom of the Cross: Essays in Honor of John Howard Yoder*, edited by Stanley Hauerwas et al., 24–42. Grand Rapids: Eerdmans, 1999.

———. "A People in the World: Theological Interpretation." In *The Concept of the Believers' Church: Addresses from the 1967 Louisville Conference*, edited by Leo Garrett Jr., 250–83. Scottdale, PA: Herald, 1969.

---. *The Politics of Jesus: Vicit Agnus Noster*. 2nd ed. Grand Rapids: Eerdmans, 1994.

---. "Power and the Powerless." *Covenant Quarterly* 36 (1978) 29–35.

---. *Preface to Theology: Christology and Theological Method*. Introduction by Stanley Hauerwas and Alex Sider. Grand Rapids: Brazos, 2002.

---. *The Priestly Kingdom: Social Ethics as Gospel*. Notre Dame: University of Notre Dame Press, 1984.

---. "Responding to Stanley Fish lecture responding to George Marsden book." Memo "to myself and potential confidential eavesdroppers." November 12, 1994.

---. Review of *Naming the Powers* by Walter Wink. *Theological Students Fellowship Bulletin* 9 (1986) 25.

---. Unpublished review of *The Simple Life*, by Vernard Eller, and *Beyond the Rat Race*, by Arthur G. Gish. December, 1973.

---. *Revolutionary Christianity: The 1966 South American Lectures*. Edited by Paul Martens, Mark Thiessen Nation, Matthew Porter, and Myles Werntz. Eugene, OR: Cascade, 2011.

---. *The Royal Priesthood: Essays Ecclesiological and Ecumenical*. Edited by Michael G. Cartwright. Grand Rapids: Eerdmans, 1994.

---. "Sacrament as Social Process: Christ the Transformer of Culture." *Theology Today* 48/3 (1991) 33–44.

---. "A Syllabus of Issues Facing the Church College." Paper presented at three Mennonite colleges prior to a workshop convened by the Mennonite Board of Education, April, 1964.

---. "Theological Perspectives on 'Growth with Equity.'" In *Growth with Equity: Strategies for Meeting Human Needs*, edited by Mary Evelyn Jegen and Charles K. Wilber, 9–16. New York: Paulist, 1979.

---. "Theological Revision and the Burden of Particular Identity." In *James M. Gustafson's Theocentric Ethics: Interpretations and Assessments*, edited by Harlan R. Beckley and Charles M. Swezey, 63–94. Macon, GA: Mercer University Press, 1988.

---. "Time and the Christian." *Christian Living* 2/3 (1955) 14–15.

---. *To Hear the Word*. Eugene, OR: Wipf & Stock, 2001.

---. *The War of the Lamb: The Ethics of Nonviolence and Peacemaking*. Edited by Glen Stassen, Mark Thiessen Nation, and Matt Hamsher. Grand Rapids: Brazos, 2009.

---. "Walk and Word: The Alternatives to Methodologism." In *Theology Without Foundations: Religious Practice and the Future of Theological Truth*, edited by Stanley Hauerwas, Nancey Murphy, and Mark Nation, 77–90. Nashville: Abingdon, 1994.

---. "What Would You Do If . . . ?: An Exercise in Situation Ethics." *The Journal of Religious Ethics* 2/2 (1974) 81–105.

---. "Why I Don't Pay All My Income Tax." *Sojourners* (1977) 11–12.

Yoder, John Howard, editor. *What Would You Do? A Serious Answer to a Standard Question*. Expanded ed. Scottdale, PA: Herald, 1992.

York, Herbert F. *The Advisors: Oppenheimer, Teller, and the Superbomb*. San Francisco: Freeman, 1976.

Zaleski, Jeff. *The Soul in Cyberspace: How New Technology is Changing our Spiritual Lives*. San Francisco: HarperEdge, 1997.

Zimmerman, Earl. *Practicing the Politics of Jesus: The Origin and Significance of John Howard Yoder's Social Ethics*. Telford, PA: Cascadia, 2007.

Index

Amish, the
   Gelassenheit, 34
   as Luddites, 30–31
   Ordnung, 34
   origins, 23n82
   as technological saints, 31–33
Aquinas, Thomas, 18–19, 117, 125n23
Arendt, Hannah, 11n34, 64n121
automobiles
   background, 77–78
   extreme views, 78–80
   ideals, 81–85
   tactics for conscientiously engaging, 188–92

Bacon, Roger, 18
Bakardjieva, Maria, 104–5
Barbour, Ian, 3–4, 5n18, 77n12
Barlow, John Perry, 104n121
Barth, Karl, 45n38, 57, 60, 62, 63n110, 64n121, 65n123
Barthes, Roland, 80
Bass, Dorothy C., 59, 201
Bender, Harold S., 45, 54, 142
Berkhof, Hendrikus, 65n123
Berners-Lee, Tim, 102
Berry, Wendell, 33–34
Billington, David P., 170
bioethics, 6–10
Boers, Arthur Paul, 22n81
Borgmann, Albert, 11n34, 20–22, 59, 68n144, 69, 107n128, 108n132, 111n139, 140–41, 177, 183–87, 190, 193

Braungart, Michael, 130n43
Brende, Eric, 23–33, 35
Brenneman, Bob, 153n129
Brunk, Conrad G., 96, 171–72
Bucciarelli, Louis, 166n51, 169, 170n70
Bury, J. B., xiv

Cahalan, Kathleen, 22n81
Cahill, Lisa Sowle, 7–8
Caldecott, Stratford, xvn12
Carter, Craig A., 42–43
Cartwright, Michael G., 172
Cavanaugh, William T., 195n64
Certeau, Michel, de, 187n38
Coles, Romand, 185–86
Cole-Turner, Ronald, 7
conscientious engagement, 51–53, 175, 177, 202–3
Consolmagno, Guy, 167n57, 174n79
Crawford, Matthew B., 190n48
Crick, F. H. C., 87
Cullman, Oscar, 45n38, 64n121, 65n123, 66

Davis, Michael, 164n38, 169
Dawn, Marva J., 22n81, 64, 141n82
Deane-Drummond, Celia, 6n19, 170n70
De Vries, George, 35n126
Dintamen, Stephen, 54
Drees, Willem, 3–5
Dueck, Irma Fast, 186n35
Durbin, Paul T., 19n69, 75n7

Dykstra, Craig, 174–75

Ellul, Jacques, xvii, 10–16, 21, 40, 61–64, 67–71, 74, 77, 82n39, 105, 128, 130, 132, 166n50
engineering
  aesthetics, 169–70
  ambiguity of, 167
  the church, 171–74
  effectiveness, properly understood, 164–67
  emotion, 168–69

Feenberg, Andrew, 22n78, 104–5
Ferguson, Eugene S., 164n38, 167–68, 170
Finger, Thomas N., 55–56
Fish, Stanley, 50n61, 124n22
Florman, Samuel, 165, 167–68
Friesen, Duane K., 50n60

Gaillardetz, Richard R., 122n17, 137n67, 141n82, 184n25
Galbraith, John Kenneth, 168
Gaud, William S., 86n53
genetically modified food
  background, 86–89
  extreme views, 89–94
  ideals, 94–100
  tactics for conscientiously engaging, 192–97
Gill, David W., 64n121, 69n146
Goetz, Thomas, 198n73
Goodenough, Ursula, 4
Graham, Mark, 27n93
Grant, George, 10, 12–14, 16, 19, 21, 22
Gustafson, James M., 2

Hall, Douglas John, 2
Harris, Nancy, 89n62
Hauerwas, Stanley, 2, 50n61, 60, 117, 118n9, 170n70, 175n84, 179n3
Hefner, Philip, 3–5
Heidegger, Martin, 2, 11, 20n73, 116n2
Himanen, Pekka, 200n77

Holland, Scott, 185
Homer-Dixon, Thomas, 11n36, 77n12
Hopper, David H., xv
Huebner, Chris K., 9n31, 39, 50n60, 191n49
Huebner, Harry J., 127n32
Hugh of St. Victor, 18

Ihde, Don, 20
Illich, Ivan, 78–79, 84
Internet, the
  background, 100–102
  ideals, 105–12
  lack of extreme views, 103–5
  tactics for conscientiously engaging, 197–201

Jacobsen, Eric O., 22n81
Jardine, Murray, 5n17
Joachim of Fiore, 18
Jonas, Hans, 38n5, 92n80

Kallenberg, Brad J., 137n65, 170
Kaufman, Gordon D., 39n5
Kingsolver, Barbara, 193–96
Klein, Eran P., 7
Koen, Billy Vaughn, 165–66
Koontz, Ted, 71n152
Kotva, Joseph J., Jr., 118n9
Kraybill, Donald B., 34n120, 34n122, 36n127
Kundera, Milan, xv, 83–84, 120

Lasch, Christopher, xv
Levinson, Paul, 32n108
Lindbeck, George A., 137, 139
Lomasky, Loren E., 81–82, 120
Lonergan, Bernard, 2
Long, D. Stephen, 116n2
Long, Tony, 31
Lysaught, M. Therese, 9n29

MacIntyre, Alasdair C., 59, 116n2, 117, 137, 138n70, 139, 141, 164
Magnus, Albertus, 18

marks of the church
  commitment, 120
  humility, 125–27
  nonconformity, 127–29
  patience, 120–21
  servanthood, 129–32
  simplicity, 134–35
  suffering, 121–22
  visibility, 133–34
  vulnerability, 123–25
Martens, Paul, 156n1
Marx, Karl, 10, 11n38, 13
McDonough, William, 130n43
McKenny, Gerald P., 9, 39, 95–96, 123
McKibben, Bill, 105n124
McLuhan, Marshall, 133
Meaton, Julia, 78
Milbank, John, 60, 114n1, 157n7
Miller, Vincent J., 137, 139–40, 186–87
Mitcham, Carl, xiin3, 2, 3n6
Molella, Arthur P., 168
Morrice, David, 78
Mumford, Lewis, 83
Murphy, Nancey, 43
Nation, Mark Thiessen, 44–46, 153n129

Negroponte, Nicholas, 105n124, 133
Niebuhr, H. Richard, 4n11, 48, 73–74
Nietzche, Friedrich, 10, 11n34
Nisbet, Robert, xivn9
Noble, David F., 11, 16–19, 21–22, 29, 30n104, 164n38, 169n66

O'Donovan, Oliver, 2, 8n26, 200
Official Catholic Teaching
  grappling theologically with technology, 25–27
  use of technology to define progress, 24–25
  view of technology as morally neutral, 27–29
Olshan, Marc C., 36n127
Ovitt, George, Jr., 18

Pacey, Arnold, 17n62
Paul (apostle), 65–66, 116–17, 146, 149–50, 179
Perry, John, 90n74
Petrini. Carlo, 192n54
Petroski, Henry, 165
Pitt, Joseph C., 75n7
Polak, Paul, 134, 135n60
Pollan, Michael, 98n96
Pope John Paul II, 24
Post, Robert C., 168
practices of the church
  baptism, 149
  binding and loosing, 147–48
  breaking bread, 148
  making disciples, 153–54
  as more than techniques, 174–75
  multiplicity of gifts, 149–50
  open meeting, 150–51
  praise, 151
  preaching, 152
  serving, 152–53
  Yoder's perspective on, 141–46
principalities and powers, 61–70, 117, 119, 123, 126, 136–37, 177–83, 202–3
Pringle, Peter, 98
progress, xiii–xvi
Prokes, Mary Timothy, 111
Pullinger, David, 110n138, 200n78

Randels, George D, Jr., 181n17
Reimer, A. James, 38n5, 54–57, 59, 178
religion and science, 3–6
Rheingold, Howard, 31–32
Roy, Rustum, 5
Russell, Robert John, 4

Sachs, Wolfgang, 80–85, 94, 119–22
Schlabach, Gerald, 41n14, 173n78
Schmeiser, Perry, 99–100
Schultze, Quentin J., 108n131, 200n77
Sclove, Richard, 33
Scott, Peter, 96n91
Segal, Howard P., 79
Shiva, Vandana, 98, 195

Shuman, Joel James, 9n29, 175
Sider, J. Alexander, 151
Smith, Cyril Stanley, 169–70
Song, Robert, 94n89
Stahl, William, 109
Stein, Janice Gross, 108
Stout, Jeffrey, 178–79
Swanson, Wesley, 77, 79–80
Swearengen, Jack Clayton, 81, 167
Szerszynski, Bronislaw, 170n70

tactics, 186–88
Taylor, Charles, 59, 137–39, 180–82
technological ideals
    autonomy, 81–82
    comfort, 84–85
    conformity, 98–100
    control, 94–95
    efficiency, 105–8
    invisibility, 108–10
    mastery, 95–97
    novelty, 110–12
    speed, 83–84
Theophilus, 18
technology
    autonomy of, 12–16
    definition of, xii–xiii
    as formative and formable, 20–22
    and practices, 137–41
    as a principality or power, 61–70
    social construction of, 16–19
Tierney, John, 79
Tillich, Paul, 2
Toole, David, 187n38
Turkle, Sherry, 109, 181, 200

Vincenti, Walter, 165, 167
Virilio, Paul, 83, 118n10
Volf, Miroslav, 60

Walter, Jennifer K., 7
Walzer, Michael, 180–81

Ward, Graham, 112n141, 181n17
Waters, Brent, xv, 8
Waterson, John H. L., 189–90
Watson, J. D., 87,
Weaver-Zercher, David, 30n102
Wells, Samuel, 75–76, 94–95, 123
White, Lynn, Jr., 11, 16–19, 164n38, 21–22
White, Susan J., 19
Wink, Walter, 65n123, 66, 182
Winner, Langdon, xii
Wood, David, 22n81

Yoder, John Howard
    analysis of the powers, 65–67
    Christian practices, 52, 59–61
    connections with Ellul, 61–64, 67–70
    conscientious engagement, 51–53
    disapproval of engineering, 156–60
    engaging technology in the particular, 73–77
    engineering the church, 160–63
    inseparability of theology and ethics, 56–59
    international and ecumenical experiences, 44–46
    marks of the church, 119–35
    Mennonite critiques of, 54–56
    mission, 49–51
    notes on reading, 40–44
    practices of the church, 141–46
    preference for particularity, 73–77
    response to the powers, 67–70
    starting with the church, 46–48
York, Herbert F., 168,

Zimmerman, Earl, 43, 45n39, 56n84, 65n123

www.ingramcontent.com/pod-product-compliance
Lightning Source LLC
Chambersburg PA
CBHW072023240426
43667CB00044B/2257